Britannica's STUDENT ATLAS

ENCYCLOPÆDIA
Britannica®

Chicago   London   New Delhi   Paris   Seoul   Sydney   Taipei   Tokyo

Published by

Copyright © 2010
by GeoNova Publishing, Inc.
All rights reserved.
Printed in Canada

ISBN: 978-1-61535-335-4
1 TC/G Beauceville, QC CANADA Sept 09

Material on the inside back cover and on pages 113–132
© Merriam-Webster, Incorporated.

Acknowledgements:

"How to use this Atlas" written by Elspeth Leacock.

Photograph on cover © Valueline/PunchStock

Photographs on pages 24–25 Copyright © 2010 Corel Corp. Except "Arid" World Landmarks and Travel/Getty Images and "Tropical Wet" World Commerce and Travel/Getty Images.

Photographs on pages 26–27 Copyright © 2010 Corel Corp. Except "Midlatitude grassland" US Landmarks and Travel/Getty Images; "Coniferous forest," "Subtropical broadleaf evergreen forest" US Landmarks and Travel 2/Getty Images and "Mixed forest," "Tropical rain forest" Nature, Wildlife and the Environment/Getty Images.

Photograph on page 40 by Nancy Yatabe.

Photograph on page 42 Library of Congress, LC-W861-35.

Photographs on pages 58–59 "Earthquakes" © Royalty-Free/Corbis, "Fall line" Copyright © 2010 Corel Corp. and "Fault" US Landmarks and Travel/Getty Images.

Photographs on pages 60–61 US Landmarks and Travel/Getty Images. Except "Tropical Wet" US Landmarks and Travel 2/Getty Images and "Mediterranean," "Tundra" Copyright © 2010 Corel Corp.

Photographs on pages 62–63 Copyright © Corel Corp. Except "Coniferous forest" Copyright © 2010 FreeStockPhotos; "Midlatitude scrubland" US Landmarks and Travel/Getty Images and "Mixed forest" Nature, Wildlife and the Environment/Getty Images.

Photograph on pages 68–69 © Royalty-Free/Corbis.

Merriam-Webster's Geographical Dictionary 2007 was used as a source of information throughout.

AN ATLAS is a collection of

maps that can be used to find information about your world. The very latest data has been collected to make these maps. Hundreds of satellite images were used to map the dramatic shrinking of Earth's forests. The latest census data from each and every country was used to build a picture of Earth's current population. The most recent scientific research was used to create thematic maps of continental drift, the ocean floor, the environment and our natural resources. Look closely and you will see that the information for the maps comes from many different sources such as NASA, the U.S. Department of the Interior or the World Bank. You can use these maps to explore your world, discover connections between places, and see relationships between places and peoples.

But this atlas is more than just a wealth of information. It is fun to look at too. You will find that these maps and photographs can evoke images of far away places. They invite you to pause and to dream. With a map you can journey the world without ever getting wet, cold, tired or hungry. You can imagine great adventures and not leave the comfort of your favorite chair!

To get the most out of this atlas you need to know how to read maps. Just as you learned to read words like the ones on this page, you can learn how to read the language of maps. The map skills you need to know are:
1. locating places
2. measuring distance
3. finding direction
4. reading map symbols

Locating Places
To find places in this atlas, you can begin with the index. To find Dallas follow these steps.

1. Look up Dallas in the index at the end of this book.
2. The index tells you that Dallas is a city in Texas and that it can be found on page 50. You will also learn that Dallas is located at 32°47'N (32 degrees 47 minutes north) and 96°48'W (96 degrees 48 minutes west.)
3. Go to page 50 and find the line of latitude nearest to the number 32°N and the line of longitude nearest to the number 96°W. You will find

Dallas close to where those two lines meet. You can learn more about latitude and longitude on pages 8-9.

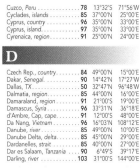

Measuring Distance
To measure distance most maps have a distance scale. You can learn more about measuring distance on page 7.

| 0 | 200 | 400 mi |
| 0 | 200 | 400 km |

Finding Direction
To find directions use the map's compass rose. You can also use lines of latitude and longitude to find direction. Every line of longitude points north and south. Every line of latitude points east and west. You can learn more about latitude and longitude on pages 8-9.

Reading Map Symbols
Every map symbol shows the location of something. It could be something as large as a continent or as small as a bird-house. A dot shows the location of a city. A blue line shows the course of a river. But map symbols are not the same on all maps. One map might show a city with a square. Map legends or keys help explain the symbols used on a map. You can find out more about legends and the map symbols used in this atlas on page 6.

Special Features of this Atlas

This atlas has been designed and organized to be easy for you to use. Here is a "road map" to your atlas.

The Blue Tab Bar
Somewhere along the top blue tab bar of each spread you will see a darker blue tab. It tells you

| Geographic Features | Climate | Land Cover |

the subject of the map or maps you are looking at. The light blue tabs tell you the subjects of the surrounding map spreads. If, for example, you are looking at the World Climate map and would like to compare it to the World Vegetation map, you can use the tabs to find that map quickly and easily.

Map Skills
Look at the blue tab bar above and you will see that you are in the map skills section. This section should be called "Read Me First" because it is here that you will find all sorts of helpful information about maps and how to read them. Even if you are a practiced map reader, read this section!

The World
In this section you will find a world political map, a world physical map, and 35 world thematic maps. The world political map shows the most up to date national boundaries. On the world physical map you can see huge deserts,

great mountain ranges, and even the sea ice that covers much of the Arctic. The thematic maps include the most up to date information on everything from the world distribution of computers and televisions to life expectancy, religion and literacy. If you want to see the ocean floor, or to find where in the world volcanoes form, this is the section to look in.

Continents

The continent units are designed to all have the same kinds of maps. This will enable you to compare and contrast one continent with another with ease and accuracy. There is a political map, a physical map, and a total of seven thematic maps per continent.

Used individually each map can provide answers to many questions. But all together, each set of maps can be used to tell a story.

Imagine a journey crossing a continent. You can see the regions visited, the mountains climbed, or the deserts crossed. You can tell if many people are passed along the way or few. You can describe the activities of the people. Will you see miners or ranchers or farmers? And you can tell about the different climates experienced along the way. All of this information and more is on the maps for every continent but Antarctica.

Environmental Issues

There is a special "Environmental Issues" feature for each continent and one for the world. To create these features the latest scientific information was gathered and organized for you. The topics cover the three major environmental issues faced by citizens today, desertification, deforestation, and acid rain.

The United States

In the section on the United States you will find a political map with two pages of political facts, a physical map with two pages of physical facts, and seven thematic map spreads.

Canada and Mexico

Canada and Mexico both have their own spreads that include a political and physical map.

Geographic Features

There are two special "Geographic Features" included in this atlas. To find out how the continents, Earth's greatest land features, have been drifting around the globe, turn to pages 22–23. To take an in depth look at fall lines, divides, and faults turn to the United States Geographic Features spread on pages 58–59.

Charts and Graphs

This atlas is filled with charts, graphs and diagrams. They are used to give more information about subjects shown on the maps. To make these charts and graphs, long lists of the most up to date data was gathered. Then all those numbers were organized into graphic displays that can be read simply and accurately.

Line graphs are used to show change in amounts over time.

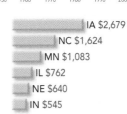

Bar graphs are used to compare amounts.

Pie charts show percentages of a total.

Glossary

There are many geographic terms found on maps such as *fjord, isthmus,* or *plateau*. You can find the meaning of these and other terms in the geographic glossary located on the inside back cover.

Legend

The following symbols are used here for general reference maps. Maps with special subjects (thematic maps) have their own unique legends.

General Reference Maps

⊛ National capital
★ Other capital
• Other city
▭ International boundary (political map)
▭ International boundary in dispute/undefined (political map)
▭ State or provincial boundary
▭ International boundary (physical map)
▭ International boundary in dispute (physical map)

▭ Nonsubject area
▲ Mountain peak
▽ Lowest point
� Perennial lake
⌢ Intermittent lake
~ Perennial river
≈ Falls

Physical Maps Legend

Pack ice
Mountains
Oceans and seas
Arid lands
Ice caps
Tundra
Forests
Grasslands

Projections

A globe is the most accurate picture of the Earth. Only a globe can show distance, direction, and the true shape and area of land and sea. Mapmakers struggle with how to show the round world on a flat map.

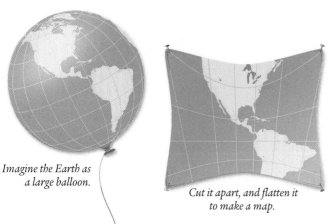

Imagine the Earth as a large balloon.

Cut it apart, and flatten it to make a map.

Mercator Projection

Gerardus Mercator, a Dutch mapmaker, wanted a map projection that showed direction and shape accurately. The problems with distortions are more obvious on this projection. You can see that the land areas are very distorted the closer to the poles that you get. So, this projection ended up greatly distorting distance and size.

To show the round Earth on flat paper, mapmakers used different **projections**, or ways of showing a round shape on a flat surface.

With every projection the shapes of places are changed somewhat. This is called distortion. To find distortion, you can compare the latitude and longitude lines of a map to those same lines on a globe.

This diagram shows how a Mercator projection distorts the sizes of places. Compare Greenland on the map and the globe.

Projections – Making the Round World Flat

Robinson Projection

Arthur Robinson, an American mapmaker, wanted to develop a map projection that "looked" right. This projection uses many distortions but none are significant. You can see this by comparing one of the large scale World maps in this atlas to a globe.

Azimuthal Projection

This is a projection used to show Antarctica and the Arctic. Azimuthal maps show direction and distance accurately, if measured from the center of the map. But, other distances, shape and size are distorted.

Map Scale

Changing Scale

The **large scale map** of New York's lower Manhattan (top) shows a small area with a large amount of detail. The **small scale map** of New York State (bottom) is a large area with a small amount of detail.

One inch represents 1 mile

One centimeter represents 10 kilometers

The map of metropolitan New York (left) covers an area nearly 50 times larger than the map of lower Manhattan, above.

The map of New York State (left) covers an area over 112 times larger than the metro New York map above, and 5,243 times the area of the lower Manhattan map.

Latitude and Longitude

Since ancient times, mapmakers, geographers, and navigators have worked to develop a system for accurately locating places on the Earth. On a sphere, such as the Earth, there are no corners or sides, no beginning or end. But since the Earth rotates on an axis, there are two fixed points: the North Pole and the South Pole. These points make a good starting place for a system of imaginary lines.

These imaginary lines form a grid over the Earth, allowing us to pinpoint the exact location of any spot on the Earth. This spherical grid is called the **graticule**. It is formed by lines called **latitude** and **longitude**.

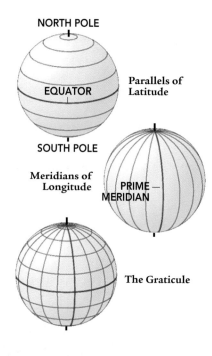

NORTH POLE

EQUATOR

SOUTH POLE

Parallels of Latitude

Meridians of Longitude

PRIME MERIDIAN

The Graticule

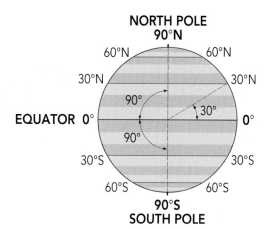

NORTH POLE
90°N

60°N   60°N

30°N   30°N

90°
30°
EQUATOR 0°   0°

90°

30°S   30°S

60°S   60°S

90°S
SOUTH POLE

Latitude

Halfway between the poles the Equator circles the globe in an east-west direction. Latitude is measured in degrees north or south of the Equator, which is 0 degrees (°). Lines of latitude are called **parallels** because they circle the globe parallel to the Equator. Parallels are numbered from 0° at the Equator to 90°N at the North Pole and 90°S at the South Pole.

Longitude

Running from pole to pole, lines of longitude—called **meridians**—circle the globe in a north-south direction. As in any circle or sphere, there are 360 degrees (°) of longitude. The meridians are numbered from the Prime Meridian which is labeled 0°. Meridians east or west of the Prime Meridian are labeled E or W up to 180°. The International Date Line generally follows the 180° meridian, making a few jogs to avoid cutting through land areas.

180°

150°W   150°E

120°W   120°E

180°

90°W   90°E

90°

Prime Meridian

60°W   60°E

30°W   30°E

0°

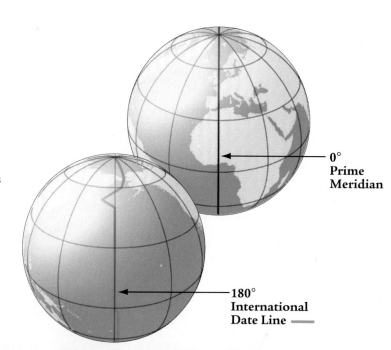

0°
Prime Meridian

180°
International Date Line ▬

Parallels and Meridians—The Facts

Parallels
- are lines of latitude used to measure location north or south of the Equator
- are always the same distance apart (about 70 miles)
- differ in length
- The Equator, the longest parallel, is almost 25,000 miles long

Meridians
- are lines of longitude used to measure location east or west of the Prime Meridian
- meet at the poles
- are all the same length

Which way north...

The geographic North and South Poles are fixed points located at each end of the Earth's axis. The Earth's magnetic fields cause the needle of a compass to point toward magnetic north, not geographic north. The north magnetic pole is located in the northern territories of Canada. The south magnetic pole is located near the coast of Antarctica. The magnetic poles are constantly moving.

Degrees, Minutes, Seconds

A degree (°) of latitude or longitude can be divided into 60 parts called minutes ('). Each minute can be divided into 60 seconds ("). The diagram at right is an example of a place located to the nearest second.

It is written as:
42° 21' 30" N   71° 03' 37" W

● This place is city center, Boston, Massachusetts.

The index at the back of this Atlas uses degrees and minutes of latitude and longitude to help you find places.

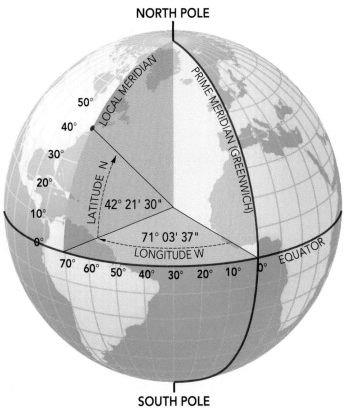

Different Kinds of Maps

Maps are special pictures of places on Earth.

All maps are alike in these important ways:
- All maps are a view from above
- All maps show selected information using symbols
- All maps are smaller than the real place on Earth that they show.

Because people want to show many different things on Earth, they create many different kinds of maps.

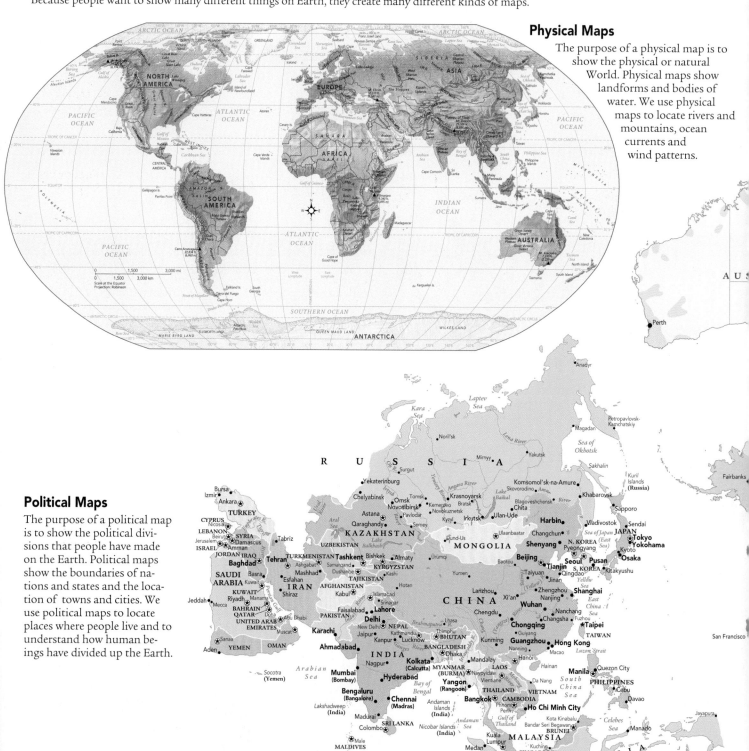

Physical Maps

The purpose of a physical map is to show the physical or natural World. Physical maps show landforms and bodies of water. We use physical maps to locate rivers and mountains, ocean currents and wind patterns.

Political Maps

The purpose of a political map is to show the political divisions that people have made on the Earth. Political maps show the boundaries of nations and states and the location of towns and cities. We use political maps to locate places where people live and to understand how human beings have divided up the Earth.

Thematic, or Special Purpose Maps

These maps show a specific subject (theme) or very limited number of subjects (such as population density, climate or historical topics). They can be used to show distributions and relationships among map features. This page contains examples of the many types of maps to be found throughout the *Student Atlas of the World*.

Locator

Historic Route Map

Population Density Map

Gross Domestic Product (GDP) Map

Vegetation Map

Land Use Map

Climate Map

Continental Drift Map

Our Solar System

SUN
Jupiter
Mercury
Venus
Earth
Mars
Asteroid belt
Saturn
Uranus

Titan
Rhea
Tethys
Mimas
Dione
Saturn
Jupiter
Miranda
Triton
Nereid
Pluto
Neptune
Uranus
Ganymede

	Pluto	Neptune	Uranus	Saturn	Jupiter
Diameter	1,485 mi (2,390 km)	30,602 mi (49,249 km)	31,518 mi (50,723 km)	72,368 mi (116,465 km)	86,882 mi (139,823 km)
Mean distance from Sun (millions of miles/millions of km)	3,670 mi (5,906 km)	2,793 mi (4,495 km)	1,785 mi (2,873 km)	891 mi (1,434 km)	484 mi (779 km)

	Approximate time to orbit the Sun	Average surface temperature
Sun	---	9,941°F (5,505°C)
Mercury	0.2 Earth year (88 days)	333°F (167°C)
Venus	0.6 Earth year (225 days)	867°F (464°C)
Earth	1 Earth year	59°F (15°C)
Mars	1.9 Earth years	-81°F (-63°C)
Jupiter	12 Earth years	-162°F (-108°C)
Saturn	29.5 Earth years	-218°F (-139°C)
Uranus	84 Earth years	-323°F (-197°C)
Neptune	165 Earth years	-330°F (-201°C)

Pluto	248 Earth years	-369°F (-223°C)

Pluto: a dwarf planet

In 2006, the International Astronomical Union revised the system of classifying bodies that orbit the Sun. These objects are now classified either as planets, dwarf planets, or small solar system bodies. Under the new method's definitions our solar system contains just 8 planets; Pluto has been designated a dwarf planet. Joining Pluto in the dwarf planet category are Ceres (orbiting within the asteroid belt) and Eris (orbiting beyond Pluto). A dozen more objects are potential dwarf planets, and that list is expected to grow.

Pluto

Neptune

Callisto

Io   Europa

Asteroid Belt   Mars

Phobos

Deimos

Moon   Earth   Venus   Mercury   SUN

Note: Distances on the lower diagram are not shown to scale, and only major satellites are shown.

Mars	Earth	Venus	Mercury	Sun
4,212 mi (6,779 km)	7,926 mi (12,756 km)	7,521 mi (12,104 km)	3,032 mi (4,879 km)	865,000 mi (1,392,000 km)
142 mi (228 km)	93 mi (150 km)	67 mi (108 km)	36 mi (58 km)	-----

Sources: JPL/NASA; World Almanac, 2006

International boundary

▲ Mountain peak

Source for elevation data:
Merriam-Webster's Geographical Dictionary, 2007

ARCTIC OCEAN

Point
Barrow

*Beaufort
Sea*

Queen Elizabeth Islands

Ellesmere
Island

Greenland

Victoria
Island

Baffin Island

*Baffin
Bay*

*Davis
Strait*

Cape
Farewell

Bering Strait

*Gulf of
Alaska*

Yukon R.

▲ Mt. McKinley
20,320 ft.
(6,194 m)

Mackenzie R.

Great Bear
Lake

Great
Slave Lake

*Hudson
Bay*

**NORTH
AMERICA**

Lake
Winnipeg

*Labrador
Sea*

Newfoundland

*Bering
Sea*

Aleutian Islands

ROCKY MOUNTAINS

GREAT PLAINS

Missouri R.

The Great Lakes

40°N

Cape
Mendocino

GREAT
BASIN

Mississippi R.

APPALACHIAN MTS.

Cape Hatteras

ATLANTIC
OCEAN

Azores

**PACIFIC
OCEAN**

SIERRA MADRE
OCCIDENTAL

TROPIC OF CANCER

20°N

Baja
California

SIERRA MADRE
ORIENTAL

*Gulf of
Mexico*

Yucatán
Pen.

Cuba

West Indies

Cape Verde
Islands

Hawaiian
Islands

Caribbean Sea

CENTRAL
AMERICA

LLANOS

GUIANA HIGHLANDS

EQUATOR

0°

Galápagos Is.

Pariñas Point

P o l y n e s i a

A M A Z O N

BASIN

Amazon R.

**SOUTH
AMERICA**

ANDES

MATO
GROSSO
PLATEAU

BRAZILIAN
HIGHLANDS

20°S

TROPIC OF CAPRICORN

Pitcairn I.

Easter I.

GRAN
CHACO

Paraná R.

PAMPAS

**PACIFIC
OCEAN**

Mt. Aconcagua ▲
22,834 ft.
(6,960 m)

ANDES

Patagonia

0   1,500   3,000 mi

0   1,500   3,000 km

Scale at the Equator
Projection: Robinson

40°S

Falkland Is.

South
Georgia

Strait of Magellan

Tierra del Fuego

Cape Horn

60°S

Drake Passage

SOUTHERN OCEAN

ANTARCTIC CIRCLE

Ross Sea

Marie Byrd Land

Ellsworth Land

Antarctic
Peninsula

*Weddell
Sea*

80°S

North Polar Region

Amur R.

STANOVOY RANGE

CENTRAL
SIBERIAN
PLATEAU

S I B E R I A

ASIA

Yenisey R.

90°E

60°E

*Barents
Sea*

EUROPE

Scandinavia

*Kara
Sea*

Novaya
Zemlya

North Cape

ARCTIC

OCEAN

*Norwegian
Sea*

Shetland Is.

Lena River

VERKHOYANSK
RANGE

Taymyr
Pen.

Severnaya
Zemlya

Franz
Josef Land

Svalbard

Faroe Is.

Ireland

*Sea of
Okhotsk*

*Laptev
Sea*

New
Siberian
Islands

Jan Mayen

PRIME MERIDIAN

ATLANTIC
OCEAN

KOLYMA RANGE

*East
Siberian
Sea*

North Pole

*Greenland
Sea*

Iceland

Denmark Strait

30°W

150°E

80°N

Greenland

Kamchatka Peninsula

Wrangel I.

*Chukchi
Sea*

Ellesmere
Island

*Baffin
Bay*

Cape Farewell

60°N

Queen Elizabeth Is.

Devon I.

*Davis
Strait*

Bering Sea

CHUKCHI PEN.

BROOKS RANGE

Point Barrow

Somerset I.

Banks
I.

Prince of
Wales I.

Baffin Island

*Labrador
Sea*

50°N

Aleutian Is.

St. Lawrence I.

SEWARD PEN.

*Beaufort
Sea*

Victoria
Island

Hudson Strait

180°

Nunivak I.

Yukon R.

▲ Mt. McKinley
20,320 ft.
(6,194 m)

Southampton

Labrador

90°W

*Hudson
Bay*

ALASKA RANGE

MACKENZIE MTS.

NORTH AMERICA

Great Bear
Lake

0   500   1,000 mi

0   500   1,000 km

150°W

**Main map labels:**

ARCTIC OCEAN

Greenland Sea · Norwegian Sea · Svalbard · Franz Josef Land · Novaya Zemlya · Severnaya Zemlya · Kara Sea · Laptev Sea · East Siberian Sea
North Cape · Barents Sea
ARCTIC CIRCLE
Iceland
Scandinavia · Lake Ladoga · SIBERIA · CENTRAL SIBERIAN PLATEAU · VERKHOYANSK RANGE · KOLYMA RANGE
North Sea · Ireland · British Isles · NORTHERN EUROPEAN PLAIN · Volga R. · URAL MTS. · WEST SIBERIAN PLAIN · Ob R. · Yenisey R. · Lena R. · ASIA
EUROPE · ALPS · Danube R. · Mt. Elbrus 18,510 ft. (5,642 m) · THE STEPPES · KAZAKH UPLANDS · ALTAY MTS. · Kamchatka Peninsula · Sea of Okhotsk
Iberian Peninsula · Black Sea · Aral Sea · Caspian Sea · TIAN SHAN · GOBI · MANCHURIAN PLAIN · Sakhalin · Kuril Is. · Hokkaido
ATLAS MOUNTAINS · Mediterranean Sea · ZAGROS MTS. · Taklimakan Desert · HINDU KUSH · NORTH CHINA PLAIN · Sea of Japan (East Sea) · Honshu · PACIFIC OCEAN
Canary Is. · Mesopotamia · Persian Gulf · PLATEAU OF TIBET · Mt. Everest 29,035 ft. (8,850 m) · HIMALAYAS · Chang (Yangtze) R. · East China Sea · Kyushu · Shikoku
SAHARA · Arabian Peninsula · Red Sea · Thar Desert · Ganges R. · Brahmaputra R. · TROPIC OF CANCER · Taiwan
AFRICA · Nile R. · SAHEL · Rub' al Khali · DECCAN PLATEAU · Bay of Bengal · Indochina Peninsula · South China Sea · Philippine Sea · Micronesia · Melanesia
ETHIOPIAN HIGHLANDS · Somali Peninsula · Arabian Sea · Cape Comorin · Sri Lanka · Malay Peninsula · Philippine Islands
Gulf of Guinea · Congo R. · Lake Victoria · Mt. Kilimanjaro 19,341 ft. (5,895 m) · INDIAN OCEAN · Sumatra · Borneo · Sulawesi (Celebes) · New Guinea · EQUATOR
CONGO BASIN · Lake Tanganyika · KATANGA PLATEAU · Lake Malawi · Java · Cape York Pen. · Coral Sea · Fiji Is.
ATLANTIC OCEAN · Mozambique Channel · Madagascar · Great Sandy Desert · GREAT DIVIDING RANGE · New Caledonia
Kalahari Desert · TROPIC OF CAPRICORN · WESTERN PLATEAU · AUSTRALIA · Great Victoria Desert · Mt. Kosciusko 7,310 ft. (2,228 m) · Tasman Sea · North Island
Cape of Good Hope · Kerguelen Is. · Tasmania · South Island
PRIME MERIDIAN · SOUTHERN OCEAN
ANTARCTIC CIRCLE
Queen Maud Land · Wilkes Land · ANTARCTICA

Compass rose: N W E S

South Polar Region

SOUTHERN OCEAN (PACIFIC) · Cape Horn · Drake Passage
Siple I. · Amundsen Sea · Thurston I. · Bellingshausen Sea · South Shetland Is.
Scott Island · Ross Sea · ROCKEFELLER PLATEAU · Marie Byrd Land · Ellsworth Land · ELLSWORTH MTS. · Alexander I. · Antarctic Peninsula
Cape Adare · Roosevelt I. · Ross Ice Shelf · Vinson Massif 16,066 ft. (4,897 m) · Ronne Ice Shelf · South Orkney Is.
Balleny Is. · McMurdo Sound · Ross I. · PRINCE ALBERT MTS. · QUEEN MAUD MTS. · PENSACOLA MTS. · Berkner I. · Weddell Sea
TRANSANTARCTIC MOUNTAINS · South Pole · Filchner Ice Shelf · Riiser-Larsen Ice Shelf · SOUTHERN OCEAN (ATLANTIC)
ANTARCTICA · Fimbul Ice Shelf · PRIME MERIDIAN
Wilkes Land · Queen Maud Land · ANTARCTIC CIRCLE
Cape Poinsett · AMERICAN HIGHLAND · PRINCE CHARLES MTS. · Amery Ice Shelf · Enderby Land
Shackleton Ice Shelf · West Ice Shelf · Davis Sea · Prydz Bay · SOUTHERN OCEAN (INDIAN)

Scale: 0 — 500 — 1,000 mi / 0 — 500 — 1,000 km

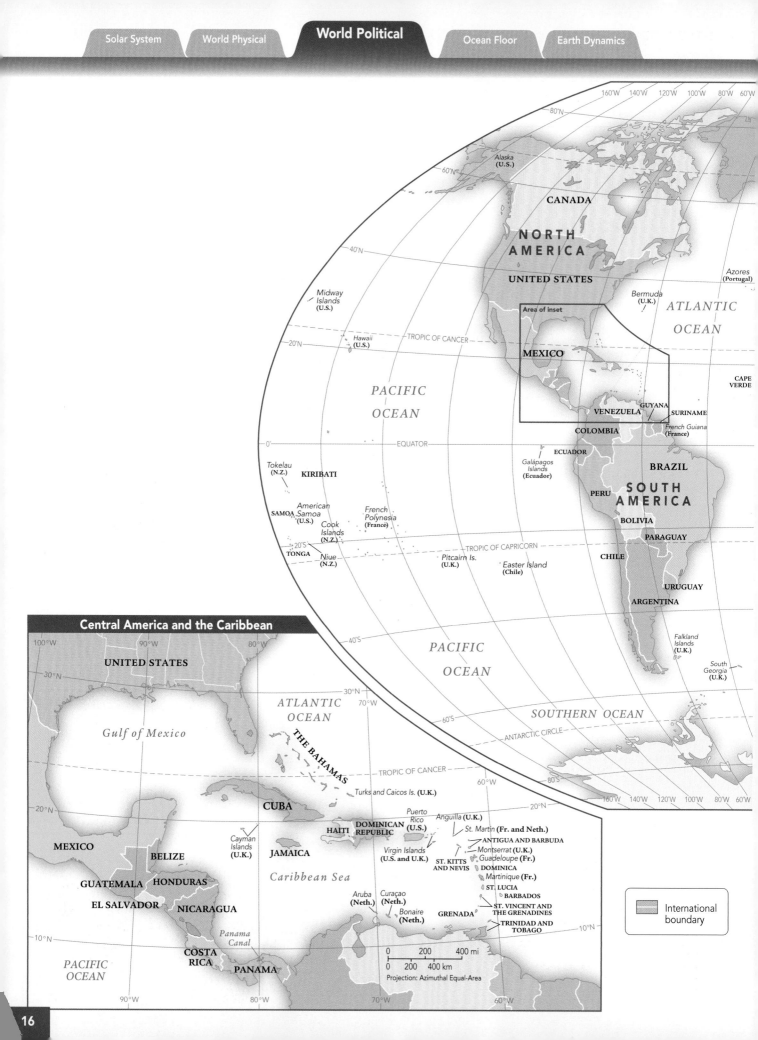

160°W 140°W 120°W 100°W 80°W 60°W

80°N

Alaska (U.S.)

60°N

CANADA

NORTH AMERICA

40°N

UNITED STATES

Midway Islands (U.S.)

Bermuda (U.K.)

ATLANTIC OCEAN

Azores (Portugal)

Area of inset

20°N   *Hawaii (U.S.)*   TROPIC OF CANCER

MEXICO

CAPE VERDE

PACIFIC OCEAN

VENEZUELA **GUYANA** **SURINAME**

French Guiana (France)

COLOMBIA

0°   EQUATOR

ECUADOR

Tokelau (N.Z.)   **KIRIBATI**

Galápagos Islands (Ecuador)

BRAZIL

SOUTH AMERICA

PERU

American Samoa (U.S.)

SAMOA   *Cook Islands (N.Z.)*   *French Polynesia (France)*

BOLIVIA

PARAGUAY

20°S

TONGA   *Niue (N.Z.)*   TROPIC OF CAPRICORN   *Pitcairn Is. (U.K.)*   *Easter Island (Chile)*

CHILE

URUGUAY

ARGENTINA

Falkland Islands (U.K.)

40°S   **PACIFIC OCEAN**

South Georgia (U.K.)

60°S   **SOUTHERN OCEAN**

ANTARCTIC CIRCLE

80°S

160°W 140°W 120°W 100°W 80°W 60°W

Central America and the Caribbean

100°W   90°W   80°W

30°N   **UNITED STATES**

ATLANTIC OCEAN

Gulf of Mexico

30°N   70°W

THE BAHAMAS

TROPIC OF CANCER

Turks and Caicos Is. (U.K.)

20°N   **CUBA**

Puerto Rico (U.S.)   *Anguilla (U.K.)*

20°N

St. Martin (Fr. and Neth.)

ANTIGUA AND BARBUDA

Cayman Islands (U.K.)   **HAITI**   **DOMINICAN REPUBLIC**

Montserrat (U.K.)

MEXICO   **JAMAICA**   *Virgin Islands (U.S. and U.K.)*   *Guadeloupe (Fr.)*

ST. KITTS AND NEVIS   **DOMINICA**

BELIZE   *Caribbean Sea*   *Martinique (Fr.)*

GUATEMALA   **HONDURAS**   **ST. LUCIA**

BARBADOS

EL SALVADOR   **NICARAGUA**   *Aruba (Neth.)*   *Curaçao (Neth.)*

ST. VINCENT AND THE GRENADINES

Bonaire (Neth.)   **GRENADA**

TRINIDAD AND TOBAGO

10°N   *Panama Canal*

COSTA RICA   **PANAMA**

10°N

PACIFIC OCEAN

90°W   80°W   70°W   60°W

0   200   400 mi

0   200   400 km

Projection: Azimuthal Equal-Area

International boundary

16

ARCTIC OCEAN

Greenland (Denmark)

ICELAND

Area of inset

EUROPE

RUSSIA

ASIA

KAZAKHSTAN

MONGOLIA

NORTH KOREA

SOUTH KOREA

JAPAN

PACIFIC OCEAN

GEORGIA
ARMENIA
AZERBAIJAN
TURKEY
TURKMENISTAN
CYPRUS
LEBANON
ISRAEL
SYRIA
IRAQ

UZBEKISTAN
KYRGYZSTAN
TAJIKISTAN

CHINA

AFGHANISTAN

IRAN

Canary Is. (Spain)

MOROCCO

TUNISIA

ALGERIA

LIBYA

EGYPT

Western Sahara (Morocco)

JORDAN
KUWAIT
BAHRAIN
QATAR
SAUDI ARABIA
U.A.E.
OMAN

PAKISTAN

BHUTAN
NEPAL

BANGLADESH

INDIA

MYANMAR (BURMA)

LAOS

TAIWAN

Northern Mariana Islands (U.S.)

Guam (U.S.)

MARSHALL ISLANDS

MAURITANIA

MALI

NIGER

CHAD

SUDAN

ERITREA

YEMEN

DJIBOUTI

THAILAND
CAMBODIA

VIETNAM

PHILIPPINES

SENEGAL
BURKINA FASO
GUINEA
SIERRA LEONE
LIBERIA
IVORY COAST
BENIN
NIGERIA

AFRICA

CENTRAL AFRICAN REPUBLIC

ETHIOPIA

SOMALIA

SRI LANKA

BRUNEI

PALAU

FEDERATED STATES OF MICRONESIA

GHANA
TOGO
GUINEA-BISSAU
EQ. GUINEA
CAMEROON
GABON
REP. CONGO

UGANDA
RWANDA
KENYA

MALDIVES

MALAYSIA

GAMBIA

SÃO TOMÉ AND PRÍNCIPE

DEM. REP. CONGO

BURUNDI

SEYCHELLES

SINGAPORE

INDONESIA

PAPUA NEW GUINEA

NAURU

KIRIBATI

Cabinda (Angola)

TANZANIA

INDIAN OCEAN

EAST TIMOR

TUVALU

ANGOLA

ZAMBIA

MALAWI

MOZAMBIQUE

COMOROS

MADAGASCAR

SOLOMON ISLANDS

VANUATU

NAMIBIA

ZIMBABWE

BOTSWANA

MAURITIUS

Réunion (France)

FIJI

New Caledonia (France)

ATLANTIC OCEAN

SOUTH AFRICA

SWAZILAND

LESOTHO

AUSTRALIA

N W E S

NEW ZEALAND

Kerguelen Islands (France)

0   1,000   2,000 mi
0   1,000   2,000 km
Scale accurate at the Equator
Projection: Winkel

SOUTHERN OCEAN

ANTARCTICA

40°W 20°W 0° 20°E 40°E 60°E 80°E 100°E 120°E 140°E 160°E

Europe

FINLAND

NORWAY

SWEDEN

ESTONIA

RUSSIA

LATVIA

LITHUANIA

Kaliningrad (Russia)

BELARUS

UNITED KINGDOM

IRELAND

North Sea

DENMARK

POLAND

NETHERLANDS

BELGIUM

GERMANY

UKRAINE

CZECH REPUBLIC

SLOVAKIA

MOLDOVA

ATLANTIC OCEAN

LUXEMBOURG

LIECHTENSTEIN

SWITZERLAND

AUSTRIA HUNGARY

SLOVENIA

ROMANIA

FRANCE

CROATIA

SAN MARINO

BOSNIA AND HERZEGOVINA

SERBIA

BULGARIA

Black Sea

0   200   400 mi
0   200   400 km
Projection: Azimuthal Equal-Area

MONACO

Corsica (Fr.)

ITALY

MONTE-NEGRO

KOSOVO

MACEDONIA

ALBANIA

TURKEY

ANDORRA

PORTUGAL

SPAIN

Balearic Islands (Sp.)

Sardinia (It.)

VATICAN CITY

Adriatic Sea

GREECE

Gibraltar (U.K.)

Mediterranean Sea

Sicily (It.)

MALTA

Crete (Gr.)

Abbreviations

DEM. REP. CONGO	DEMOCRATIC REPUBLIC OF THE CONGO
EQ. GUINEA	EQUATORIAL GUINEA
FR.	FRANCE
GR.	GREECE
IT.	ITALY
NETH.	NETHERLANDS
N.Z.	NEW ZEALAND
REP. CONGO	REPUBLIC OF THE CONGO
SP.	SPAIN
U.A.E.	UNITED ARAB EMIRATES
U.K.	UNITED KINGDOM
U.S.	UNITED STATES

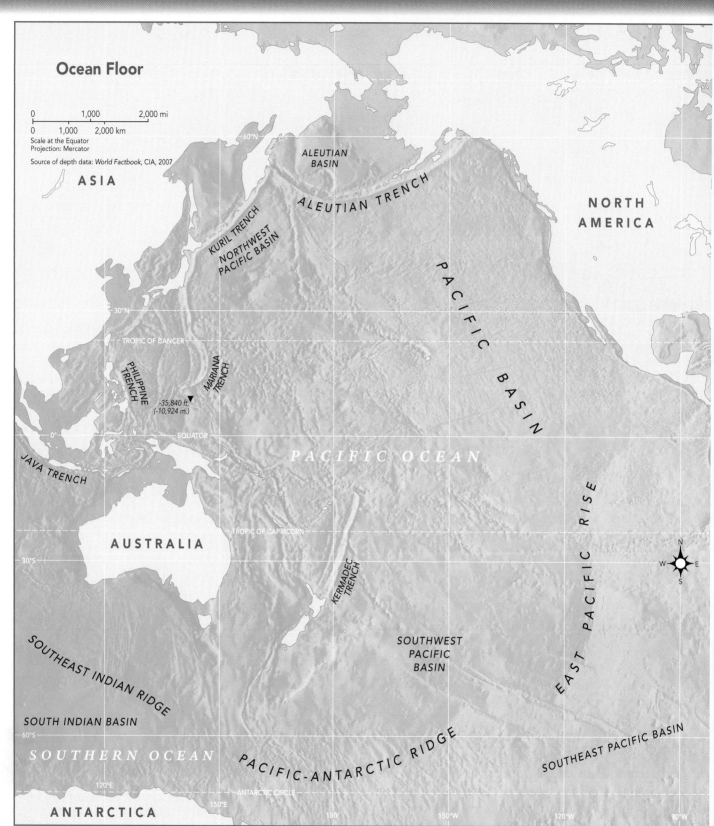

Ocean Floor

0   1,000   2,000 mi
0   1,000   2,000 km
Scale at the Equator
Projection: Mercator

Source of depth data: *World Factbook*, CIA, 2007

ASIA

60°N

ALEUTIAN BASIN

ALEUTIAN TRENCH

NORTH AMERICA

KURIL TRENCH

NORTHWEST PACIFIC BASIN

30°N

PACIFIC BASIN

TROPIC OF CANCER

PHILIPPINE TRENCH

MARIANA TRENCH

-35,840 ft. (-10,924 m.)

0°

EQUATOR

PACIFIC OCEAN

JAVA TRENCH

N
W · E
S

TROPIC OF CAPRICORN

AUSTRALIA

KERMADEC TRENCH

EAST PACIFIC RISE

30°S

SOUTHWEST PACIFIC BASIN

SOUTHEAST INDIAN RIDGE

SOUTH INDIAN BASIN

60°S

SOUTHERN OCEAN

PACIFIC-ANTARCTIC RIDGE

SOUTHEAST PACIFIC BASIN

120°E

150°E

ANTARCTIC CIRCLE

180°

150°W

120°W

90°W

ANTARCTICA

Surrounding most of the continents are gently sloping areas called continental shelves, which reach depths of about 650 ft. (200 m). At the edges of the continental shelves lie steeper continental slopes leading down to the deep ocean basin, or abyss. The abyss contains many of the same features we see on land, including plains, mountains ranges (ridges), isolated mountains (known as sea mounts or guyots), and trenches. The Mid-Ocean Ridge system marks the areas where crustal plates are moving apart, and is very active geologically, as molten rock rises and erupts to create new crust. Earthquakes and volcanoes are common along many undersea trenches and ridges.

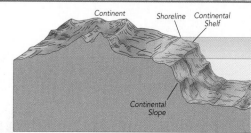

Continent   Shoreline   Continental Shelf

Continental Slope

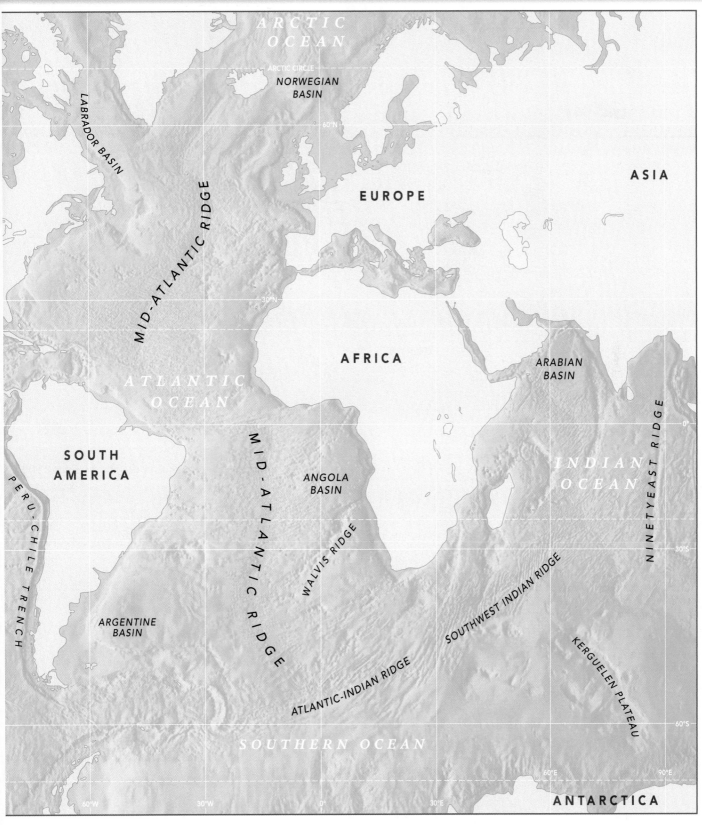

ARCTIC OCEAN

ARCTIC CIRCLE

NORWEGIAN BASIN

60°N

LABRADOR BASIN

ASIA

EUROPE

30°N

MID-ATLANTIC RIDGE

AFRICA

ARABIAN BASIN

ATLANTIC OCEAN

0°

SOUTH AMERICA

INDIAN OCEAN

MID-ATLANTIC RIDGE

ANGOLA BASIN

NINETYEAST RIDGE

PERU-CHILE TRENCH

WALVIS RIDGE

30°S

ARGENTINE BASIN

SOUTHWEST INDIAN RIDGE

KERGUELEN PLATEAU

ATLANTIC-INDIAN RIDGE

60°S

SOUTHERN OCEAN

60°W 30°W 0° 30°E 60°E 90°E

ANTARCTICA

Undersea Volcanoes

Mid-Ocean Ridge

Oceanic Trench

Continent

Abyssal Plain

Guyots

Plate Boundaries and Earthquakes

- 🔲 Earthquake region
- • Location of major earthquake
- 〜 Plate boundary
- → Direction of plate movement

The movement of Earth's crustal plates causes the phenomena known as earthquakes. The surface of the Earth actually moves or quakes. An **earthquake** can have the destructive energy of an atomic bomb. However, thousands of earthquakes occur each day all over the world without most people realizing it.

The majority of earthquakes occur along a **fault.** A fault is usually a weak or broken area in the rocks beneath the surface of the Earth, but some, like the *San Andreas Fault* in California, can be seen on the surface. See pages 58–59 to learn more about faults.

The Richter Scale measures the energy of an earthquake. This measurement is obtained from the focus, or hypocenter, the spot where the first break in the rock layers occurs. The spot on the surface of the Earth, directly above the focus and nearest to the source of energy is called the epicenter.

Earthquake damage is caused by this energy, called seismic energy, moving through the rocks or along the surface. Many geographic factors, both physical and human, determine how much damage is done by these seismic waves of energy.

Largest Earthquakes in the World Since 1900

Date	Location	Richter Scale Magnitude
May 22, 1960	Arauco, Chile	9.5
March 27, 1964	Prince William Sound, Alaska	9.2
Dec. 26, 2004	off west coast of Sumatra, Indonesia	9.0
Nov. 4, 1952	Kamchatka, Russia	9.0
Jan. 31, 1906	off coast of Ecuador	8.8
March 28, 2005	northern Sumatra, Indonesia	8.7
Feb. 4, 1965	Rat Islands, Alaska	8.7
March 9, 1957	Andreanof Islands, Alaska	8.6
Aug. 15, 1950	Assam, India	8.6
April 4, 1905	Kangra, India	8.6
Oct. 13, 1963	Kuril Islands, Russia	8.5
Feb. 1, 1938	Banda Sea, Indonesia	8.5
Nov. 11, 1922	border of Argentina-Chile	8.5

Other Significant Earthquakes Since 1900

Date	Location	Richter Scale Magnitude
Sept. 19, 1985	Mexico City, Mexico	8.0
May 12, 2008	eastern Sichuan, China	7.9
May 22, 1927	Tsinghai, China	7.9
Sept. 1, 1923	Kanto, Japan	7.9
Dec. 16, 1920	Gansu, China	7.8
April 18, 1906	San Francisco, California	7.8
Jan. 26, 2001	Ahmadabad, India	7.7
June 20, 1990	western Iran, near Qazvin	7.7
July 27, 1976	Tangshan, China	7.5
May 30, 1935	Quetta, Pakistan	7.5
Oct. 5, 1948	Ashgabat, Turkmenistan	7.3

Source: National Earthquake Information Center, U.S.G.S

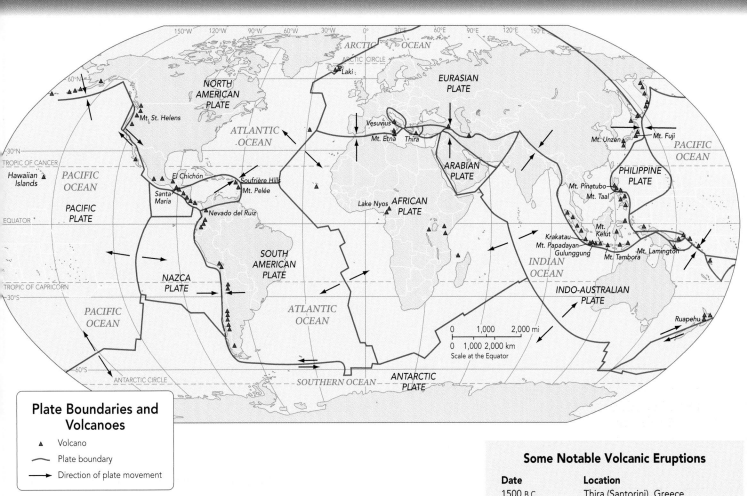

Plate Boundaries and Volcanoes

▲ Volcano

⌒ Plate boundary

→ Direction of plate movement

A **volcano** is an opening in the Earth's crust often capped by a cone-shaped hill or mountain formed from erupted lava and ash.

Volcanoes are associated with plate boundaries. Powerful forces occurring far beneath the surface at the edges of plates cause rock to melt and, at the same time, open cracks in the crust. An eruption occurs when magma (melted rock) flows, and many times explodes, through a weakness, such as a crack in the Earth's crust. Once magma is flowing on the Earth's surface it is called lava. Flowing lava can be several thousand degrees Fahrenheit.

In a few cases, volcanoes exist without being near the edge of a plate. In these cases, such as the Hawaiian Islands, a powerful and persistent flow of magma has broken through the crust.

Some Notable Volcanic Eruptions

Date	Location
1500 B.C.	Thira (Santorini), Greece
Aug. 24, A.D. 79	Vesuvius, Italy
1169	Mt. Etna, Italy
1586	Mt. Kelut, Java, Indonesia
Dec. 15, 1631	Vesuvius, Italy
March–July, 1669	Mt. Etna, Italy
Aug. 12, 1772	Mt. Papandayan, Java, Indonesia
June 8, 1783	Laki, Iceland
May 21, 1792	Mt. Unzen, Japan
Apr. 10–12, 1815	Mt. Tambora, Sumbawa, Indonesia
Oct. 8, 1822	Galunggung, Java, Indonesia
Aug. 26–28, 1883	Krakatau, Indonesia
Apr. 24, 1902	Santa Maria, Guatemala
May 8, 1902	Mt. Pelée, Martinique
Jan. 30, 1911	Mt. Taal, Philippines
May 19, 1919	Mt. Kelut, Java, Indonesia
Jan. 17–21, 1951	Mt. Lamington, New Guinea
May 18, 1980	Mt. St. Helens, United States
Mar. 28, 1982	El Chichon, Mexico
Nov. 13, 1985	Nevado del Ruiz, Colombia
Aug. 21, 1986	Lake Nyos, Cameroon
June 15, 1991	Mt. Pinatubo, Philippines
June–Sept., 1997	Soufrière Hills, Montserrat

Crater

Branch Pipe

Buried Dome

Lava Flow

Fissure Flows

Pyroclastic Layers

Sill

Magma Chamber

237 Million Years Ago

SIBERIA

ASIA

URAL MOUNTAINS

Greenland

EUROPE

PALEO-TETHYS
OCEAN

CHINA

NORTH
AMERICA

SPAIN

ITALY

TURKEY

IRAN

TIBET

PANTHALASSIC

OCEAN

PANGAEA

AFRICA

TETHYS OCEAN

ARABIA

SOUTH
AMERICA

MADAGASCAR

INDIA

NEW
GUINEA

AUSTRALIA

ANDES
MOUNTAINS

GONDWANA

ANTARCTICA

This peculiar—to our eyes—arrangement of continents with its unfamiliar oceans and seas, mountains and plains, and peninsulas and islands reminds us that the dinosaurs lived in a far different landscape than our own. As the last dinosaurs receded into memory, the future Atlantic Ocean and Mediterranean Sea were becoming more substantial

and recognizable, and the continents, except for Australia and Antarctica, were nearing their present latitudes. Within the last 65 million years, most continents nestled unhurriedly into their current positions. However, the Indian sub-continent "sprinted" north, crashing into Asia and bulldozing up the Himalayas, earth's loftiest mountain range.

237

94

65

Age of Dinosaurs

300   250   200   150   100

Millions of Years Ago

DECEMBER						
1	2	3	4	5	6	7
8	9	10	11	12	13	14
15	16	17	18	19	20	21
22	23	24	25	26	27	28
29	30	31	JANUARY			

NOVEMBER
OCTOBER
SEPTEMBER

94 Million Years Ago

ARCTIC OCEAN

ROCKY MOUNTAINS

NORTH AMERICA

Greenland

EUROPE

ASIA

ITALY   TURKEY

PHILIPPINES

PACIFIC OCEAN

ATLANTIC OCEAN

SAUDI ARABIA

PACIFIC OCEAN

SOUTH AMERICA

AFRICA

TETHYS OCEAN

NEW GUINEA

INDIA

MADAGASCAR

AUSTRALIA

ANTARCTICA

The highly controversial theory of Continental Drift was proposed in 1915 by Alfred Wegener to explain both geologic and fossil discoveries. Although supported by strong data and seemingly obvious visual evidence—most notably, the close fit of the coastlines of Africa and South America—the theory was rejected by other scientists. By the 1960s, further studies, especially those that discovered that some rocks contained a record of the alignment of the Earth's magnetic field, resurrected the theory, which was redefined under the term Plate Tectonics. Few scientists now dispute its general premise, that continental and oceanic plates move atop a layer of hot and semi-solid rock below them, although many details, particularly the causes and mechanics of the motion, are still not well understood.

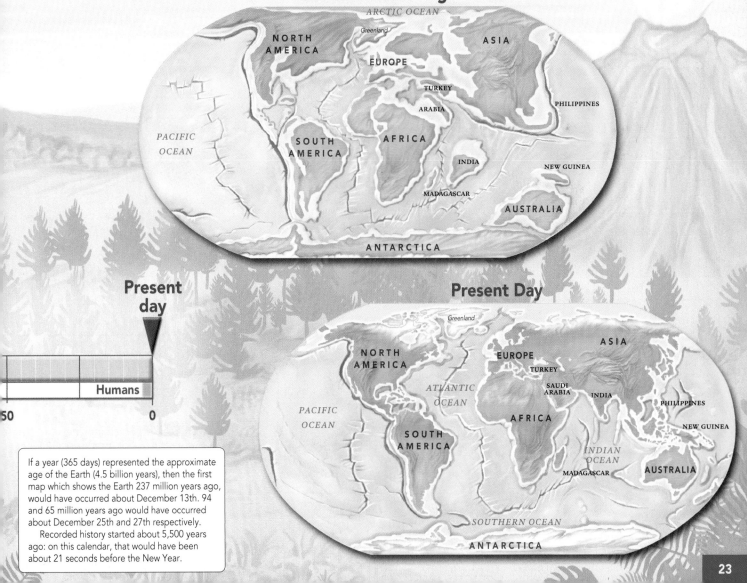

65 Million Years Ago

ARCTIC OCEAN

NORTH AMERICA

Greenland

EUROPE

ASIA

TURKEY

PHILIPPINES

ARABIA

PACIFIC OCEAN

SOUTH AMERICA

AFRICA

INDIA

NEW GUINEA

MADAGASCAR

AUSTRALIA

ANTARCTICA

Present day

Humans

50   0

Present Day

Greenland

NORTH AMERICA

EUROPE

ASIA

TURKEY

SAUDI ARABIA

INDIA

ATLANTIC OCEAN

PHILIPPINES

PACIFIC OCEAN

AFRICA

NEW GUINEA

SOUTH AMERICA

INDIAN OCEAN

AUSTRALIA

MADAGASCAR

SOUTHERN OCEAN

ANTARCTICA

If a year (365 days) represented the approximate age of the Earth (4.5 billion years), then the first map which shows the Earth 237 million years ago, would have occurred about December 13th. 94 and 65 million years ago would have occurred about December 25th and 27th respectively.

Recorded history started about 5,500 years ago: on this calendar, that would have been about 21 seconds before the New Year.

Climate

- Tropical wet
- Tropical wet and dry
- Arid
- Semiarid
- Mediterranean
- Humid subtropical
- Marine
- Humid continental
- Subarctic
- Tundra
- Icecap
- Highland

💧 Highest average annual precipitation

💧 Lowest average annual preciptation

🌡 Highest recorded temperature

🌡 Lowest recorded temperature

Major Ocean Currents

← Cool currents

← Warm currents

NORTH AMERICA

Fairbanks
Iqaluit
Nuuk
Edmonton
Vancouver
Toronto
St. John's
Denver
Chicago
San Francisco
New York City
Phoenix
Atlanta
Miami
Mexico City
San Juan

ATLANTIC OCEAN

PACIFIC OCEAN

Caracas
Bogotá
Lima

SOUTH AMERICA

Recife

Arica 0.03" (0.08 cm)

São Paulo
Rio de Janeiro
Santiago
Buenos Aires

Punta Arenas

SOUTHERN OCEAN

80°N
60°N
40°N
TROPIC OF CANCER
20°N
0° EQUATOR
20°S
TROPIC OF CAPRICORN
40°S
60°S
ANTARCTIC CIRCLE
80°S

160°W 140°W 120°W 100°W 80°W 60°W 40°W

Arid

Highland

Humid continental

Icecap

Marine

Mediterranean

Semiarid

ARCTIC OCEAN

80°N

20°W   0°   20°E   40°E   60°E   80°E   100°E   120°E   140°E   160°E

Tromsø
Murmansk
ARCTIC CIRCLE
Yakutsk
Reykjavík
60°N
Stockholm
London
Moscow
Novosibirsk
EUROPE
Paris
ASIA
Rome
Istanbul
40°N
Beijing
Seoul
Tehran
Kabul
Tokyo
Casablanca
Baghdad
New Delhi
El Azizia 136°F
(58°C)
Cairo
Shanghai
PACIFIC OCEAN
Riyadh
Karachi
Mawsynram 467" (1,186 cm)
TROPIC OF CANCER
Dakar
Kolkata
(Calcutta)
Hong Kong
20°N
Mumbai
(Bombay)
AFRICA
Bangkok
Manila
Lagos
Addis Ababa
Ho Chi Minh
City
0°
Nairobi
Kinshasa
INDIAN OCEAN
Jakarta
Brisbane
20°S
Johannesburg
TROPIC OF CAPRICORN
AUSTRALIA
Perth
Sydney
Cape
Town
Melbourne
Auckland
40°S

0   1,000   2,000 mi
0   1,000   2,000 km
Scale at the Equator
Projection: Robinson

N
W   E
S

60°S

SOUTHERN OCEAN

Vostok –129°F (–89°C)

ANTARCTICA
80°S

20°W   0°   20°E   40°E   60°E   80°E   100°E   120°E   140°E   160°E

Humid subtropical

Subarctic   Tropical wet   Tropical wet and dry   Tundra

25

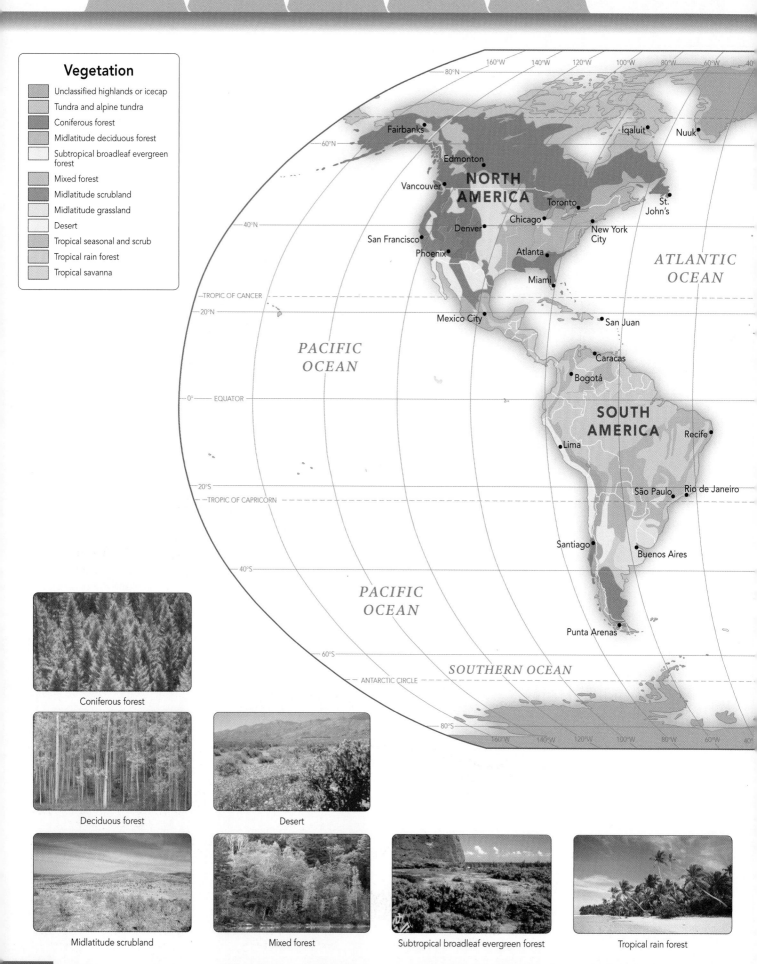

Vegetation

- Unclassified highlands or icecap
- Tundra and alpine tundra
- Coniferous forest
- Midlatitude deciduous forest
- Subtropical broadleaf evergreen forest
- Mixed forest
- Midlatitude scrubland
- Midlatitude grassland
- Desert
- Tropical seasonal and scrub
- Tropical rain forest
- Tropical savanna

Coniferous forest

Deciduous forest

Desert

Midlatitude scrubland

Mixed forest

Subtropical broadleaf evergreen forest

Tropical rain forest

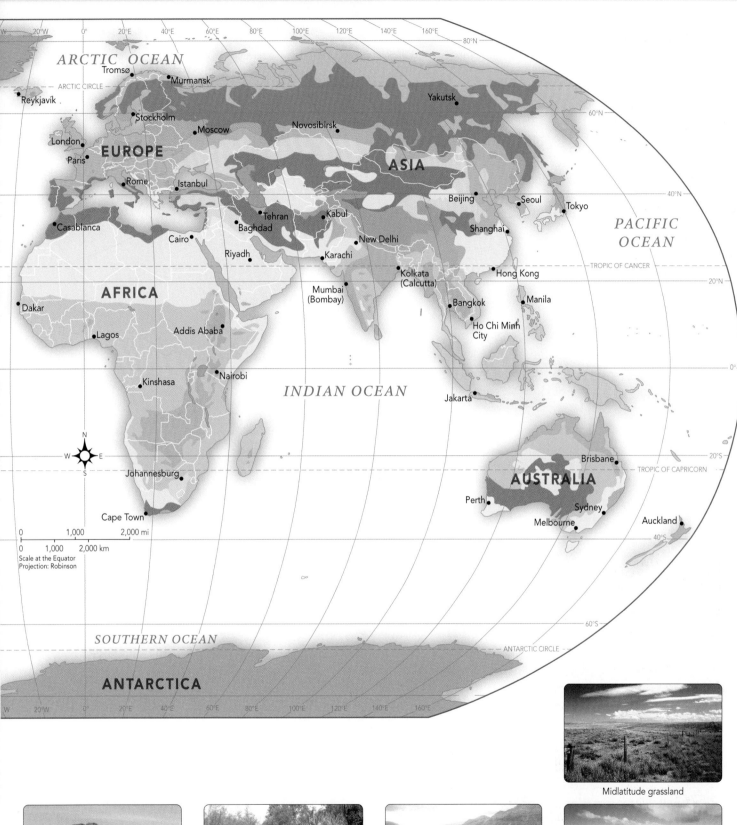

ARCTIC OCEAN

Tromsø
Murmansk
ARCTIC CIRCLE
Reykjavík
Yakutsk
Stockholm
Moscow
Novosibirsk
London
EUROPE
ASIA
Paris
Rome
Istanbul
Beijing
Seoul
Tokyo
PACIFIC OCEAN
Casablanca
Tehran
Kabul
Shanghai
Cairo
Baghdad
New Delhi
Riyadh
Karachi
Hong Kong
TROPIC OF CANCER
Kolkata (Calcutta)
AFRICA
Mumbai (Bombay)
Bangkok
Manila
Dakar
Ho Chi Minh City
Lagos
Addis Ababa
Kinshasa
Nairobi
INDIAN OCEAN
Jakarta
Johannesburg
Brisbane
AUSTRALIA
TROPIC OF CAPRICORN
Cape Town
Perth
Sydney
Melbourne
Auckland

1,000   2,000 mi
1,000   2,000 km
Scale at the Equator
Projection: Robinson

SOUTHERN OCEAN

ANTARCTICA

Tropical savanna

Tropical seasonal and scrub

Tundra and alpine tundra

Midlatitude grassland

Unclassified highlands or icecap

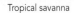

World Forest Cover

Forests help regulate climate by storing huge amounts of carbon dioxide, while providing habitats for countless animal and plant species. Environmentalists have voiced concern over a long-term decrease in forest cover, as forest lands have been cleared for such purposes as farming, logging, mining, and urban expansion.

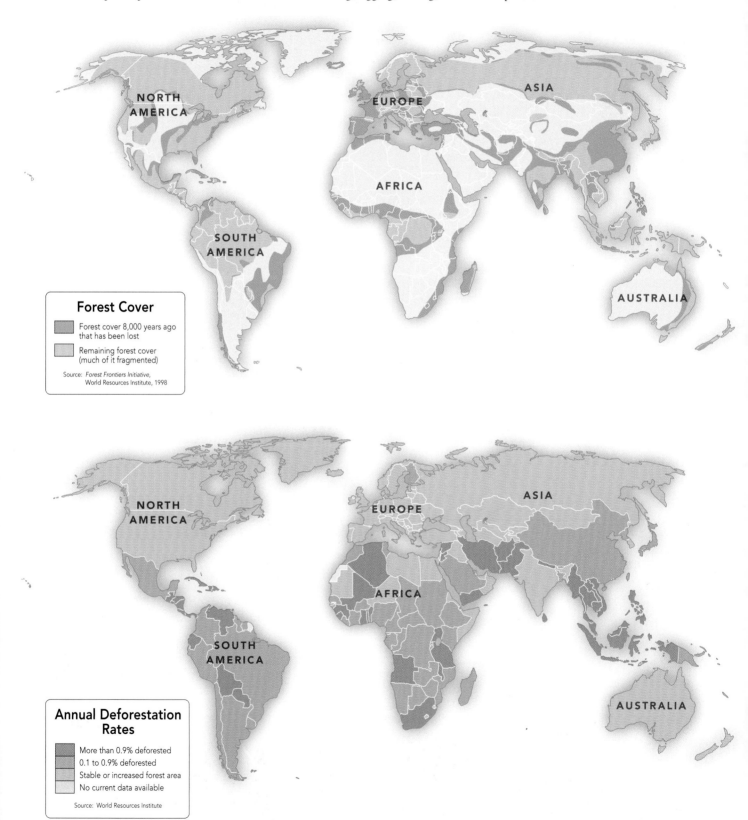

Forest Cover

- Forest cover 8,000 years ago that has been lost
- Remaining forest cover (much of it fragmented)

Source: *Forest Frontiers Initiative,* World Resources Institute, 1998

Annual Deforestation Rates

- More than 0.9% deforested
- 0.1 to 0.9% deforested
- Stable or increased forest area
- No current data available

Source: World Resources Institute

Tropical Rain Forests

Tropical rain forests, found around the Earth within 10 degrees of the Equator, contain more than half of all the world's plants and animal species, besides being home to many indigenous peoples. They are vital to the balance of nature. In the past 40 years alone, about one-fifth of the acreage has been cleared for logging and other purposes. These rain forests, including the major forests pinpointed here, remain under serious threat.

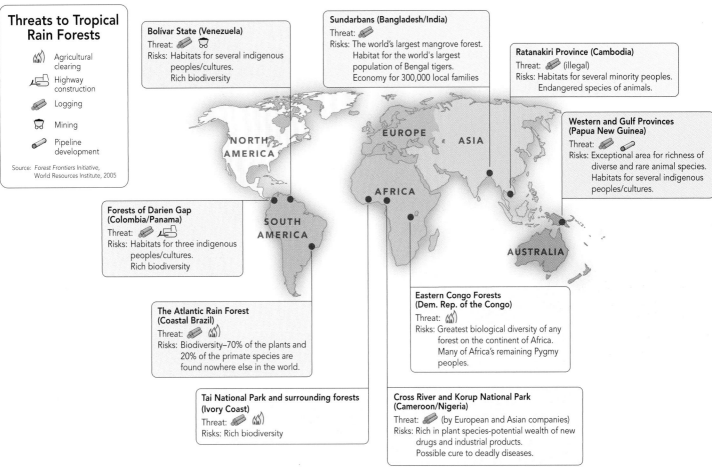

Threats to Tropical Rain Forests

- Agricultural clearing
- Highway construction
- Logging
- Mining
- Pipeline development

Source: *Forest Frontiers Initiative, World Resources Institute, 2005*

Bolívar State (Venezuela)
Threat:
Risks: Habitats for several indigenous peoples/cultures. Rich biodiversity

Sundarbans (Bangladesh/India)
Threat:
Risks: The world's largest mangrove forest. Habitat for the world's largest population of Bengal tigers. Economy for 300,000 local families

Ratanakiri Province (Cambodia)
Threat: (illegal)
Risks: Habitats for several minority peoples. Endangered species of animals.

Western and Gulf Provinces (Papua New Guinea)
Threat:
Risks: Exceptional area for richness of diverse and rare animal species. Habitats for several indigenous peoples/cultures.

Forests of Darien Gap (Colombia/Panama)
Threat:
Risks: Habitats for three indigenous peoples/cultures. Rich biodiversity

The Atlantic Rain Forest (Coastal Brazil)
Threat:
Risks: Biodiversity–70% of the plants and 20% of the primate species are found nowhere else in the world.

Eastern Congo Forests (Dem. Rep. of the Congo)
Threat:
Risks: Greatest biological diversity of any forest on the continent of Africa. Many of Africa's remaining Pygmy peoples.

Tai National Park and surrounding forests (Ivory Coast)
Threat:
Risks: Rich biodiversity

Cross River and Korup National Park (Cameroon/Nigeria)
Threat: (by European and Asian companies)
Risks: Rich in plant species-potential wealth of new drugs and industrial products. Possible cure to deadly diseases.

Percentage of Frontier Forest Under Moderate or High Threat of Destruction
(through 2030)

Source: *Forest Frontiers Initiative, World Resources Institute, 1998*

According to the World Resources Institute, only about one-fifth of the Earth's forest cover of 8,000 years ago survives unfragmented, in the large unspoiled tracts it calls *frontier forests*. These forests are big enough to provide stable habitats for a rich diversity of plant and animal species.

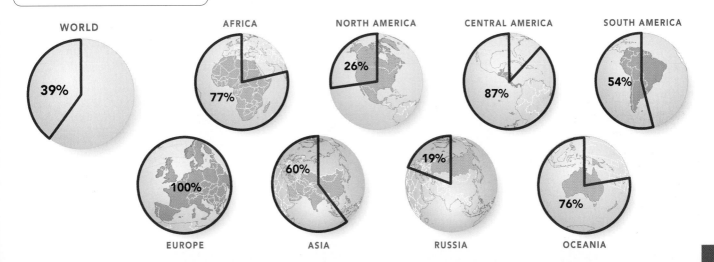

WORLD 39%
AFRICA 77%
NORTH AMERICA 26%
CENTRAL AMERICA 87%
SOUTH AMERICA 54%
EUROPE 100%
ASIA 60%
RUSSIA 19%
OCEANIA 76%

Population Density 2003

Persons per sq. mile	Persons per sq. km
Over 520	Over 200
260 to 519	100 to 199
130 to 259	50 to 99
25 to 129	10 to 49
1 to 24	1 to 9
0	0

● Urban agglomerations with over 10,000,000 inhabitants

World population total as of Sept 9, 2005:
6,465,434,433
(Every day it increases by about 202,419)

Source: International Programs Center,
U.S. Bureau of the Census

Largest Cities (urban agglomerations)

	2000		2015 (projected)
1	Tokyo 26,444,000	1	Tokyo 36,200,000
2	Mexico City 18,131,000	2	Mumbai 22,600,000
3	Mumbai 18,066,000	3	Delhi......... 20,900,000
4	São Paulo 17,755,000	4	Mexico City 20,600,000
5	New York 16,640,000	5	São Paulo 20,000,000
6	Lagos 13,427,000	6	New York...... 19,700,000
7	Los Angeles 13,140,000	7	Dhaka 17,900,000
8	Kolkata 12,918,000	8	Jakarta 17,500,000
9	Shanghai....... 12,887,000	9	Kolkata 16,800,000
10	Buenos Aires ... 12,560,000	10	Lagos 17,000,000
11	Dhaka 12,317,000	11	Karachi........ 16,200,000
12	Karachi 11,794,000	12	Buenos Aires ... 14,600,000
13	Delhi.......... 11,695,000	13	Los Angeles.... 12,900,000
14	Jakarta 11,018,000	14	Shanghai....... 12,700,000
15	Osaka......... 11,013,000	15	Manila 12,600,000

Source: United Nations Population Division, 2003

New York City
Los Angeles
Mexico City
São Paulo
Rio de Janeiro
Buenos Aires

Population Projections by Continent

YEAR
2006 2025 2050

Source: U.S. Bureau of the Census,
International Data Division

ARCTIC OCEAN

NORTH AMERICA
480,545,000
618,802,000
731,814,000

PACIFIC OCEAN

ATLANTIC OCEAN

EUROPE*
644,922,000
711,526,000
728,982,000

ASIA
3,688,072,000
4,753,366,000
5,331,884,000

PACIFIC OCEAN

AFRICA
1,981,116,000
1,327,429,000
805,243,000

SOUTH AMERICA
346,504,000
447,181,000
490,094,000

Equator

ATLANTIC OCEAN

INDIAN OCEAN

AUSTRALIA & PACIFIC IS.
30,795,000
39,685,000
44,545,000

*Including Russia

SOUTHERN OCEAN

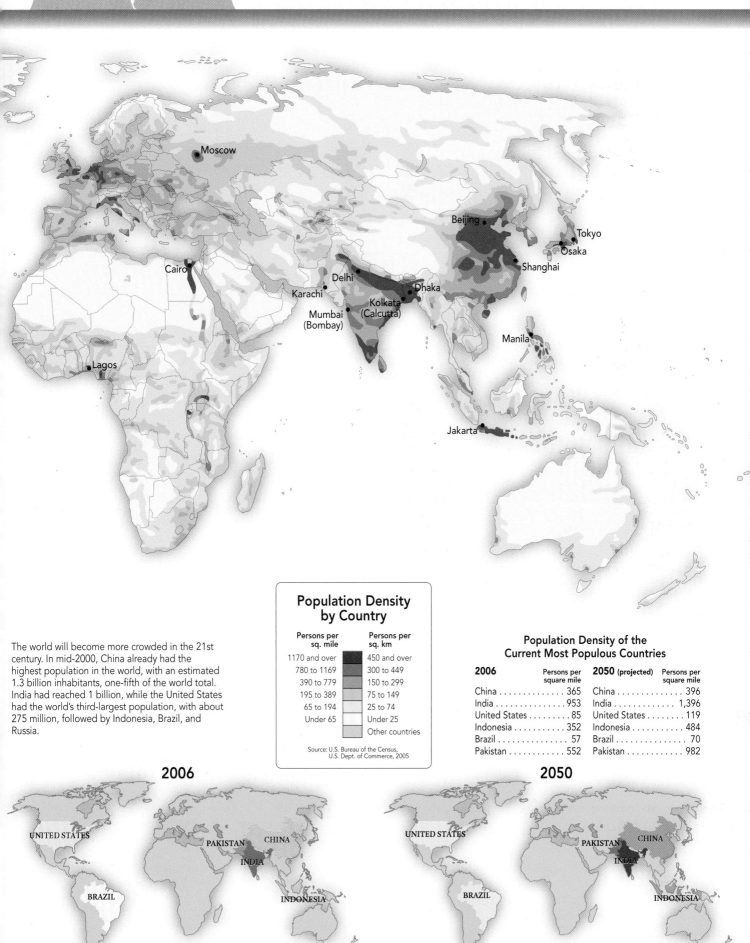

Population Density by Country

Persons per sq. mile	Persons per sq. km
1170 and over	450 and over
780 to 1169	300 to 449
390 to 779	150 to 299
195 to 389	75 to 149
65 to 194	25 to 74
Under 65	Under 25
	Other countries

Source: U.S. Bureau of the Census,
U.S. Dept. of Commerce, 2005

The world will become more crowded in the 21st century. In mid-2000, China already had the highest population in the world, with an estimated 1.3 billion inhabitants, one-fifth of the world total. India had reached 1 billion, while the United States had the world's third-largest population, with about 275 million, followed by Indonesia, Brazil, and Russia.

Population Density of the Current Most Populous Countries

2006	Persons per square mile	2050 (projected)	Persons per square mile
China	365	China	396
India	953	India	1,396
United States	85	United States	119
Indonesia	352	Indonesia	484
Brazil	57	Brazil	70
Pakistan	552	Pakistan	982

2006

2050

Life Expectancy

Life expectancy at birth is a common measure of the number of years a person may expect to live. There are many factors, such as nutrition, sanitation, health and medical services, that contribute to helping people live longer.

As some of the above factors improve in the develop-ing countries, life expectancy there should increase. But most of sub-Saharan Africa will have less than average life expectancies.

Although it is not included here, females almost always have a longer life expectancy than males.

2000

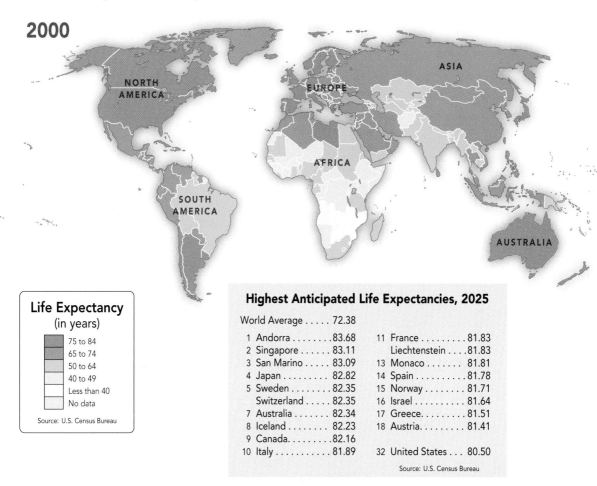

Life Expectancy
(in years)

- 75 to 84
- 65 to 74
- 50 to 64
- 40 to 49
- Less than 40
- No data

Source: U.S. Census Bureau

Highest Anticipated Life Expectancies, 2025

World Average 72.38

1 Andorra 83.68	11 France 81.83
2 Singapore 83.11	Liechtenstein 81.83
3 San Marino 83.09	13 Monaco 81.81
4 Japan 82.82	14 Spain 81.78
5 Sweden 82.35	15 Norway 81.71
Switzerland 82.35	16 Israel 81.64
7 Australia 82.34	17 Greece. 81.51
8 Iceland 82.23	18 Austria. 81.41
9 Canada. 82.16	
10 Italy 81.89	32 United States . . . 80.50

Source: U.S. Census Bureau

2025

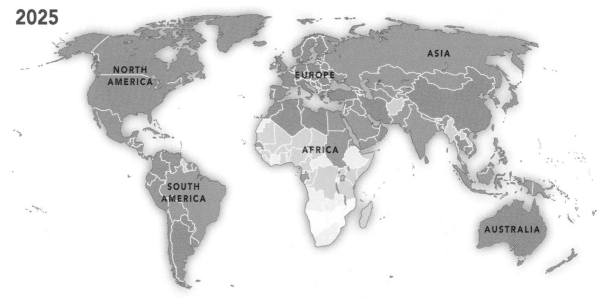

Youthful Population

A country with a youthful population often reflects a high birthrate and a short life expectancy. The youthful component of a country's population should be the healthiest and the most energetic. In countries where there is a good system of education, the standards of living can only benefit from a large, educated youthful population. Furthermore, large numbers of young workers offer a means for provid-ing financial and social support for the older members of the population. Unfortunately, a country's economic and physical resources may not be able to absorb a ballooning youthful population. A lack of opportunity in rural regions encourages migration to over-crowded cities where, in turn, a lack of jobs or space in schools leads to swelling numbers of unemployed.

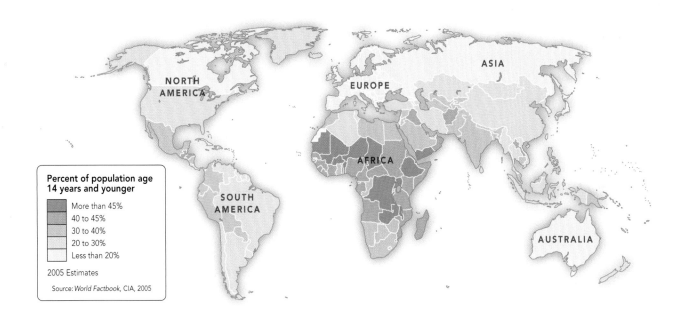

Percent of population age 14 years and younger

- More than 45%
- 40 to 45%
- 30 to 40%
- 20 to 30%
- Less than 20%

2005 Estimates

Source: *World Factbook*, CIA, 2005

Food and Nutrition

There has been a general trend towards better nutrition, but sub-Saharan Africa remains a problem area: increasing numbers of people will be suffering from undernutrition.

On a worldwide basis, the food supply seems adequate. Unfortunately the availability of food and the distribution of people don't always match up.

UNITED STATES 3,772
HAITI 2,056
BOLIVIA 2,218
ARGENTINA 3,181
AUSTRIA 3,757
BULGARIA 2,467
ISRAEL 3,562
EGYPT 3,346
AFGHANISTAN 1,539
DEMOCRATIC REPUBLIC OF THE CONGO 1,514
PAPUA NEW GUINEA 2,175
NEW ZEALAND 3,252

Average Daily per Capita Calorie Supply, 1998–2000

Within each continent, the countries with the highest per capita calorie supply are labeled in green, while the countries with the lowest per capital calorie supply are labeled in red.

Source: UN Food and Agriculture Organization

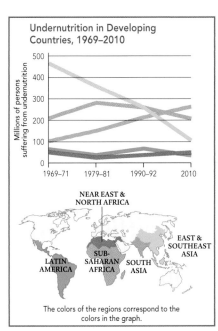

Undernutrition in Developing Countries, 1969–2010

Millions of persons suffering from undernutrition

1969–71   1979–81   1990–92   2010

NEAR EAST & NORTH AFRICA
LATIN AMERICA
SUB-SAHARAN AFRICA
SOUTH ASIA
EAST & SOUTHEAST ASIA

The colors of the regions correspond to the colors in the graph.

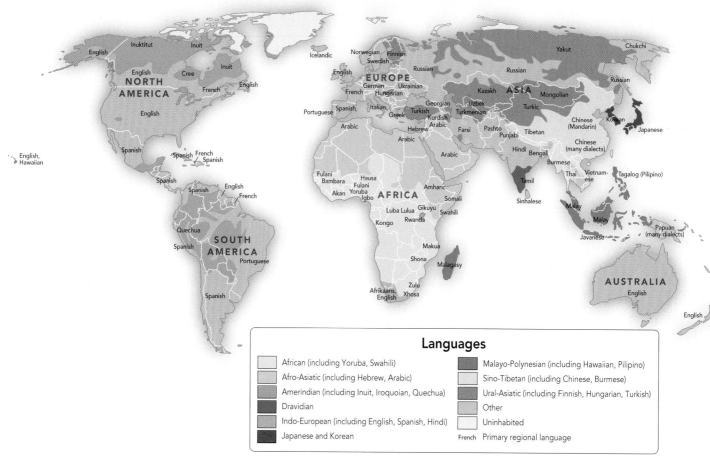

Languages

African (including Yoruba, Swahili)	Malayo-Polynesian (including Hawaiian, Pilipino)
Afro-Asiatic (including Hebrew, Arabic)	Sino-Tibetan (including Chinese, Burmese)
Amerindian (including Inuit, Iroquoian, Quechua)	Ural-Asiatic (including Finnish, Hungarian, Turkish)
Dravidian	Other
Indo-European (including English, Spanish, Hindi)	Uninhabited
Japanese and Korean	French Primary regional language

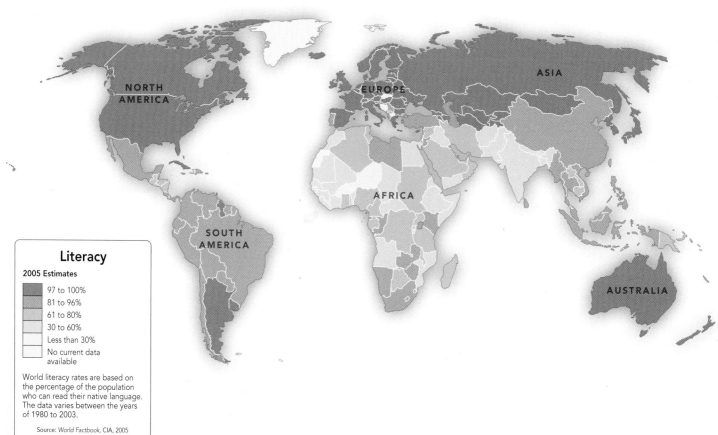

Literacy

2005 Estimates

- 97 to 100%
- 81 to 96%
- 61 to 80%
- 30 to 60%
- Less than 30%
- No current data available

World literacy rates are based on the percentage of the population who can read their native language. The data varies between the years of 1980 to 2003.

Source: *World Factbook*, CIA, 2005

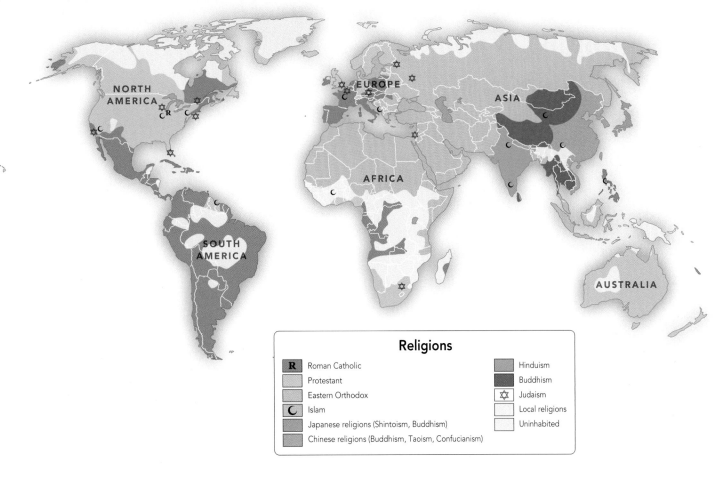

NORTH
AMERICA

EUROPE

ASIA

AFRICA

SOUTH
AMERICA

AUSTRALIA

Religions

R	Roman Catholic			Hinduism
	Protestant			Buddhism
	Eastern Orthodox		✡	Judaism
☾	Islam			Local religions
	Japanese religions (Shintoism, Buddhism)			Uninhabited
	Chinese religions (Buddhism, Taoism, Confucianism)			

Historical Spread of Religions

- Buddhism
- Christianity
- Hinduism
- Islam
- Judaism (Jewish diaspora)

Present-day boundaries

500s
300s
1500s
600s–900s
400s
1300s
1400s
1500s
500s
500s
900s
800s
600s
500s
1200s
1500s
700s
600s
1400s
600s
300s
1800s

Land Use

- Commercial agriculture
- Dairying
- Livestock ranching
- Nomadic herding
- Subsistence agriculture
- Primarily forestland
- Limited agricultural activity
- ● Major manufacturing and trade centers

Shares of the World's GDP 2004

Source: *World Factbook*, CIA, 2005

Rest of the world 32%

United States 21%

India 6%

Japan 7%

China 13%

European Union 21%

The Gross Domestic Product (GDP) is the value of goods and services produced by a political entity in any given period. These values help indicate how well the economy is doing.

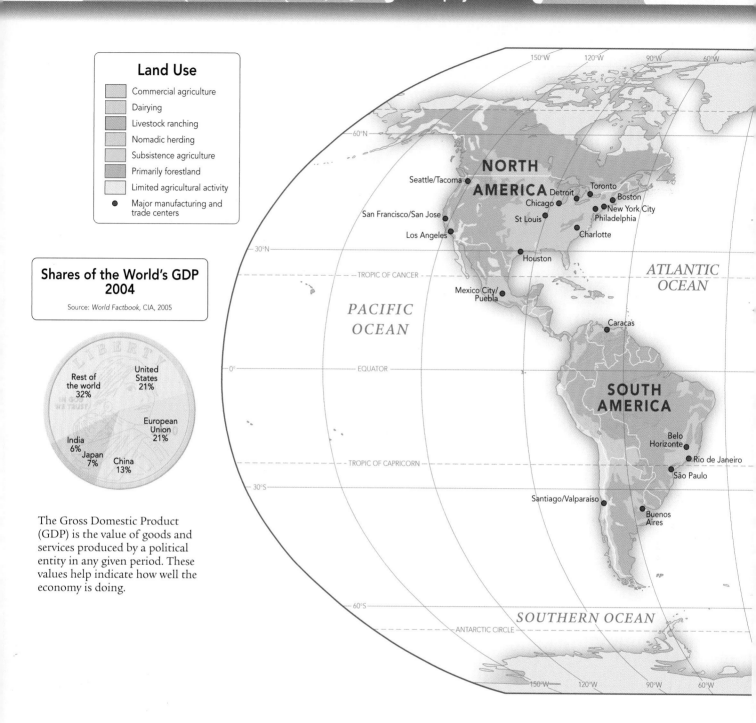

NORTH AMERICA

Seattle/Tacoma

Detroit
Toronto
Boston
Chicago
New York City
St Louis
Philadelphia
San Francisco/San Jose
Charlotte
Los Angeles

Houston

Mexico City/ Puebla

ATLANTIC OCEAN

PACIFIC OCEAN

Caracas

SOUTH AMERICA

Belo Horizonte
Rio de Janeiro
São Paulo

Santiago/Valparaíso

Buenos Aires

SOUTHERN OCEAN

TROPIC OF CANCER

EQUATOR

TROPIC OF CAPRICORN

ANTARCTIC CIRCLE

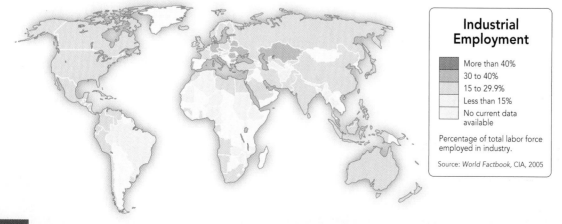

Industrial Employment

- More than 40%
- 30 to 40%
- 15 to 29.9%
- Less than 15%
- No current data available

Percentage of total labor force employed in industry.

Source: *World Factbook*, CIA, 2005

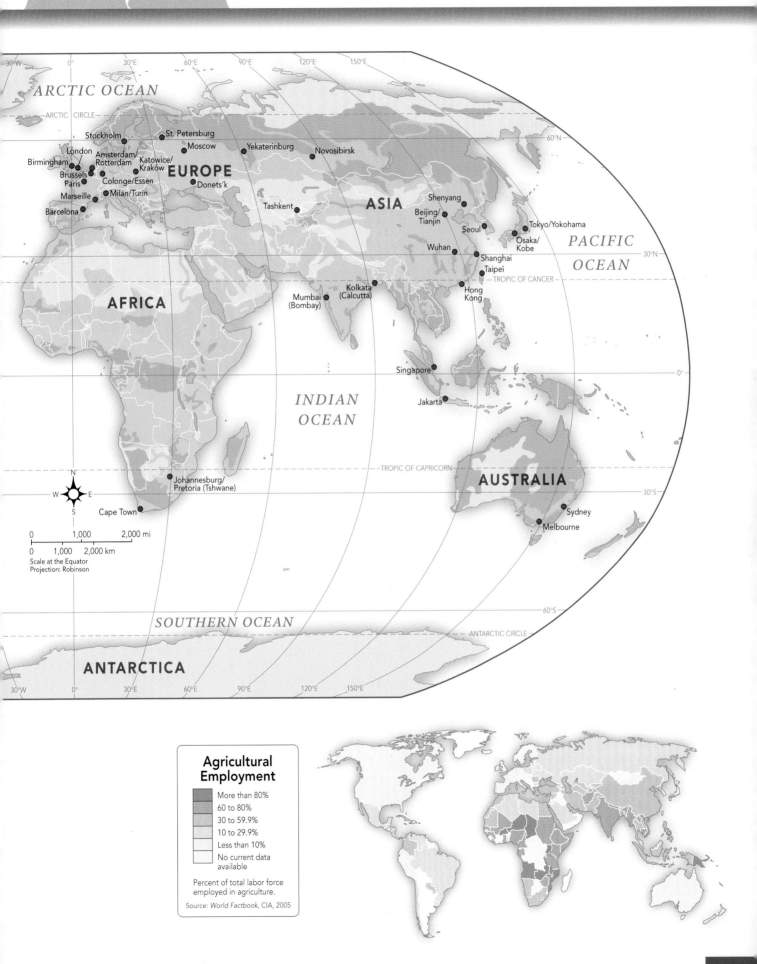

ARCTIC OCEAN

ARCTIC CIRCLE

Stockholm
St. Petersburg
London   Moscow
Amsterdam/   Yekaterinburg   Novosibirsk
Birmingham   Rotterdam   Katowice/
Brussels   Colonge/Essen   Kraków   EUROPE
Paris   Donets'k
Marseille   Milan/Turin
Barcelona

Tashkent   ASIA
                                      Shenyang
                            Beijing/   Seoul   Tokyo/Yokohama
                            Tianjin   Osaka/   PACIFIC
                                  Wuhan   Kobe   OCEAN
                                      Shanghai
AFRICA   Taipei
                        Kolkata   Hong
                Mumbai   (Calcutta)   Kong
                (Bombay)

TROPIC OF CANCER

Singapore

Jakarta
INDIAN
OCEAN

AUSTRALIA

TROPIC OF CAPRICORN

Johannesburg/
Pretoria (Tshwane)   Sydney
Cape Town   Melbourne

0   1,000   2,000 mi
0   1,000   2,000 km
Scale at the Equator
Projection: Robinson

SOUTHERN OCEAN

ANTARCTIC CIRCLE

ANTARCTICA

30°W   0°   30°E   60°E   90°E   120°E   150°E

Agricultural Employment

- More than 80%
- 60 to 80%
- 30 to 59.9%
- 10 to 29.9%
- Less than 10%
- No current data available

Percent of total labor force
employed in agriculture.

Source: *World Factbook*, CIA, 2005

Oil, Natural Gas, and Coal

- Major oil fields
- Other oil fields
- Natural gas fields
- Coal deposits

0 1,500 3,000 mi
0 1,500 3,000 km
Scale at the Equator
Projection: Robinson

Major Minerals

- Al Bauxite
- Cr Chromium
- Cu Copper
- Diamonds
- Au Gold
- Fe Iron
- Pb Lead
- Mn Manganese
- Ni Nickel
- Pt Platinum
- Ag Silver
- Sn Tin
- Ti Titanium
- Zn Zinc

0 1,500 3,000 mi
0 1,500 3,000 km
Scale at the Equator
Projection: Robinson

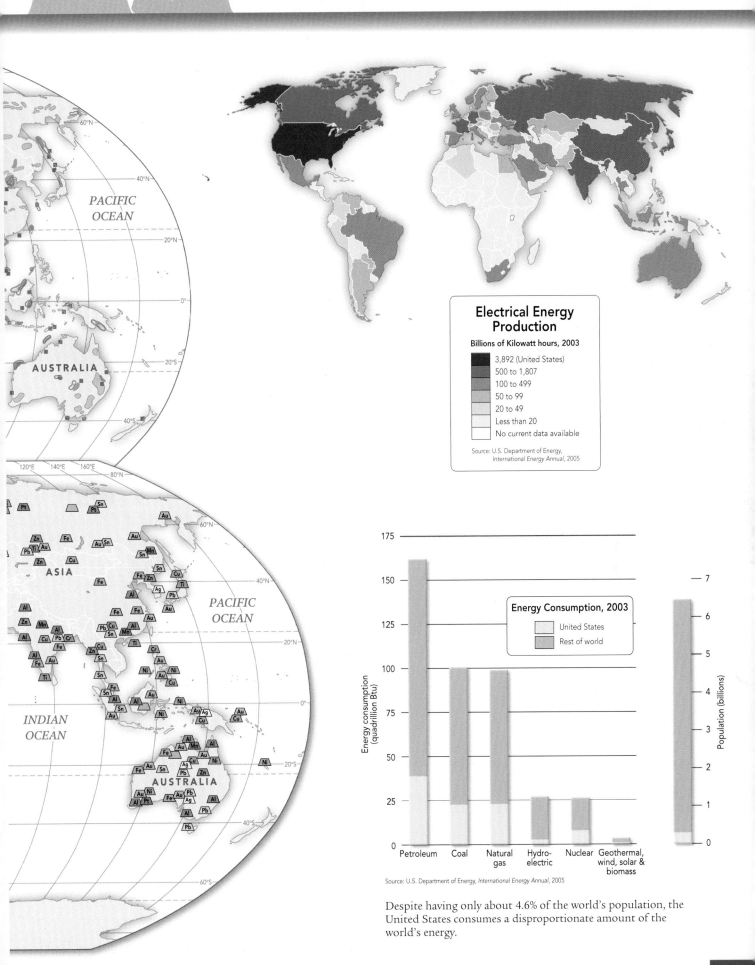

Electrical Energy Production

Billions of Kilowatt hours, 2003

- 3,892 (United States)
- 500 to 1,807
- 100 to 499
- 50 to 99
- 20 to 49
- Less than 20
- No current data available

Source: U.S. Department of Energy, *International Energy Annual*, 2005

Energy Consumption, 2003

- United States
- Rest of world

Energy consumption (quadrillion Btu)

Population (billions)

Petroleum   Coal   Natural gas   Hydro-electric   Nuclear   Geothermal, wind, solar & biomass

Source: U.S. Department of Energy, *International Energy Annual*, 2005

Despite having only about 4.6% of the world's population, the United States consumes a disproportionate amount of the world's energy.

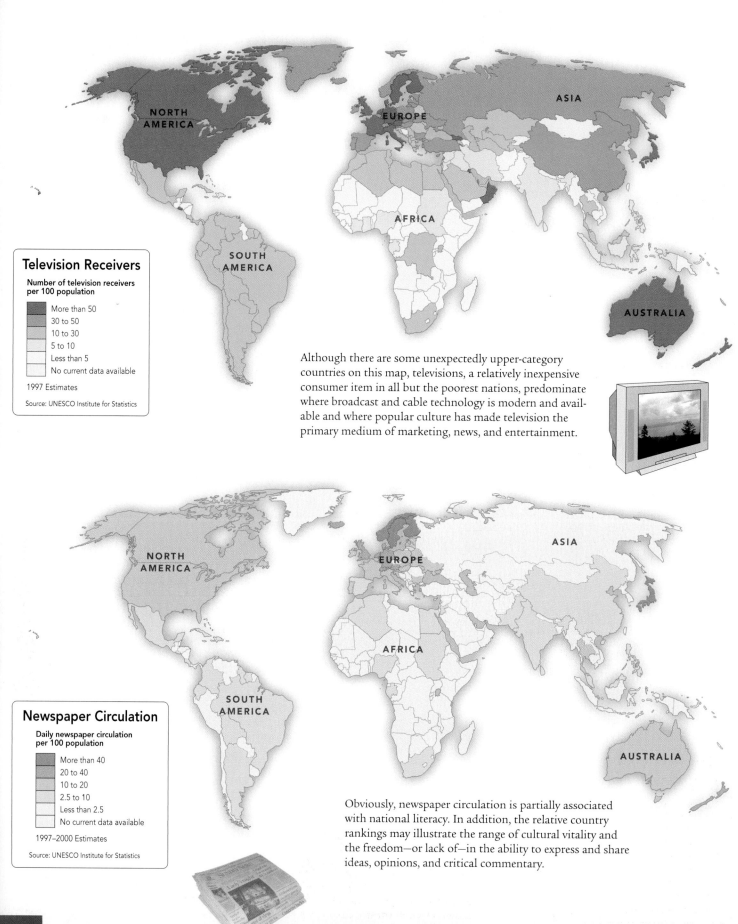

Television Receivers

Number of television receivers per 100 population

- More than 50
- 30 to 50
- 10 to 30
- 5 to 10
- Less than 5
- No current data available

1997 Estimates

Source: UNESCO Institute for Statistics

Although there are some unexpectedly upper-category countries on this map, televisions, a relatively inexpensive consumer item in all but the poorest nations, predominate where broadcast and cable technology is modern and available and where popular culture has made television the primary medium of marketing, news, and entertainment.

Newspaper Circulation

Daily newspaper circulation per 100 population

- More than 40
- 20 to 40
- 10 to 20
- 2.5 to 10
- Less than 2.5
- No current data available

1997–2000 Estimates

Source: UNESCO Institute for Statistics

Obviously, newspaper circulation is partially associated with national literacy. In addition, the relative country rankings may illustrate the range of cultural vitality and the freedom—or lack of—in the ability to express and share ideas, opinions, and critical commentary.

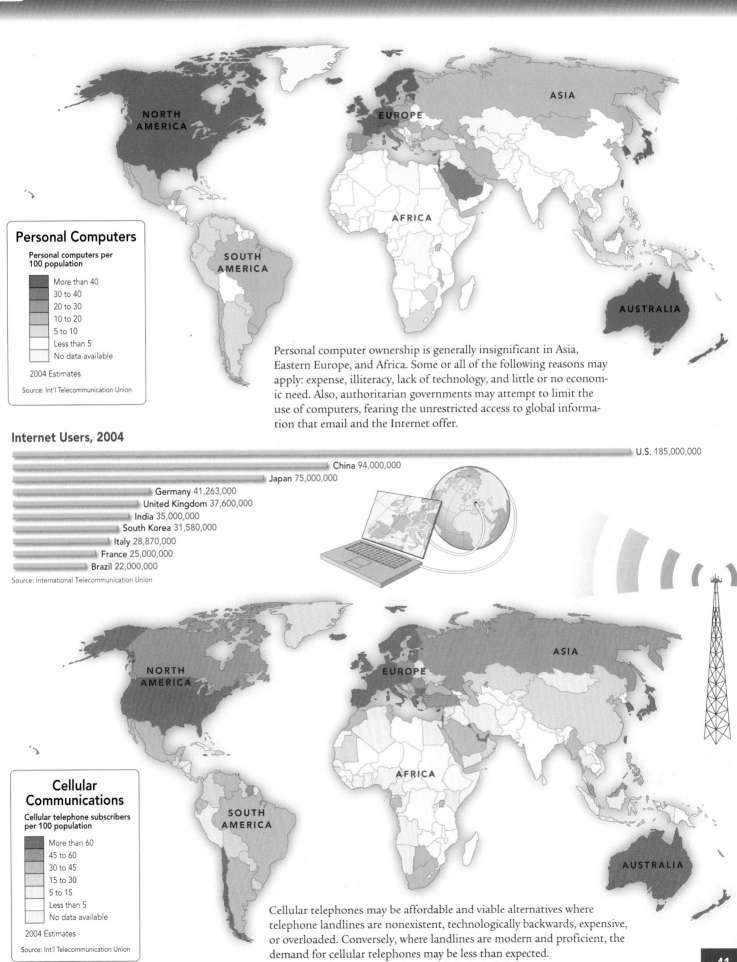

Personal Computers

Personal computers per 100 population

- More than 40
- 30 to 40
- 20 to 30
- 10 to 20
- 5 to 10
- Less than 5
- No data available

2004 Estimates

Source: Int'l Telecommunication Union

Personal computer ownership is generally insignificant in Asia, Eastern Europe, and Africa. Some or all of the following reasons may apply: expense, illiteracy, lack of technology, and little or no economic need. Also, authoritarian governments may attempt to limit the use of computers, fearing the unrestricted access to global information that email and the Internet offer.

Internet Users, 2004

- U.S. 185,000,000
- China 94,000,000
- Japan 75,000,000
- Germany 41,263,000
- United Kingdom 37,600,000
- India 35,000,000
- South Korea 31,580,000
- Italy 28,870,000
- France 25,000,000
- Brazil 22,000,000

Source: International Telecommunication Union

Cellular Communications

Cellular telephone subscribers per 100 population

- More than 60
- 45 to 60
- 30 to 45
- 15 to 30
- 5 to 15
- Less than 5
- No data available

2004 Estimates

Source: Int'l Telecommunication Union

Cellular telephones may be affordable and viable alternatives where telephone landlines are nonexistent, technologically backwards, expensive, or overloaded. Conversely, where landlines are modern and proficient, the demand for cellular telephones may be less than expected.

41

Time Zones

Non-standard times

| 11 P.M. | Mid-night | 1 A.M. | 2 A.M. | 3 A.M. | 4 A.M. | 5 A.M. | 6 A.M. | 7 A.M. | 8 A.M. | 9 A.M. | 10 A.M. | 11 A.M. | Noon | 1 P.M. | 2 P.M. | 3 P.M. | 4 P.M. | 5 P.M. | 6 P.M. | 7 P.M. | 8 P.M. | 9 P.M. | 10 P.M. |

NORTH AMERICA · Anchorage · Montreal · Chicago · San Francisco · Los Angeles · Washington, D.C. · Mexico City
SOUTH AMERICA · Lima · Buenos Aires
EUROPE · Dublin · Paris · Moscow
AFRICA · Cairo · Johannesburg
ASIA · **CHINA** · Beijing · Delhi
AUSTRALIA · Sydney

International Date Line · Prime Meridian

−3½ · −4½ · +14 · +13 · −9½ · +11½ · +13 · +10½ · +12¾ · +3½ · +4½ · +5¾ · +5½ · +6½ · +5½ · +6 · +6½ · +9½

Hours

| +11 | +12 | −12 | −11 | −10 | −9 | −8 | −7 | −6 | −5 | −4 | −3 | −2 | −1 | 0 | +1 | +2 | +3 | +4 | +5 | +6 | +7 | +8 | +9 | +10 |

The World is divided into 24 time zones, beginning at the Prime Meridian, which runs through Greenwich, England. The twelve zones east and twelve zones west of the Prime Meridian meet halfway around the globe at the International Date Line.

Traveling in an easterly direction, the time of day moves ahead one hour for each zone crossed. Traveling west, time falls behind one hour per zone. At the International Date Line a traveler gains one day crossing it in an easterly direction, and loses one day traveling west.

Note that the times shown are "standard time." Adjustments are necessary when "daylight saving time" is used.

Average Speeds of Some Passenger Transportation

Walking 3–4 mph/5-6 kph

Bicycle 10 mph/16 kph

Ocean liner, *Queen Elizabeth II* 33 mph/53 kph

Intercity bus, Greyhound; U.S. 54 mph/87 kph

Air cushion vehicle, United Kingdom 69 mph/111kph

Electric train, Amtrak *Acela Express*; Eastern U.S. 150 mph/241 kph (top speed)

High-speed train, *Shinkansen* (Bullet Train); Japan 164 mph/263 kph (average speed between stations)

Jet airliner, Boeing 737 500 mph/805 kph

Ocean Travel, New York City to London

1854, Clipper ship 14 days

1883, Steamship 6 days

2000, Ocean liner, *Queen Elizabeth II,* 5 days

Air Travel, New York City to Paris

1927, *Spirit of St. Louis,* single-engine propeller plane 33 hours 30 minutes

1958, Boeing 707, four-engine jet 8 hours 41 minutes

1977, Concorde SST, supersonic jet 3 hours 44 minutes

Famous Airplane Flights

1903
Orville and Wilbur Wright made the first engine-powered flight in a heavier-than-air craft at Kitty Hawk, NC. The flight lasted less than 12 seconds.

1908
Glenn Curtiss made the first official flight of more than 1 kilometer (0.62 miles).

1926
Floyd Bennett (pilot) and Richard E. Byrd (navigator) claimed to have circled the North Pole.

1927
Charles A. Lindbergh made the first solo, nonstop, transatlantic flight. He flew from Garden City, NY to Paris in 33 hours 30 minutes.

1929
Richard E. Byrd established an Antarctic base at Little America. On November 28 and 29, Byrd and his pilot, Bernt Balchen, left the base and flew to the South Pole.

1932
Amelia Earhart was the first woman to fly across the Atlantic Ocean. She flew from Harbour Grace, Newfoundland to Northern Ireland, a distance of 2,026 miles (3,260 kilometers) in 15 hours 18 minutes.

1933
Wiley Post made the first solo, round-the-world flight. He flew from Floyd Bennett Field in Brooklyn, NY and covered 15,596 miles (25,099 kilometers) in 7 days 18 hours 49 minutes.

1949
An Air Force crew made the first nonstop, round-the-world flight. Using a B-50A bomber, they traveled 23,452 miles (37,742 kilometers) in 3 days 22 hours 1 minute.

1992
French pilots flew the supersonic Concorde around the world, east-to-west, in a record setting 32 hours 49 minutes 3 seconds.

Passengers at Major Airports 2004

✈ More than 50 million
✈ 40 to 50 million
✈ 30 to 40 million

Source: Airports Council International

Note: Only the ten busiest U.S. airports are shown.

see Europe inset below

North America

Legend
- International boundary
- State or provincial boundary
- ⊛ National capital

Symbol and label sizes indicate relative sizes of cities:
- ● **New York**
- ● Baltimore
- • Charlotte

Facts

- Area: 8,260,174 square miles (21,393,762 square kilometers)
- Highest Point: Mt. McKinley, United States, 20,320 ft. (6,194 m)
- Lowest Point: Death Valley, United States, 282 ft. (86 m) below sea level
- Longest River: Mississippi-Missouri, 3,877 mi. (6,238 km)
- Largest Lake: Lake Superior, United States/Canada, 31,700 sq. mi. (82,103 sq. km)
- Largest Country: Canada, 3,851,809 sq. mi. (9,976,185 sq. km)
- Largest Urban Concentration: Mexico City, Mexico, and New York City, United States [A]

Nations of the Lesser Antilles

Country	Capital	Country	Capital
Antigua and Barbuda	St. John's	St. Vincent and the Grenadines	Kingstown
St. Kitts and Nevis	Basseterre	Grenada	St. George's
Dominica	Roseau	Trinidad and Tobago	Port-of-Spain
St. Lucia	Castries		
Barbados	Bridgetown		

ASIA

ARCTIC OCEAN

Cape Morris Jesup

North Pole

EUROPE

ARCTIC OCEAN

NORTH AMERICA
ATLANTIC OCEAN
EUROPE
ASIA
PACIFIC OCEAN
AFRICA
SOUTH AMERICA
INDIAN OCEAN
AUSTRALIA
Equator
PACIFIC OCEAN
ANTARCTICA
SOUTHERN OCEAN
Robinson Projection

Chukchi Sea

Bering Sea

Point Barrow

Beaufort Sea

Greenland

Ellesmere Island

Queen Elizabeth Islands

Devon I.

Baffin Bay

Denmark Strait

Bering Strait

Mt. McKinley 20,320 ft. (6,194 m)

BROOKS RANGE

Yukon River

ALASKA RANGE

Banks Island

Victoria Island

Great Bear Lake

Mackenzie River

MACKENZIE MTS.

Baffin Island

Davis Strait

Cape Farewell

Gulf of Alaska

Mt. Logan 19,551 ft. (5,959 m)

Southampton I.

Alexander Archipelago

COAST MOUNTAINS

ROCKY

Great Slave Lake

Peace River

Athabasca River

Lake Athabasca

Hudson Bay

Belcher Is.

Ungava Peninsula

Labrador Sea

Labrador

Queen Charlotte Is.

PACIFIC OCEAN

Vancouver I.

Fraser River

Columbia River

Nelson R.

Saskatchewan River

CANADIAN SHIELD

Anticosti I.

Newfoundland

Gulf of St. Lawrence

Miquelon Is.

Cape Breton I.

Mt. Rainier 14,411 ft. (4,392 m)

CASCADE RANGE

MOUNTAINS

Snake River

GREAT PLAINS

Lake Winnipeg

Lake Superior

Lake Huron

Lake Ontario

St. Lawrence River

Cape Sable

Cape Mendocino

SIERRA NEVADA

COAST RANGES

GREAT BASIN

Great Salt Lake

Black Hills

Lake Michigan

Niagara Falls

Lake Erie

Cape Cod

ATLANTIC OCEAN

Mt. Whitney 14,494 ft. (4,418 m)

Death Valley 282 ft. (86 m) below sea level

COLORADO PLATEAU

L. Mead

Colorado River

Mt. Elbert 14,433 ft. (4,399 m)

Arkansas

Missouri River

Platte River

River

OZARK PLATEAU

Ohio River

Tennessee River

Mt. Mitchell 6,684 ft. (2,037 m)

APPALACHIAN MTS.

ATLANTIC COASTAL PLAIN

Cape Hatteras

Bermuda

Red River

Mississippi River

Alabama R.

Baja California

SIERRA MADRE OCCIDENTAL

Brazos River

Colorado River

Rio Grande

GULF COASTAL PLAIN

TROPIC OF CANCER

False Cape

Gulf of California

SIERRA MADRE ORIENTAL

Gulf of Mexico

Bay of Campeche

Yucatán Peninsula

Straits of Florida

Bahamas

Cuba

Cayman Is.

Greater Antilles

Jamaica

Puerto Rico

Hispaniola

Leeward Is.

Lesser Antilles

Windward Is.

International boundary
Mountain peak
Lowest point
Falls

Sources for elevation data:
Natural Resources Canada
Merriam-Webster's
Geographical Dictionary, 2007

Pico de Orizaba 18,700 ft. (5,700 m)

Caribbean Sea

Aruba

Bonaire

Curaçao

Trinidad

N
W E
S

Lake Nicaragua

Panama Canal

Isthmus of Panama

SOUTH AMERICA

Elevation Profile

110°W | 100°W | 90°W | 80°W | 70°W

Baja California | Rocky Mountains | Great Plains | Lake Michigan | Lake Huron | St. Lawrence River | Newfoundland

12,500 ft.

7,500 ft.

2,500 ft.
Sea level

A   B

45

Major Metropolitan Areas

Antigua & Barbuda
St. John's — 22,000

Bahamas
Nassau — 211,000

Barbados
Bridgetown — 6,000

Belize
Belize City — 49,000
Belmopan — 8,000

Canada
Toronto — 4,683,000
Montréal — 3,426,000
Vancouver — 1,987,000
Ottawa — 1,064,000
Calgary — 951,000
Edmonton — 938,000
Québec — 683,000
Winnipeg — 671,000
Hamilton — 662,000

Costa Rica
San José — 1,305,000

Cuba
Havana — 2,192,000

Dominica
Roseau — 16,000

Dominican Republic
Santo Domingo — 2,677,000

El Salvador
San Salvador — 1,909,000

Grenada
St. George's — 5,000

Guatemala
Guatemala City — 1,007,000

Haiti
Port-au-Prince — 991,000

Honduras
Tegucigalpa — 835,000

Jamaica
Kingston — 578,000

Mexico
Mexico City — 16,203,000
Guadalajara — 3,349,000
Monterrey — 3,131,000
Puebla — 1,272,000
Ciudad Juárez — 1,187,000
Tijuana — 1,149,000
León — 1,021,000

Nicaragua
Managua — 1,148,000

Panama
Panama City — 1,002,000

Puerto Rico
San Juan — 2,450,000

St. Kitts & Nevis
Basseterre — 13,000

St. Lucia
Castries — 11,000

St. Vincent & Grenadines
Kingstown — 15,000

Trinidad & Tobago
Port of Spain — 48,000

United States
New York-Newark — 21,200,000
Los Angeles — 16,374,000
Chicago — 9,158,000
Washington-Baltimore — 7,608,000
San Francisco-Oakland-San Jose — 7,039,000
Philadelphia — 6,188,000
Boston — 5,819,000
Detroit — 5,456,000
Dallas-Ft. Worth — 5,222,000
Houston — 4,670,000
Atlanta — 4,112,000
Miami — 3,876,000
Seattle-Tacoma — 3,555,000
Phoenix — 3,252,000
Minneapolis-St. Paul — 2,969,000
Cleveland-Akron — 2,946,000
San Diego — 2,814,000
St. Louis — 2,604,000
Denver — 2,582,000
Tampa-St. Petersburg — 2,396,000
Pittsburgh — 2,359,000
Portland — 2,265,000
Cincinnati — 1,979,000
Sacramento — 1,797,000
Kansas City — 1,776,000
Milwaukee — 1,690,000

International comparability of population data is limited by varying census methods. Where metropolitan population is unavailable, core city population is shown.

Population

Persons per sq. mile	Persons per sq. km
Over 520	Over 200
260 to 519	100 to 199
130 to 259	50 to 99
25 to 129	10 to 49
1 to 24	1 to 9
0	0

Major metropolitan areas
● Over 2 million
● 1 million to 2 million
• Under 1 million

Estimated 2005 Population (in millions)

United States 296
Mexico 106
Canada 33
Guatemala 12
Cuba 11
All others 54

Source: U.S. Census Bureau

46

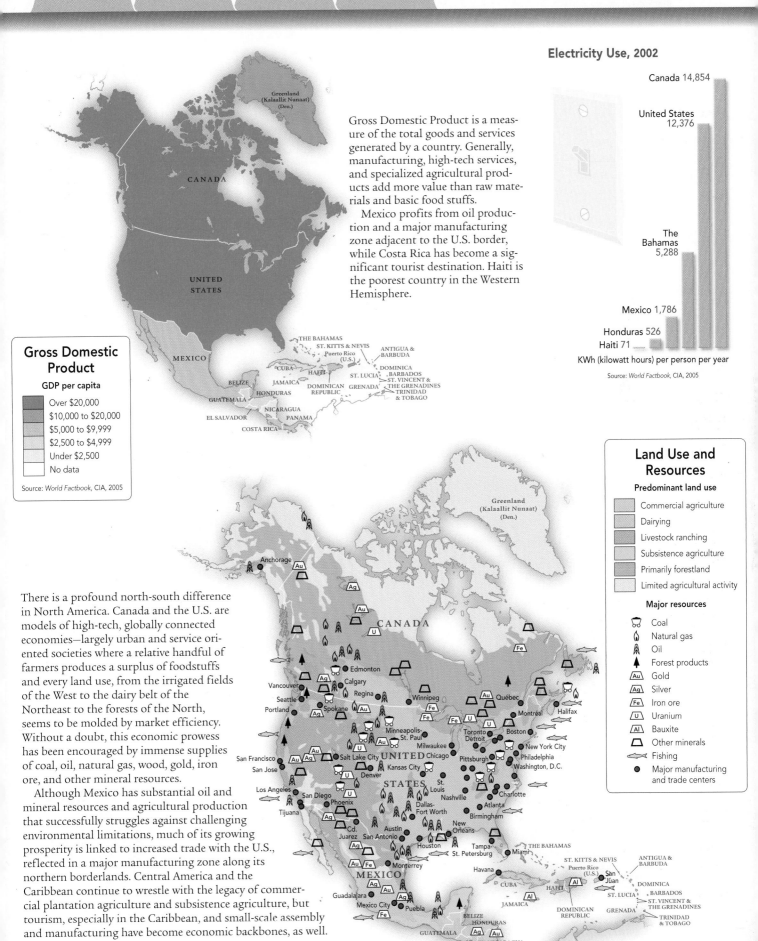

Electricity Use, 2002

Canada 14,854
United States 12,376
The Bahamas 5,288
Mexico 1,786
Honduras 526
Haiti 71

KWh (kilowatt hours) per person per year

Source: *World Factbook*, CIA, 2005

Gross Domestic Product is a measure of the total goods and services generated by a country. Generally, manufacturing, high-tech services, and specialized agricultural products add more value than raw materials and basic food stuffs.

Mexico profits from oil production and a major manufacturing zone adjacent to the U.S. border, while Costa Rica has become a significant tourist destination. Haiti is the poorest country in the Western Hemisphere.

Gross Domestic Product

GDP per capita

- Over $20,000
- $10,000 to $20,000
- $5,000 to $9,999
- $2,500 to $4,999
- Under $2,500
- No data

Source: *World Factbook*, CIA, 2005

Land Use and Resources

Predominant land use
- Commercial agriculture
- Dairying
- Livestock ranching
- Subsistence agriculture
- Primarily forestland
- Limited agricultural activity

Major resources
- Coal
- Natural gas
- Oil
- Forest products
- Au Gold
- Ag Silver
- Fe Iron ore
- U Uranium
- Al Bauxite
- Other minerals
- Fishing
- Major manufacturing and trade centers

There is a profound north-south difference in North America. Canada and the U.S. are models of high-tech, globally connected economies—largely urban and service oriented societies where a relative handful of farmers produces a surplus of foodstuffs and every land use, from the irrigated fields of the West to the dairy belt of the Northeast to the forests of the North, seems to be molded by market efficiency. Without a doubt, this economic prowess has been encouraged by immense supplies of coal, oil, natural gas, wood, gold, iron ore, and other mineral resources.

Although Mexico has substantial oil and mineral resources and agricultural production that successfully struggles against challenging environmental limitations, much of its growing prosperity is linked to increased trade with the U.S., reflected in a major manufacturing zone along its northern borderlands. Central America and the Caribbean continue to wrestle with the legacy of commercial plantation agriculture and subsistence agriculture, but tourism, especially in the Caribbean, and small-scale assembly and manufacturing have become economic backbones, as well.

47

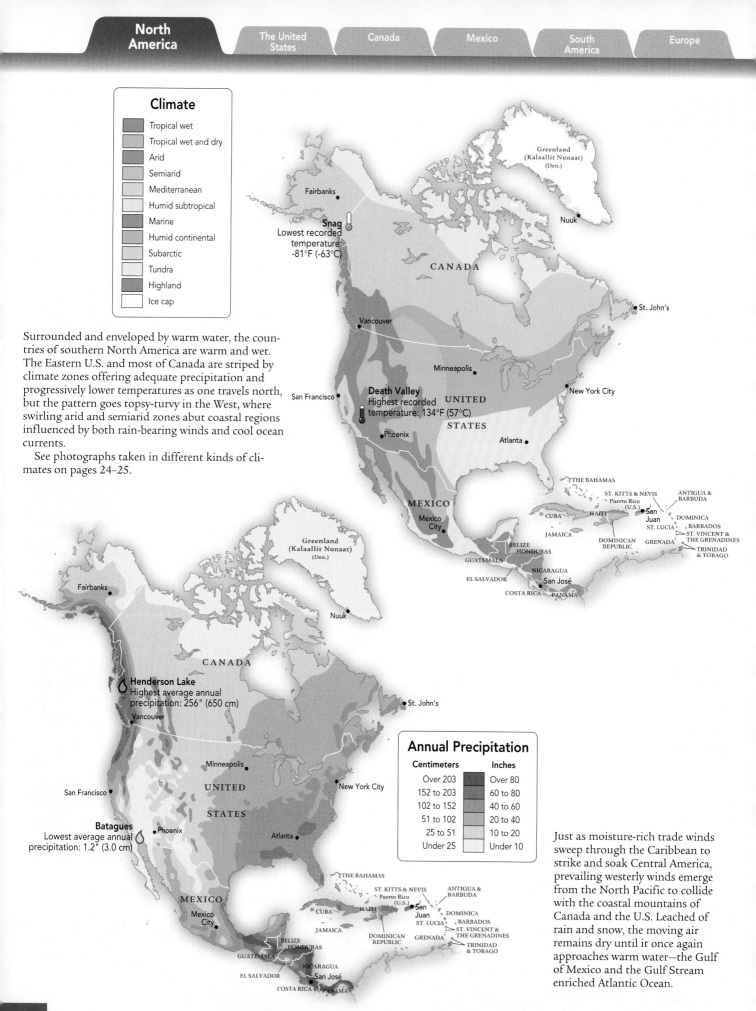

Climate

- Tropical wet
- Tropical wet and dry
- Arid
- Semiarid
- Mediterranean
- Humid subtropical
- Marine
- Humid continental
- Subarctic
- Tundra
- Highland
- Ice cap

Surrounded and enveloped by warm water, the countries of southern North America are warm and wet. The Eastern U.S. and most of Canada are striped by climate zones offering adequate precipitation and progressively lower temperatures as one travels north, but the pattern goes topsy-turvy in the West, where swirling arid and semiarid zones abut coastal regions influenced by both rain-bearing winds and cool ocean currents.

See photographs taken in different kinds of climates on pages 24–25.

Snag
Lowest recorded temperature: -81°F (-63°C)

Death Valley
Highest recorded temperature: 134°F (57°C)

Henderson Lake
Highest average annual precipitation: 256" (650 cm)

Batagues
Lowest average annual precipitation: 1.2" (3.0 cm)

Annual Precipitation

Centimeters	Inches
Over 203	Over 80
152 to 203	60 to 80
102 to 152	40 to 60
51 to 102	20 to 40
25 to 51	10 to 20
Under 25	Under 10

Just as moisture-rich trade winds sweep through the Caribbean to strike and soak Central America, prevailing westerly winds emerge from the North Pacific to collide with the coastal mountains of Canada and the U.S. Leached of rain and snow, the moving air remains dry until it once again approaches warm water—the Gulf of Mexico and the Gulf Stream enriched Atlantic Ocean.

Climate Graphs

Average daily temperature range (in °F) | Average monthly precipitation (in inches)

100° High
65° Low
32°
0°   20° / 10° / 0°

ATLANTA, USA
FAIRBANKS, USA
(Temp. Range -21 to -1)
MEXICO CITY, Mexico
MINNEAPOLIS, USA
NUUK, Greenland
NEW YORK CITY, USA
PHOENIX, USA
ST. JOHN'S, Canada
SAN FRANCISCO, USA
SAN JOSÉ, Costa Rica
SAN JUAN, Puerto Rico
VANCOUVER, Canada

Vegetation

- Unclassified highlands or ice cap
- Tundra and alpine tundra
- Coniferous forest
- Midlatitude deciduous forest
- Subtropical broadleaf evergreen forest
- Mixed forest
- Midlatitude scrubland
- Midlatitude grassland
- Desert
- Tropical seasonal and scrub
- Tropical rain forest

Deserts spanning the U.S./Mexico border join the tropical plant life of Central America and southern Mexico to the temperate and arctic vegetation of Canada and the U.S.—vegetation predominately forest land but split by the arc of the Great Plains and interwoven with scrublands able to endure infrequent rainfall.

See photographs of different the kinds of vegetation on page 26–27.

In the U.S. and Canada, heavy consumption of energy and other resources is a source of many environmental problems. Environmental laws and regulations have helped, but air pollutants and gases continue to cause health problems and may contribute to global warming.

In the western U.S. and parts of Mexico, large areas are susceptible to desertification from overgrazing and agriculture.

Deforestation is a major issue in Latin America and the Caribbean. In Haiti, for example, all the native rain forests have been destroyed, causing irreversible harm to ecosystems.

Environmental Issues

- Current forest
- Cleared forest
- Area at highest risk of desertification
- Areas most affected by acid rain
- • Poor air quality*

*Cities exceeding at least one of the World Health Organization's (WHO) annual mean guidelines for air quality

Sources: Global Distribution of Original and Remaining Forests, UNEP-WCMC, 2002
World Soil Resources Map Index, USDA/NRCS, 2002
World Development Indicators, World Bank, 1999

United States

Alabama

Alaska

Arizona

Arkansas

California

Hawaii

Idaho

Iowa

Kansas

Maine

Maryland

Minnesota

Mississippi

Nebraska

Nevada

New Mexico

New York

Ohio

Oklahoma

Rhode Island

South Carolina

South Dakota

Tennessee

Texas

Utah

United States

Map labels:
Seattle, Olympia, Tacoma, Spokane, WASHINGTON, Portland, Columbia River, Salem, Eugene, OREGON, Medford, Great Falls, Helena, MONTANA, Billings, Yellowstone R., IDAHO, Boise, Snake River, WYOMING, Pocatello, Casper, NORTH DAKOTA, Grand Forks, Bismarck, Fargo, SOUTH DAKOTA, Pierre, Rapid City, Sioux Falls, Missouri River, Ogden, Cheyenne, NEBRASKA, Lake Tahoe, Reno, NEVADA, Great Salt Lake, Salt Lake City, Provo, Fort Collins, Lincoln, Platte River, Sacramento, Carson City, UTAH, Denver, San Francisco, Oakland, San Jose, COLORADO, Colorado Springs, KANSAS, Salinas, Fresno, Las Vegas, St. George, Pueblo, Arkansas River, Wichita, CALIFORNIA, Colorado River, Bakersfield, OKLAHOMA, Santa Barbara, Oxnard, Flagstaff, Santa Fe, Oklahoma City, Los Angeles, San Bernardino, Riverside, Albuquerque, Amarillo, Lawton, San Diego, ARIZONA, NEW MEXICO, Lubbock, Red R., Yuma, Phoenix, Roswell, Fort Worth, Tucson, Abilene, Dallas, Las Cruces, El Paso, Odessa, Waco, TEXAS, Austin, Rio Grande, San Antonio, Laredo, Corpus Christi, Brownsville

Barrow, ARCTIC CIRCLE, Nome, ALASKA, Yukon River, Fairbanks, Anchorage, Juneau, Ketchikan

0 400 mi / 0 400 km

Honolulu, HAWAII, Hilo

0 100 mi / 0 100 km

Colorado

Connecticut

Delaware

District of Columbia

Florida

Georgia

Illinois

Indiana

Kentucky

Louisiana

Massachusetts

Michigan

Missouri

Montana

New Hampshire

New Jersey

North Carolina

North Dakota

Oregon

Pennsylvania

Map

Scale:
0 — 150 — 300 mi
0 — 150 — 300 km

MINNESOTA — Duluth — Sault Sainte Marie
St. Paul — Green Bay — MICHIGAN — MAINE — Augusta
Minneapolis — WISCONSIN — Grand Rapids — Flint — VERMONT — Burlington — Montpelier — NEW HAMPSHIRE — Portland
Rochester — Madison — Milwaukee — Lansing — Detroit — Erie — NEW YORK — Concord — Manchester — Boston
Sioux City — IOWA — Rockford — Toledo — Cleveland — Syracuse — Rochester — Worcester — MASSACHUSETTS — Providence
Cedar Rapids — Chicago — South Bend — Akron — PENNSYLVANIA — Albany — Hartford — RHODE ISLAND
Des Moines — Davenport — ILLINOIS — Gary — OHIO — Wheeling — Pittsburgh — Buffalo — Newark — CONNECTICUT
Omaha — Peoria — INDIANA — Columbus — Harrisburg — Trenton — New York City — NEW JERSEY
Decatur — Dayton — Philadelphia
Springfield — Indianapolis — Cincinnati — WEST VIRGINIA — Baltimore — Wilmington — DELAWARE
Kansas City — Louisville — Frankfort — Charleston — Annapolis — Dover
Topeka — Kansas City — Jefferson City — Evansville — Lexington — VIRGINIA — MARYLAND — Washington, D.C.
MISSOURI — KENTUCKY — Richmond — Newport News
Springfield — Roanoke — Norfolk — Virginia Beach
Tulsa — Nashville — Knoxville — Winston-Salem — Greensboro — Raleigh
ARKANSAS — TENNESSEE — Charlotte — NORTH CAROLINA
Memphis — Chattanooga — SOUTH CAROLINA
Fort Smith — Huntsville — Atlanta — Columbia
Little Rock — Birmingham — GEORGIA — Augusta — Charleston
Meridian — Macon — Savannah
Shreveport — ALABAMA — Columbus
Jackson — Montgomery
MISSISSIPPI — Mobile — Jacksonville
Beaumont — Biloxi — Tallahassee — FLORIDA
Baton Rouge — Orlando
Houston — New Orleans — Tampa — West Palm Beach
St. Petersburg — Lake Okeechobee — Fort Lauderdale
Miami

Lake of the Woods — Lake Superior — Lake Huron — Lake Michigan — Lake Ontario — Lake Erie — Ohio River — Missouri River — Mississippi River — Arkansas River — Red River — Tennessee River

Legend

State boundary
⊛ National capital
★ State capital

Symbol and label sizes indicate relative sizes of cities:

● **New York City**
● St. Louis
• Carson City

Source:
[A] U.S. Census Bureau, metropolitan area, 2006 estimate

Facts

- Total Area: 3,620,067 square miles (9,375,974 square kilometers)
- Highest Point: Mt. McKinley, Alaska, 20,320 ft. (6,194 m)
- Lowest Point: Death Valley, California, 282 ft. (86 m) below sea level
- Longest River: Mississippi-Missouri, 3,877 mi. (6,238 km)
- Largest Lake (within U.S.): Lake Michigan, 22,300 sq. mi. (57,757 sq. km)
- Largest State: Alaska, 591,004 sq. mi. (1,530,700 sq. km)
- Largest Urban Concentration: New York City, New York 18,818,536 [A]

Vermont

Virginia

Washington

West Virginia

Wisconsin

Wyoming

State	2000 Population and Rank		Capital	Largest City	Abbreviation		Nickname
					Traditional	Postal Service	
Alabama	4,447,100	23rd	Montgomery	Birmingham	ALA.	AL	Heart of Dixie
Alaska	626,932	48th	Juneau	Anchorage	(none)	AK	The Last Frontier
Arizona	5,130,632	20th	Phoenix	Phoenix	ARIZ.	AZ	Grand Canyon State
Arkansas	2,673,400	33rd	Litttle Rock	Little Rock	ARK.	AR	Land of Opportunity
California	33,871,648	1st	Sacramento	Los Angeles	CALIF.	CA	Golden State
Colorado	4,301,261	24th	Denver	Denver	COLO.	CO	Centennial State
Connecticut	3,405,565	29th	Hartford	Bridgeport	CONN.	CT	Constitution State, Nutmeg State
Delaware	783,600	45th	Dover	Wilmington	DEL.	DE	First State, Diamond State
Florida	15,982,378	4th	Tallahassee	Jacksonville	FLA.	FL	Sunshine State
Georgia	8,186,453	10th	Atlanta	Atlanta	GA.	GA	Empire State of the South, Peach State
Hawaii	1,211,537	42nd	Honolulu	Honolulu	(none)	HI	Aloha State
Idaho	1,293,953	39th	Boise	Boise	IDA.	ID	Gem State
Illinois	12,419,293	5th	Springfield	Chicago	ILL.	IL	Prairie State
Indiana	6,080,485	14th	Indianapolis	Indianapolis	IND.	IN	Hoosier State
Iowa	2,926,324	30th	Des Moines	Des Moines	(none)	IA	Hawkeye State
Kansas	2,688,418	32nd	Topeka	Wichita	KANS.	KS	Sunflower State
Kentucky	4,041,769	25th	Frankfort	Louisville	KY. or KEN.	KY	Bluegrass State
Louisiana	4,468,976	22nd	Baton Rouge	New Orleans	LA.	LA	Pelican State
Maine	1,274,923	40th	Augusta	Portland	(none)	ME	Pine Tree State
Maryland	5,296,486	19th	Annapolis	Baltimore	MD.	MD	Old Line State, Free State
Massachusetts	6,349,097	13th	Boston	Boston	MASS.	MA	Bay State, Old Colony
Michigan	9,938,444	8th	Lansing	Detroit	MICH.	MI	Wolverine State
Minnesota	4,919,479	21st	St. Paul	Minneapolis	MINN.	MN	North Star State, Gopher State
Mississippi	2,844,658	31st	Jackson	Jackson	MISS.	MS	Magnolia State
Missouri	5,595,211	17th	Jefferson City	Kansas City	MO.	MO	Show Me State

State	2000 Population and Rank		Capital	Largest City	Abbreviation		Nickname
					Traditional	Postal Service	
Montana	902,195	44th	Helena	Billings	MONT.	MT	Treasure State
Nebraska	1,711,265	38th	Lincoln	Omaha	NEBR.	NE	Cornhusker State
Nevada	1,998,257	35th	Carson City	Las Vegas	NEV.	NV	Silver State
New Hampshire	1,235,786	41st	Concord	Manchester	N.H.	NH	Granite State
New Jersey	8,414,350	9th	Trenton	Newark	N.J.	NJ	Garden State
New Mexico	1,819,046	36th	Santa Fe	Albuquerque	N. MEX. or N.M.	NM	Land of Enchantment
New York	18,976,457	3rd	Albany	New York City	N.Y.	NY	Empire State
North Carolina	8,049,313	11th	Raleigh	Charlotte	N.C.	NC	Tar Heel State
North Dakota	642,200	47th	Bismarck	Fargo	N. DAK. or N.D.	ND	Peace Garden State, Flickertail State
Ohio	11,353,140	7th	Columbus	Columbus	(none)	OH	Buckeye State
Oklahoma	3,450,654	27th	Oklahoma City	Oklahoma City	OKLA.	OK	Sooner State
Oregon	3,421,399	28th	Salem	Portland	ORE.	OR	Beaver State
Pennsylvania	12,281,054	6th	Harrisburg	Philadelphia	PA. or PENN.	PA	Keystone State
Rhode Island	1,048,319	43rd	Providence	Providence	R.I.	RI	Ocean State
South Carolina	4,012,012	26th	Columbia	Columbia	S.C.	SC	Palmetto State
South Dakota	754,844	46th	Pierre	Sioux Falls	S. DAK. or S.D.	SD	Mt. Rushmore State
Tennessee	5,689,283	16th	Nashville	Memphis	TENN.	TN	Volunteer State
Texas	20,851,820	2nd	Austin	Houston	TEX.	TX	Lone Star State
Utah	2,233,169	34th	Salt Lake City	Salt Lake City	(none)	UT	Beehive State
Vermont	608,827	49th	Montpelier	Burlington	VT.	VT	Green Mountain State
Virginia	7,078,515	12th	Richmond	Virginia Beach	VA.	VA	Old Dominion
Washington	5,894,121	15th	Olympia	Seattle	WASH.	WA	Evergreen State
West Virginia	1,808,344	37th	Charleston	Charleston	W. VA.	WV	Mountain State
Wisconsin	5,363,675	18th	Madison	Milwaukee	WIS.	WI	Badger State
Wyoming	493,782	50th	Cheyenne	Cheyenne	WYO.	WY	Equality State

Strait of Juan de Fuca
Cape Flattery

International boundary
State boundary
▲ Mountain peak
▽ Lowest point

Source for elevation data:
U.S. Geological Survey

PACIFIC OCEAN

Puget Sound
Mt. Rainier 14,411 ft. (4,392 m)
Mt. St. Helens 8,364 ft. (2,549 m)
Mt. Hood 11,239 ft. (3,425 m)

COAST RANGES
CASCADE RANGE
COLUMBIA
Columbia River
Snake River
Salmon River
Columbia

Milk River
Missouri River
Fort Peck Lake
Clark Fork
BITTERROOT RANGE
ROCKY

Yellowstone River
Granite Peak 12,799 ft. (3,901 m)
Little Missouri River
Lake Sakakawea

Yellowstone Lake
Bighorn River
Powder River
Black Hills
Lake Oahe

Cape Mendocino
Mt. Shasta 14,162 ft. (4,316 m)

COLUMBIA PLATEAU
Snake River Plain
Snake River
Owyhee River

Great Salt Lake
Great Salt Lake Desert
Green River
N. Platte River
GREAT
Cheyenne River
White R.
Niobrara River
Sand Hills

San Francisco Bay
Sacramento River
Central Valley
SIERRA NEVADA
Lake Tahoe

GREAT BASIN

WASATCH RANGE
Kings Peak 13,528 ft. (4,123 m)
MOUNTAINS
S. Platte River
FRONT RANGE

PLAINS

Monterey Bay
San Joaquin River
COAST RANGES

Mt. Whitney 14,494 ft. (4,418 m)
282 ft. (86 m) below sea level
Death Valley

Lake Mead
Colorado River
Lake Powell
Grand Canyon

Colorado River
COLORADO PLATEAU
Mt. Elbert 14,433 ft. (4,399 m)
Pikes Peak 14,110 ft. (4,300 m)
Arkansas River
SANGRE DE CRISTO

Point Conception
Mojave Desert

Humphreys Peak 12,633 ft. (3,851 m)
Verde River
Wheeler Peak 13,161 ft. (4,011 m)

San Juan River
Rio Grande
Pecos River
LLANO ESTACADO

Channel Islands
Salton Sea
Sonoran Desert
Colorado River
Gila River
Salt River

Guadalupe Peak 8,749 ft. (2,667 m)

EDWARDS PLATEAU

RUSSIA
Pt. Barrow
ARCTIC OCEAN
Bering Strait
BROOKS RANGE
Seward Peninsula
Yukon River
St. Lawrence Island
ARCTIC CIRCLE
RANGE
ALASKA RANGE
Mt. McKinley 20,320 ft. (6,194 m)
CANADA
Kenai Peninsula
Gulf of Alaska
Bering Sea
Kodiak Island
ALEUTIAN RANGE
Aleutian Is.

N
W E
S

0   250   500 mi
0   250   500 km

PACIFIC OCEAN
Kaua'i
Ni'ihau
O'ahu
Moloka'i
Lāna'i
Maui
Kaho'olawe
Hawaiian Islands
Hawai'i
Mauna Kea 13,796 ft. (4,205 m)

N
W E
S

0   100   200 mi
0   100   200 km

MEXICO

Coast Ranges | Sierra Nevada | Great Basin | Wasatch Range | Mount Elbert | Pikes Peak

15,000 ft.
10,000 ft.
Lake Tahoe
5,000 ft.
Sea level
A

CANADA

Lake of the Woods

Isle Royale

MESABI RANGE

Lake Superior

Upper Peninsula

Red River of the North

St. Croix River

Minnesota River

James River

Mississippi

Wisconsin River

Lake Michigan

Lake Huron

Lower Peninsula

Grand River

Lake St. Clair

Lake Erie

Lake Ontario

St. Lawrence River

Lake Champlain

WHITE MTS.

Mt. Washington
6,288 ft.
(1,917 m)

GREEN MTS.

Merrimack R.

ADIRONDACK MTS.

Hudson River

Connecticut River

Gulf of Maine

Cape Cod

Saint John River

Penobscot River

Quoddy Head

Des Moines River

Cedar River

Iowa River

Rock River

Illinois River

CENTRAL LOWLAND

Wabash River

Scioto River

Genesee R.

Allegheny R.

ALLEGHENY PLATEAU

Susquehanna River

Delaware River

Long Island Sound

Long Island

Delaware Bay

Loup R.

Platte River

Republican River

Smoky Hill R.

Kansas River

Missouri River

FLINT HILLS

Kaskaskia River

White River

Ohio River

Kentucky R.

Green River

Cumberland River

ALLEGHENY MOUNTAINS

CUMBERLAND PLATEAU

APPALACHIAN MOUNTAINS

BLUE RIDGE

Potomac River

James River

Roanoke River

Chesapeake Bay

PIEDMONT

ATLANTIC COASTAL PLAIN

Cape Hatteras

ATLANTIC OCEAN

OZARK PLATEAU

Lake of the Ozarks

BOSTON MTS.

OUACHITA MOUNTAINS

Cimarron River

Canadian River

Arkansas River

Ouachita River

White River

Mississippi River

Tennessee River

Mt. Mitchell
6,684 ft.
(2,037 m)

Pee Dee R.

Savannah River

Oconee River

Ocmulgee River

Altamaha River

Cape Fear

Red River

Sabine River

Yazoo River

Pearl River

Tombigbee River

Alabama River

Chattahoochee River

Flint River

Appalachicola River

St. Johns River

Cape Canaveral

Brazos River

Trinity River

Colorado River

GULF COASTAL PLAIN

Lake Pontchartrain

Mobile Bay

Mississippi Delta

Tampa Bay

Lake Okeechobee

THE BAHAMAS

Nueces River

Rio Grande

Padre Island

Galveston Bay

Gulf of Mexico

N
W   E
S

0   150   300 mi
0   150   300 km

Florida Keys

Straits of Florida

95°W   90°W   85°W   80°W   75°W   70°W

50°N

40°N

35°N

30°N

25°N

70°W

Great Plains   Mississippi River   Central Lowland   Appalachian Mountains

A ——— B

Chesapeake Bay

Delaware Bay

B

State	Total Area and Rank		Highest Point		Temperature °F		Annual Precipitation	
					Highest Recorded	Lowest Recorded	Highest Recorded	Lowest Recorded
Alabama	52,419 sq mi 135,765 sq km	30th	Cheaha Mtn.	2,407 ft 734 m	112°	−27°	106.57"	22.00"
Alaska	591,004 sq mi 1,530,700 sq km	1st	Mt. McKinley	20,320 ft 6,194 m	100°	−80°	332.29"	1.61"
Arizona	113,998 sq mi 295,254 sq km	6th	Humphreys Peak	12,633 ft 3,851 m	128°	−40°	58.92"	0.07"
Arkansas	53,179 sq mi 137,732 sq km	29th	Magazine Mtn.	2,753 ft 839 m	120°	−29°	98.55"	19.11"
California	163,696 sq mi 423,970 sq km	3rd	Mt. Whitney	14,494 ft 4,418 m	134°	−45°	153.54"	0.00"
Colorado	104,094 sq mi 269,601 sq km	8th	Mt. Elbert	14,433 ft 4,399 m	118°	−61°	92.84"	1.69"
Connecticut	5,543 sq mi 14,357 sq km	48th	Mt. Frissell on south slope at state line	2,380 ft 725 m	105°	−32°	78.53"	23.60"
Delaware	2,489 sq mi 6,447 sq km	49th	On Ebright Road at DE-PA border	448 ft 137 m	110°	−17°	72.75"	21.38"
Florida	65,755 sq mi 170,304 sq km	22nd	Britton Hill	345 ft 105 m	109°	−2°	112.43"	21.16"
Georgia	59,425 sq mi 153,909 sq km	24th	Brasstown Bald	4,784 ft 1,458 m	112°	−17°	112.16"	17.14"
Hawaii	10,931 sq mi 28,311 sq km	43rd	Pu'u Wekiu, Mauna Kea	13,796 ft 4,205 m	100°	12°	704.83"	0.19"
Idaho	83,570 sq mi 216,446 sq km	14th	Borah Peak	12,662 ft 3,859 m	118°	−60°	81.05"	2.09"
Illinois	57,914 sq mi 149,998 sq km	25th	Charles Mound	1,235 ft 376 m	117°	−35°	74.58"	16.59"
Indiana	36,418 sq mi 94,321 sq km	38th	Hoosier Hill	1,257 ft 383 m	116°	−35°	97.38"	18.67"
Iowa	56,272 sq mi 145,743 sq km	26th	Hawkeye Point	1,670 ft 509 m	118°	−47°	74.50"	12.11"
Kansas	82,277 sq mi 213,096 sq km	15th	Mt. Sunflower	4,039 ft 1,231 m	121°	−40°	67.02"	4.77"
Kentucky	40,409 sq mi 104,659 sq km	37th	Black Mtn.	4,145 ft 1,263 m	114°	−34°	79.68"	14.51"
Louisiana	51,840 sq mi 134,264 sq km	31st	Driskill Mtn.	535 ft 163 m	114°	−16°	113.74"	26.44"
Maine	35,385 sq mi 91,646 sq km	39th	Mt. Katahdin	5,268 ft 1,606 m	105°	−48°	75.64"	23.06"
Maryland	12,407 sq mi 32,133 sq km	42nd	Hoye Crest (point on Backbone Mtn.	3,360 ft 1,024 m	109°	−40°	72.59"	17.76"
Massachusetts	10,555 sq mi 27,336 sq km	44th	Mt. Greylock	3,491 ft 1,064 m	107°	−35°	72.19"	21.76"
Michigan	96,716 sq mi 250,494 sq km	11th	Mt. Arvon	1,979 ft 603 m	112°	−51°	64.01"	15.64"
Minnesota	86,939 sq mi 225,171 sq km	12th	Eagle Mtn.	2,301 ft 701 m	114°	−59°	51.53"	7.81"
Mississippi	48,430 sq mi 125,434 sq km	32nd	Woodall Mtn.	806 ft 246 m	115°	−19°	104.36"	25.97"
Missouri	69,704 sq mi 180,533 sq km	21st	Taum Sauk Mtn.	1,772 ft 540 m	118°	−40°	92.77"	16.14"

State	Total Area and Rank		Highest Point		Temperature °F		Annual Precipitation	
					Highest Recorded	Lowest Recorded	Highest Recorded	Lowest Recorded
Montana	147,042 sq mi 380,838 sq km	4th	Granite Peak	12,799 ft 3,901 m	117°	−70°	55.51"	2.97"
Nebraska	77,354 sq mi 200,345 sq km	16th	Panorama Point	5,424 ft 1,653 m	118°	−47°	64.52"	6.30"
Nevada	110,567 sq mi 286,368 sq km	7th	Boundary Peak	13,140 ft 4,005 m	125°	−50°	59.03"	Trace
New Hampshire	9,350 sq mi 24,216 sq km	46th	Mt. Washington	6,288 ft 1,917 m	106°	−46°	130.14"	22.31"
New Jersey	8,721 sq mi 22,588 sq km	47th	High Point	1,803 ft 550 m	110°	−34°	85.99"	19.85"
New Mexico	121,589 sq mi 314,915 sq km	5th	Wheeler Peak	13,161 ft 4,011 m	122°	−50°	62.45"	1.00"
New York	54,556 sq mi 141,299 sq km	27th	Mt. Marcy	5,344 ft 1,629 m	108°	−52°	82.06"	17.64"
North Carolina	53,819 sq mi 139,389 sq km	28th	Mt. Mitchell	6,684 ft 2,037 m	110°	−34°	129.60"	22.69"
North Dakota	70,700 sq mi 183,112 sq km	19th	White Butte	3,506 ft 1,069 m	121°	−60°	37.98"	4.02"
Ohio	44,825 sq mi 116,096 sq km	34th	Campbell Hill	1,550 ft 472 m	113°	−39°	70.82"	16.96"
Oklahoma	69,898 sq mi 181,036 sq km	20th	Black Mesa	4,973 ft 1,516 m	120°	−27°	84.47"	6.53"
Oregon	98,381 sq mi 254,805 sq km	9th	Mt. Hood	11,239 ft 3,426 m	119°	−54°	168.88"	3.33"
Pennsylvania	46,055 sq mi 119,283 sq km	33rd	Mt. Davis	3,213 ft 979 m	111°	−42°	81.64"	15.71"
Rhode Island	1,545 sq mi 4,002 sq km	50th	Jerimoth Hill	812 ft 247 m	104°	−23°	70.21"	24.08"
South Carolina	32,020 sq mi 82,932 sq km	40th	Sassafras Mtn.	3,560 ft 1,085 m	111°	−19°	101.65"	20.73"
South Dakota	77,116 sq mi 199,731 sq km	17th	Harney Peak	7,242 ft 2,207 m	120°	−58°	48.42"	2.89"
Tennessee	42,143 sq mi 109,151 sq km	36th	Clingmans Dome	6,643 ft 2,025 m	113°	−32°	114.88"	25.23"
Texas	268,581 sq mi 695,621 sq km	2nd	Guadalupe Peak	8,749 ft 2,667 m	120°	−23°	109.38"	1.64"
Utah	84,899 sq mi 219,887 sq km	13th	Kings Peak	13,528 ft 4,123 m	117°	−69°	108.54"	1.34"
Vermont	9,614 sq mi 24,901 sq km	45th	Mt. Mansfield	4,393 ft 1,339 m	105°	−50°	92.88"	22.98"
Virginia	42,774 sq mi 110,785 sq km	35th	Mt. Rogers	5,729 ft 1,746 m	110°	−30°	81.78"	12.52"
Washington	71,300 sq mi 184,665 sq km	18th	Mt. Rainier	14,411 ft 4,392 m	118°	−48°	184.56"	2.61"
West Virginia	24,230 sq mi 62,755 sq km	41st	Spruce Knob	4,863 ft 1,482 m	112°	−37°	94.01"	9.50"
Wisconsin	65,498 sq mi 169,639 sq km	23rd	Timms Hill	1,951 ft 595 m	114°	−54°	62.07"	12.00"
Wyoming	97,814 sq mi 253,336 sq km	10th	Gannett Peak	13,804 ft 4,207 m	114°	−63°	55.46"	1.28"

Divide

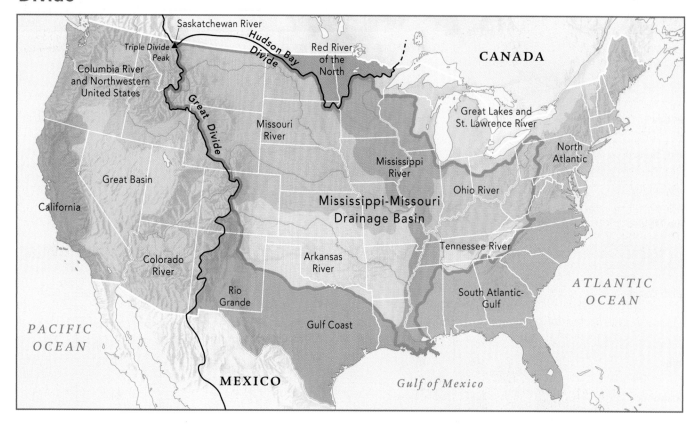

DIVIDE: *The boundary or high ground between river systems.* Streams on one side of the divide flow in a different direction and into a different drainage basin from the streams on the other side. A continental divide is the boundary that separates the rivers flowing toward opposite sides of a continent.

In North America a continental divide called the **Great Divide** runs along the crest of the Rocky Mountains, dividing rivers that flow to the Gulf of Mexico and the Atlantic Ocean from those that flow into the Pacific Ocean. Another much lower divide separates those rivers that flow north through Hudson Bay to the Arctic Ocean. Triple Divide Peak in Montana is located on both these divides. Water from one side of this mountain flows east to the Atlantic or Gulf of Mexico; from another side water flows west to the Pacific; and from the north face, water flows to the Arctic Ocean.

Earthquakes

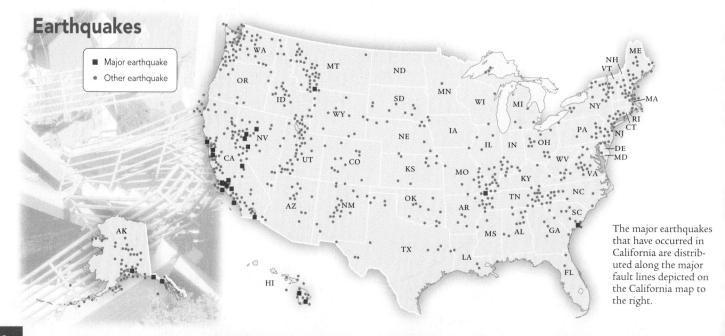

- ■ Major earthquake
- • Other earthquake

The major earthquakes that have occurred in California are distributed along the major fault lines depicted on the California map to the right.

Fall Line

FALL LINE: *A geologic feature where uplands meet lowlands and a series of waterfalls and rapids occur.* Fall lines are formed where a region of hard rock borders softer rock, and the softer rock has eroded away. The erosion creates a ledge that water flows over.

A major fall line exists in the eastern United States. It marks the boundary between the Coastal Plain and the Piedmont and runs between New York and Alabama. Cities have grown into industrial and commercial hubs around each waterfall on the fall line for two reasons. First, the energy of the falling water can be captured and used by industry. Second, the fall line is often the farthest point reachable by ships carrying goods up river, which means that goods are transferred to land-based transport at that point. Some fall line cities on the East Coast include Trenton, Philadelphia, Baltimore, Washington, D.C., Richmond, Petersburg, Columbia, Macon, and Montgomery. If you draw a line on a map connecting these city dots, you will have drawn the Eastern Fall Line.

Fault

FAULT: *A break in the Earth's crust caused by movement.* Solid rock on one side of the fault no longer matches the solid rock on the other side. The movement may take place in any direction—up, down, or sideways. The movement may be a few inches or thousands of feet.

A fault that moves up or down is called a **dip-slip fault**. Niagara Falls cascades over an escarpment caused by this kind of movement.

A fault that moves sideways is called a **strike-slip fault**. The San Andreas fault is an example of this kind. Horizontal movement along this fault caused the devastating San Francisco earthquake in 1906 and will cause more earthquakes in the future. This happens because this fault marks the boundary between the Pacific Plate and the North American Plate (see page 20).

Where two parallel faults pull away from each other, they create a long, sunken valley between them called a **rift**. The Great Rift Valley in Africa is the world's most visible example (see page 91). Underwater, the huge Mid-Ocean Ridge is the longest rift on Earth (see pages 18–19).

North America

The United States

Canada

Mexico

South America

Europe

Arid

Highland

Humid continental

Climate

- Tropical wet
- Tropical wet and dry
- Arid
- Semiarid
- Mediterranean
- Humid subtropical
- Marine
- Humid continental
- Subarctic
- Tundra
- Highland

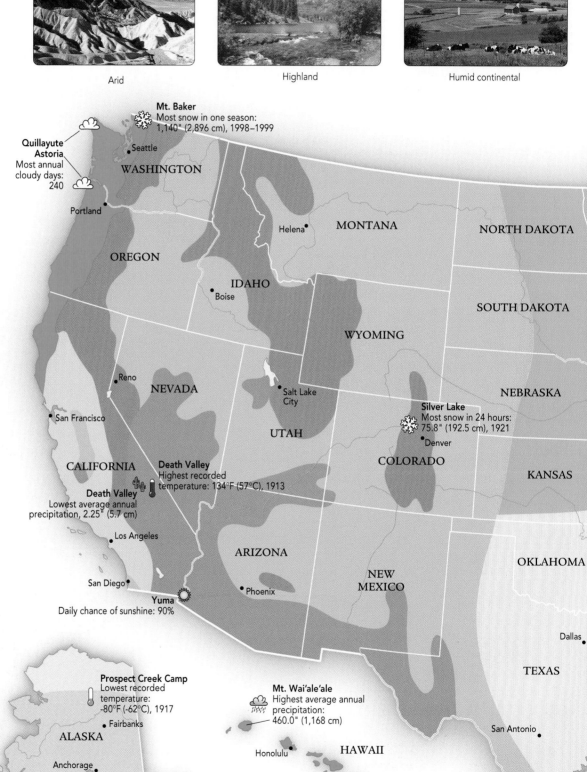

Mt. Baker Most snow in one season: 1,140" (2,896 cm), 1998–1999

Quillayute Astoria Most annual cloudy days: 240

Seattle

WASHINGTON

Portland

MONTANA

Helena

NORTH DAKOTA

OREGON

IDAHO

Boise

WYOMING

SOUTH DAKOTA

Reno

NEVADA

Salt Lake City

UTAH

Silver Lake Most snow in 24 hours: 75.8" (192.5 cm), 1921

San Francisco

Denver

NEBRASKA

COLORADO

KANSAS

CALIFORNIA

Death Valley Highest recorded temperature: 134°F (57°C), 1913

Death Valley Lowest average annual precipitation, 2.25" (5.7 cm)

Los Angeles

ARIZONA

NEW MEXICO

OKLAHOMA

San Diego

Phoenix

Yuma Daily chance of sunshine: 90%

Dallas

TEXAS

Prospect Creek Camp Lowest recorded temperature: -80°F (-62°C), 1917

Fairbanks

ALASKA

Anchorage

Mt. Wai'ale'ale Highest average annual precipitation: 460.0" (1,168 cm)

Honolulu

HAWAII

San Antonio

Hilo

Hilo Most days of rain: 277

Humid subtropical

Marine

Mediterranean

Semiarid

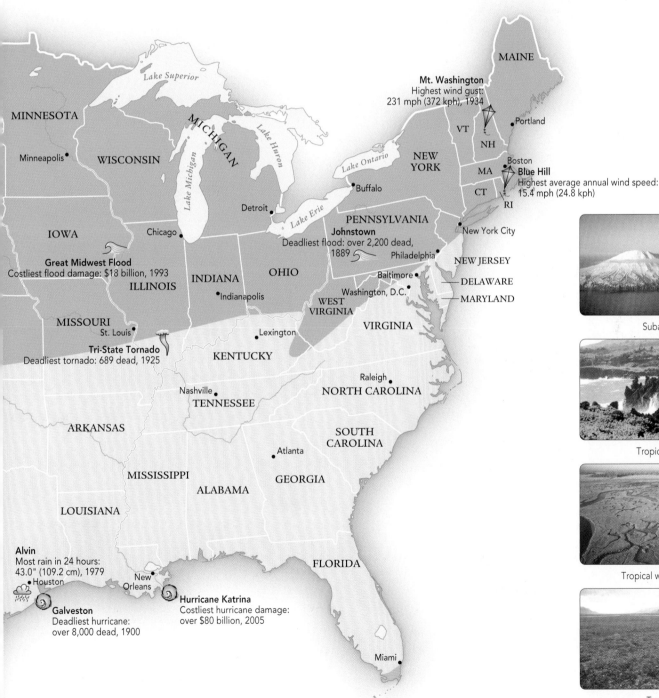

MINNESOTA

Lake Superior

Minneapolis •

WISCONSIN

MICHIGAN

Lake Michigan

Lake Huron

Mt. Washington
Highest wind gust:
231 mph (372 kph), 1934

MAINE

VT
• Portland

NH

Boston
Blue Hill
Highest average annual wind speed:
15.4 mph (24.8 kph)

MA

CT

RI

NEW
YORK

Lake Ontario

IOWA

Chicago •

Detroit •

Lake Erie

Buffalo •

Great Midwest Flood
Costliest flood damage: $18 billion, 1993

ILLINOIS

INDIANA

• Indianapolis

OHIO

PENNSYLVANIA

Johnstown
Deadliest flood: over 2,200 dead,
1889

Philadelphia •

• New York City

NEW JERSEY

Baltimore •

DELAWARE

Washington, D.C. •

MARYLAND

MISSOURI
St. Louis •

WEST
VIRGINIA

VIRGINIA

Tri-State Tornado
Deadliest tornado: 689 dead, 1925

KENTUCKY

• Lexington

Raleigh •

NORTH CAROLINA

Nashville •

TENNESSEE

ARKANSAS

SOUTH
CAROLINA

MISSISSIPPI

• Atlanta

GEORGIA

ALABAMA

LOUISIANA

Alvin
Most rain in 24 hours:
43.0" (109.2 cm), 1979
• Houston

New
Orleans •

FLORIDA

Galveston
Deadliest hurricane:
over 8,000 dead, 1900

Hurricane Katrina
Costliest hurricane damage:
over $80 billion, 2005

Miami •

Subarctic

Tropical wet

Tropical wet and dry

Tundra

Vegetation

- Tundra and alpine tundra
- Coniferous forest
- Midlatitude deciduous forest
- Subtropical broadleaf evergreen forest
- Mixed forest
- Midlatitude scrubland
- Midlatitude grassland
- Desert
- Tropical rain forest

Coniferous forest

Desert

Midlatitude deciduous forest

Midlatitude grassland

Midlatitude scrubland

Mixed forest

Subtropical broadleaf evergreen forest

Tropical rain forest

Tundra and alpine tundra

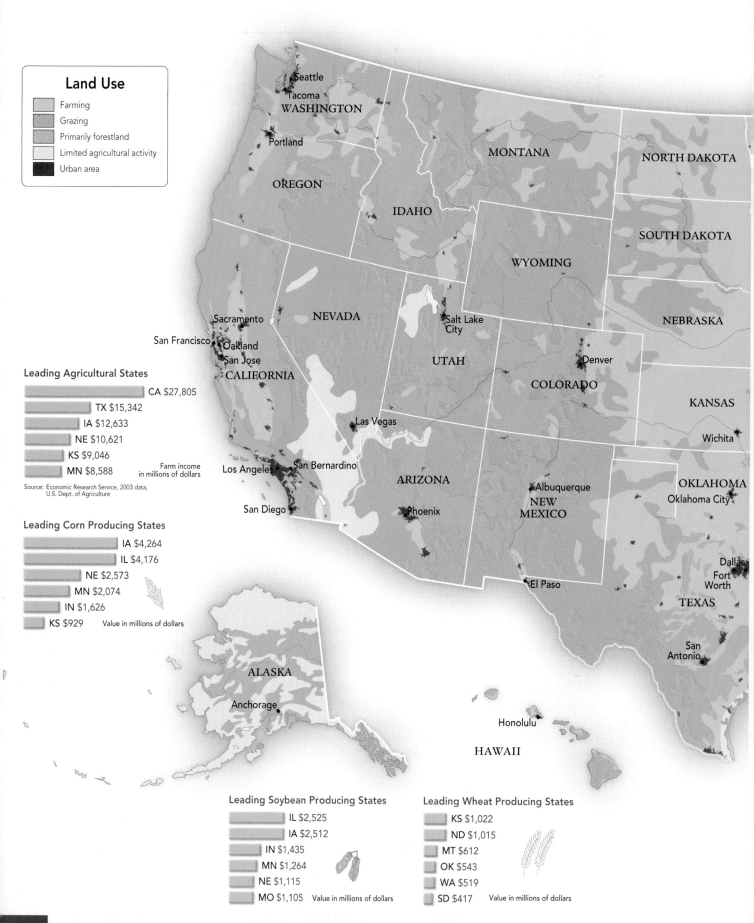

Land Use

- Farming
- Grazing
- Primarily forestland
- Limited agricultural activity
- Urban area

Leading Agricultural States

CA	$27,805
TX	$15,342
IA	$12,633
NE	$10,621
KS	$9,046
MN	$8,588

Farm income in millions of dollars

Source: Economic Research Service, 2003 data, U.S. Dept. of Agriculture

Leading Corn Producing States

IA	$4,264
IL	$4,176
NE	$2,573
MN	$2,074
IN	$1,626
KS	$929

Value in millions of dollars

Leading Soybean Producing States

IL	$2,525
IA	$2,512
IN	$1,435
MN	$1,264
NE	$1,115
MO	$1,105

Value in millions of dollars

Leading Wheat Producing States

KS	$1,022
ND	$1,015
MT	$612
OK	$543
WA	$519
SD	$417

Value in millions of dollars

Seattle
Tacoma
WASHINGTON
Portland
OREGON
MONTANA
NORTH DAKOTA
IDAHO
SOUTH DAKOTA
WYOMING
Sacramento
San Francisco
Oakland
San Jose
CALIFORNIA
NEVADA
Salt Lake City
UTAH
Denver
COLORADO
NEBRASKA
KANSAS
Wichita
Las Vegas
Los Angeles
San Bernardino
ARIZONA
Albuquerque
NEW MEXICO
OKLAHOMA
Oklahoma City
San Diego
Phoenix
El Paso
Dallas
Fort Worth
TEXAS
San Antonio
ALASKA
Anchorage
Honolulu
HAWAII

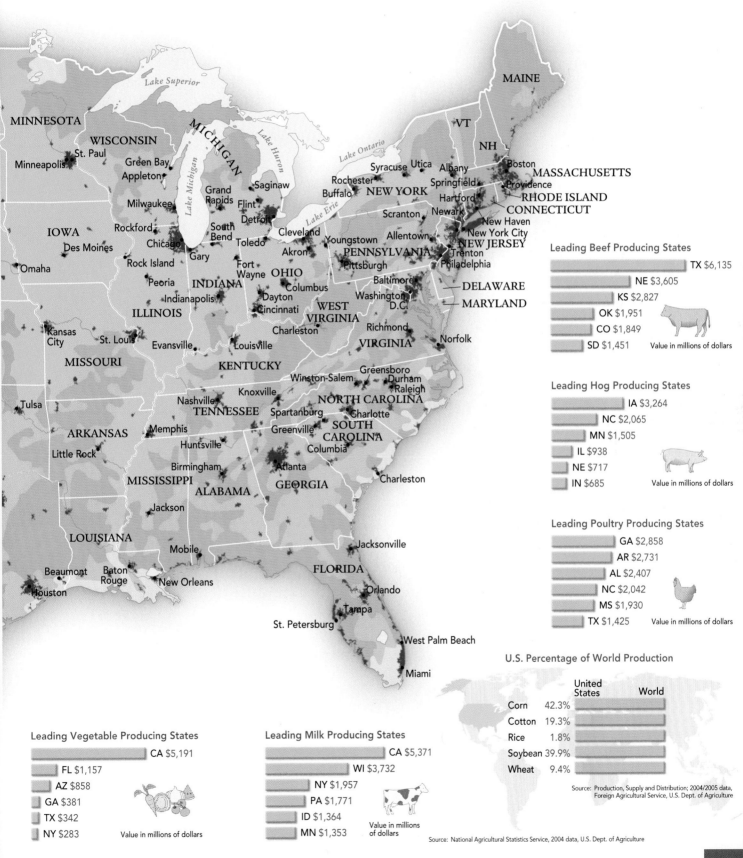

MAINE

MINNESOTA

WISCONSIN

St. Paul
Minneapolis

Green Bay
Appleton

MICHIGAN

Lake Superior

Lake Huron

Lake Michigan

VT

NH

Boston
Providence

MASSACHUSETTS

Milwaukee

Grand Rapids

Saginaw

Lake Ontario

Syracuse Utica

Albany
Springfield
Hartford

RHODE ISLAND
CONNECTICUT

IOWA

Rockford

Flint
Detroit

South Bend

Cleveland

Rochester
Buffalo

NEW YORK

Scranton

Newark
New Haven
New York City

Des Moines

Chicago

Toledo

Youngstown
Akron

Allentown

NEW JERSEY
Trenton
Philadelphia

Omaha

Rock Island

Gary

Fort Wayne

PENNSYLVANIA
Pittsburgh

Baltimore

DELAWARE

Peoria

INDIANA

Columbus

Washington D.C.

MARYLAND

Indianapolis

OHIO

Dayton
Cincinnati

WEST VIRGINIA

ILLINOIS

Kansas City

St. Louis

Evansville

Louisville

Charleston

Richmond

Norfolk

MISSOURI

KENTUCKY

VIRGINIA

Tulsa

Nashville
Knoxville

Winston-Salem

Greensboro Durham
Raleigh

ARKANSAS

Memphis

TENNESSEE

Spartanburg
Greenville

Charlotte

NORTH CAROLINA

Little Rock

Huntsville

SOUTH CAROLINA
Columbia

Birmingham

Atlanta

Charleston

MISSISSIPPI

ALABAMA

GEORGIA

Jackson

LOUISIANA

Mobile

Jacksonville

Beaumont

Baton Rouge

New Orleans

FLORIDA

Houston

Orlando

Tampa

St. Petersburg

West Palm Beach

Miami

Leading Beef Producing States

TX $6,135
NE $3,605
KS $2,827
OK $1,951
CO $1,849
SD $1,451

Value in millions of dollars

Leading Hog Producing States

IA $3,264
NC $2,065
MN $1,505
IL $938
NE $717
IN $685

Value in millions of dollars

Leading Poultry Producing States

GA $2,858
AR $2,731
AL $2,407
NC $2,042
MS $1,930
TX $1,425

Value in millions of dollars

U.S. Percentage of World Production

	United States	World
Corn	42.3%	
Cotton	19.3%	
Rice	1.8%	
Soybean	39.9%	
Wheat	9.4%	

Source: Production, Supply and Distribution; 2004/2005 data, Foreign Agricultural Service, U.S. Dept. of Agriculture

Leading Vegetable Producing States

CA $5,191
FL $1,157
AZ $858
GA $381
TX $342
NY $283

Value in millions of dollars

Leading Milk Producing States

CA $5,371
WI $3,732
NY $1,957
PA $1,771
ID $1,364
MN $1,353

Value in millions of dollars

Source: National Agricultural Statistics Service, 2004 data, U.S. Dept. of Agriculture

65

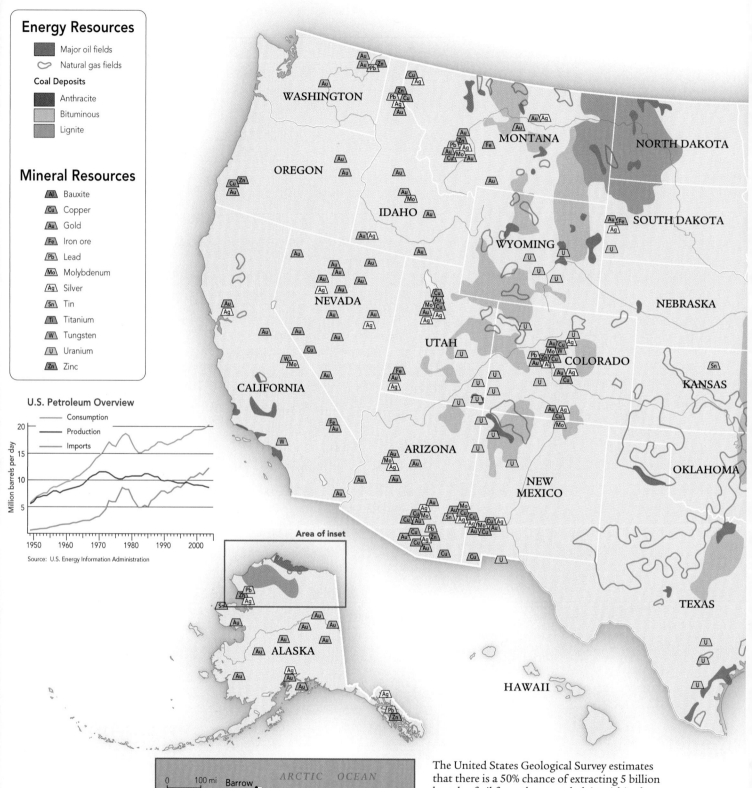

Energy Resources

- � Major oil fields
- ⬭ Natural gas fields

Coal Deposits
- ▮ Anthracite
- ▮ Bituminous
- ▮ Lignite

Mineral Resources

Al	Bauxite
Cu	Copper
Au	Gold
Fe	Iron ore
Pb	Lead
Mo	Molybdenum
Ag	Silver
Sn	Tin
Ti	Titanium
W	Tungsten
U	Uranium
Zn	Zinc

U.S. Petroleum Overview

Consumption
Production
Imports

Million barrels per day

20
15
10
5

1950 1960 1970 1980 1990 2000

Source: U.S. Energy Information Administration

Area of inset

WASHINGTON
OREGON
IDAHO
NEVADA
CALIFORNIA
ARIZONA
MONTANA
WYOMING
UTAH
NEW MEXICO
NORTH DAKOTA
SOUTH DAKOTA
NEBRASKA
COLORADO
KANSAS
OKLAHOMA
TEXAS
HAWAII
ALASKA

The United States Geological Survey estimates that there is a 50% chance of extracting 5 billion barrels of oil from the coastal plain within the Arctic National Wildlife Refuge. Debate surrounds the issue of drilling and production and its impact on the environment.

ARCTIC OCEAN
0 100 mi
0 100 km
Barrow
Prudhoe Bay
Beaufort Sea
TRANS-ALASKA PIPELINE
ARCTIC NATIONAL WILDLIFE REFUGE
NOATAK NATL. PRES.
KOBUK VALLEY N.P.
GATES OF THE ARCTIC N.P. AND PRES.
CANADA
U.S.

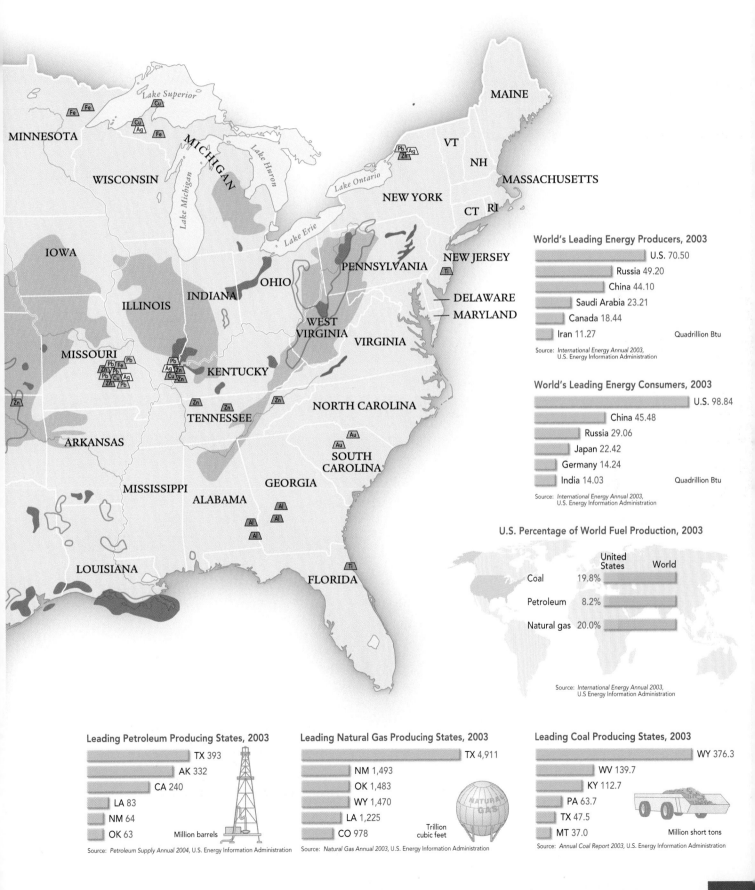

MAINE

MINNESOTA

WISCONSIN

MICHIGAN

Lake Superior

Lake Michigan

Lake Huron

Lake Ontario

Lake Erie

VT

NH

MASSACHUSETTS

NEW YORK

CT   RI

IOWA

OHIO

PENNSYLVANIA

NEW JERSEY

ILLINOIS

INDIANA

DELAWARE

MARYLAND

WEST
VIRGINIA

VIRGINIA

MISSOURI

KENTUCKY

NORTH CAROLINA

TENNESSEE

ARKANSAS

SOUTH
CAROLINA

GEORGIA

MISSISSIPPI

ALABAMA

LOUISIANA

FLORIDA

World's Leading Energy Producers, 2003

U.S. 70.50
Russia 49.20
China 44.10
Saudi Arabia 23.21
Canada 18.44
Iran 11.27   Quadrillion Btu

Source: *International Energy Annual 2003*,
U.S. Energy Information Administration

World's Leading Energy Consumers, 2003

U.S. 98.84
China 45.48
Russia 29.06
Japan 22.42
Germany 14.24
India 14.03   Quadrillion Btu

Source: *International Energy Annual 2003*,
U.S. Energy Information Administration

U.S. Percentage of World Fuel Production, 2003

	United States	World
Coal	19.8%	
Petroleum	8.2%	
Natural gas	20.0%	

Source: *International Energy Annual 2003*,
U.S Energy Information Administration

Leading Petroleum Producing States, 2003

TX 393
AK 332
CA 240
LA 83
NM 64
OK 63   Million barrels

Source: *Petroleum Supply Annual 2004*, U.S. Energy Information Administration

Leading Natural Gas Producing States, 2003

TX 4,911
NM 1,493
OK 1,483
WY 1,470
LA 1,225
CO 978   Trillion
                         cubic feet

Source: *Natural Gas Annual 2003*, U.S. Energy Information Administration

Leading Coal Producing States, 2003

WY 376.3
WV 139.7
KY 112.7
PA 63.7
TX 47.5
MT 37.0   Million short tons

Source: *Annual Coal Report 2003*, U.S. Energy Information Administration

67

North America

The United States

Canada

Mexico

South America

Europe

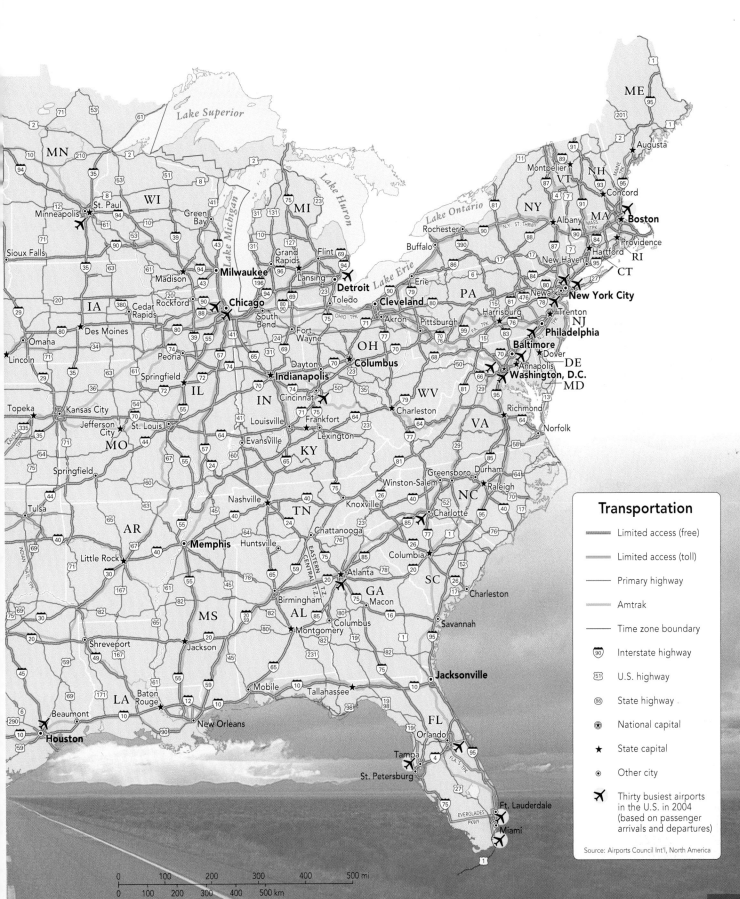

Transportation

━━━━ Limited access (free)

──── Limited access (toll)

──── Primary highway

──── Amtrak

──── Time zone boundary

(90) Interstate highway

(51) U.S. highway

(86) State highway

⊛ National capital

★ State capital

⊙ Other city

✈ Thirty busiest airports in the U.S. in 2004 (based on passenger arrivals and departures)

Source: Airports Council Int'l, North America

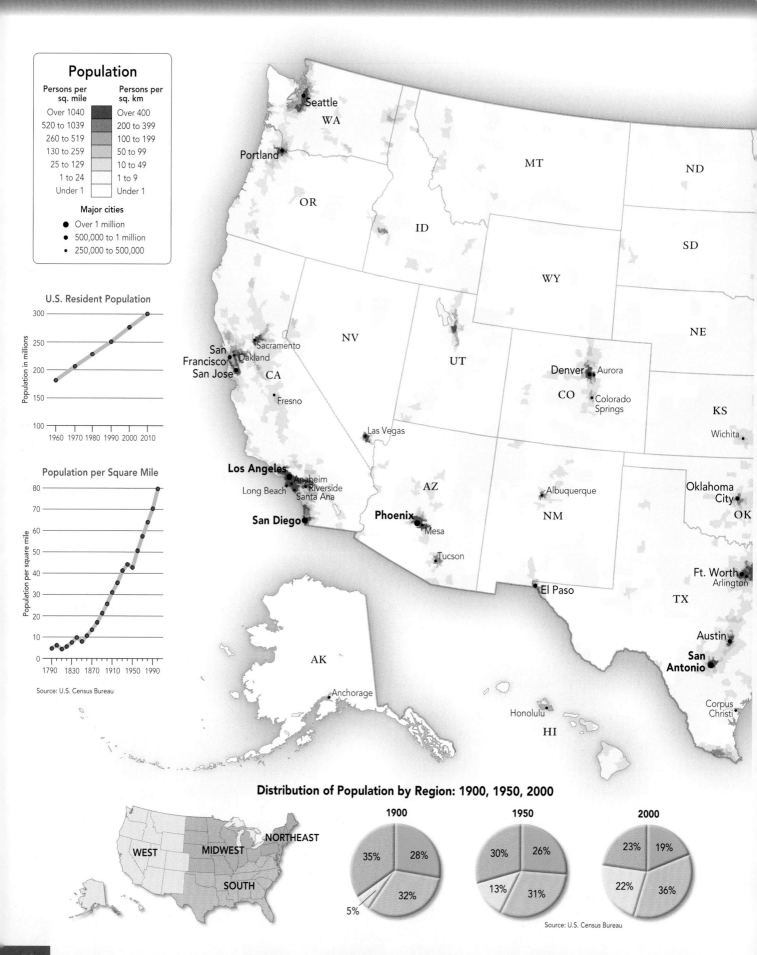

Population

Persons per sq. mile	Persons per sq. km
Over 1040	Over 400
520 to 1039	200 to 399
260 to 519	100 to 199
130 to 259	50 to 99
25 to 129	10 to 49
1 to 24	1 to 9
Under 1	Under 1

Major cities
- Over 1 million
- 500,000 to 1 million
- 250,000 to 500,000

U.S. Resident Population

Population in millions

300
250
200
150
100

1960 1970 1980 1990 2000 2010

Population per Square Mile

Population per square mile

80
70
60
50
40
30
20
10
0

1790 1830 1870 1910 1950 1990

Source: U.S. Census Bureau

Distribution of Population by Region: 1900, 1950, 2000

WEST · MIDWEST · NORTHEAST · SOUTH

1900
35% | 28% | 32% | 5%

1950
30% | 26% | 13% | 31%

2000
23% | 19% | 22% | 36%

Source: U.S. Census Bureau

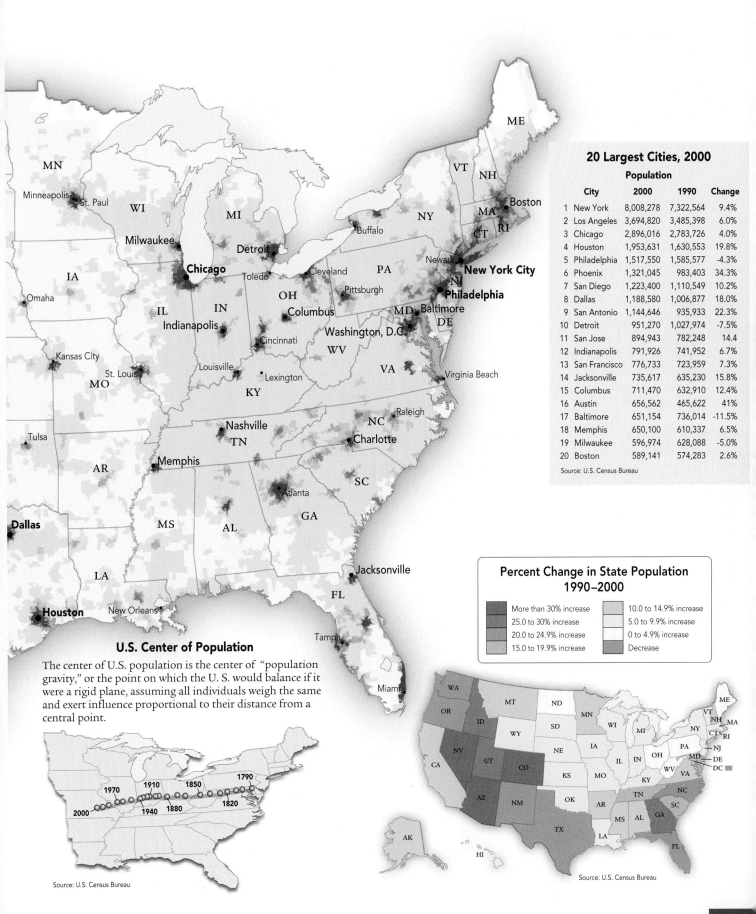

20 Largest Cities, 2000

Population

	City	2000	1990	Change
1	New York	8,008,278	7,322,564	9.4%
2	Los Angeles	3,694,820	3,485,398	6.0%
3	Chicago	2,896,016	2,783,726	4.0%
4	Houston	1,953,631	1,630,553	19.8%
5	Philadelphia	1,517,550	1,585,577	-4.3%
6	Phoenix	1,321,045	983,403	34.3%
7	San Diego	1,223,400	1,110,549	10.2%
8	Dallas	1,188,580	1,006,877	18.0%
9	San Antonio	1,144,646	935,933	22.3%
10	Detroit	951,270	1,027,974	-7.5%
11	San Jose	894,943	782,248	14.4
12	Indianapolis	791,926	741,952	6.7%
13	San Francisco	776,733	723,959	7.3%
14	Jacksonville	735,617	635,230	15.8%
15	Columbus	711,470	632,910	12.4%
16	Austin	656,562	465,622	41%
17	Baltimore	651,154	736,014	-11.5%
18	Memphis	650,100	610,337	6.5%
19	Milwaukee	596,974	628,088	-5.0%
20	Boston	589,141	574,283	2.6%

Source: U.S. Census Bureau

Percent Change in State Population 1990–2000

More than 30% increase	10.0 to 14.9% increase
25.0 to 30% increase	5.0 to 9.9% increase
20.0 to 24.9% increase	0 to 4.9% increase
15.0 to 19.9% increase	Decrease

U.S. Center of Population

The center of U.S. population is the center of "population gravity," or the point on which the U. S. would balance if it were a rigid plane, assuming all individuals weigh the same and exert influence proportional to their distance from a central point.

Source: U.S. Census Bureau

Source: U.S. Census Bureau

71

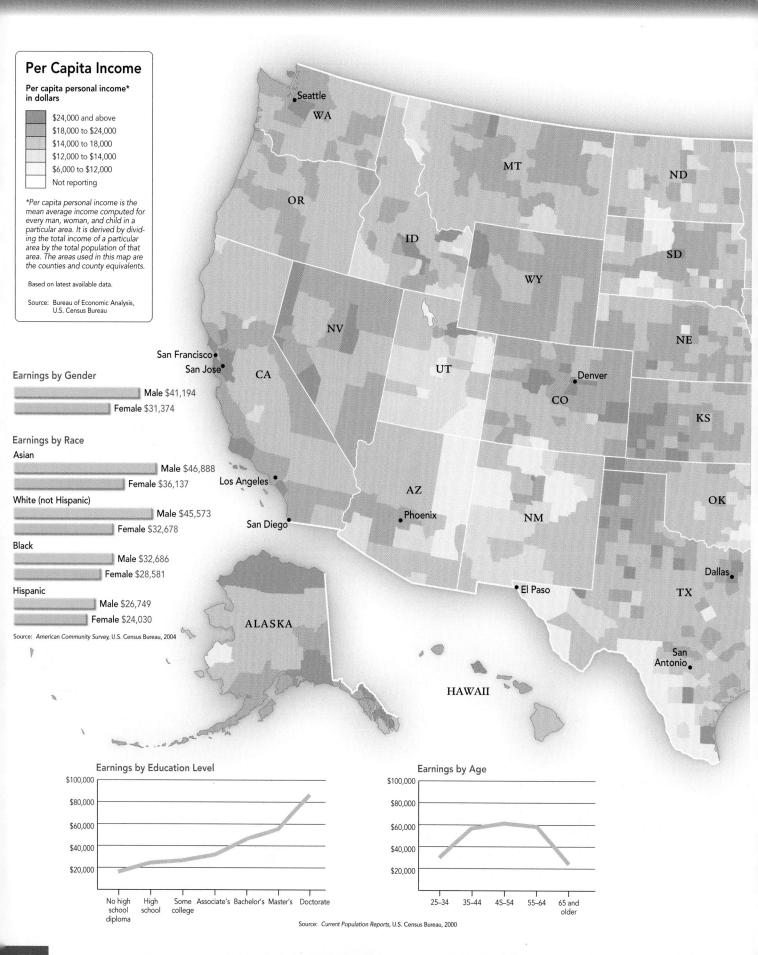

Per Capita Income

Per capita personal income* in dollars

- $24,000 and above
- $18,000 to $24,000
- $14,000 to 18,000
- $12,000 to $14,000
- $6,000 to $12,000
- Not reporting

*Per capita personal income is the mean average income computed for every man, woman, and child in a particular area. It is derived by dividing the total income of a particular area by the total population of that area. The areas used in this map are the counties and county equivalents.

Based on latest available data.

Source: Bureau of Economic Analysis, U.S. Census Bureau

Earnings by Gender
- Male $41,194
- Female $31,374

Earnings by Race
Asian
- Male $46,888
- Female $36,137

White (not Hispanic)
- Male $45,573
- Female $32,678

Black
- Male $32,686
- Female $28,581

Hispanic
- Male $26,749
- Female $24,030

Source: American Community Survey, U.S. Census Bureau, 2004

Earnings by Education Level
$100,000 / $80,000 / $60,000 / $40,000 / $20,000

No high school diploma | High school | Some college | Associate's | Bachelor's | Master's | Doctorate

Earnings by Age
$100,000 / $80,000 / $60,000 / $40,000 / $20,000

25–34 | 35–44 | 45–54 | 55–64 | 65 and older

Source: Current Population Reports, U.S. Census Bureau, 2000

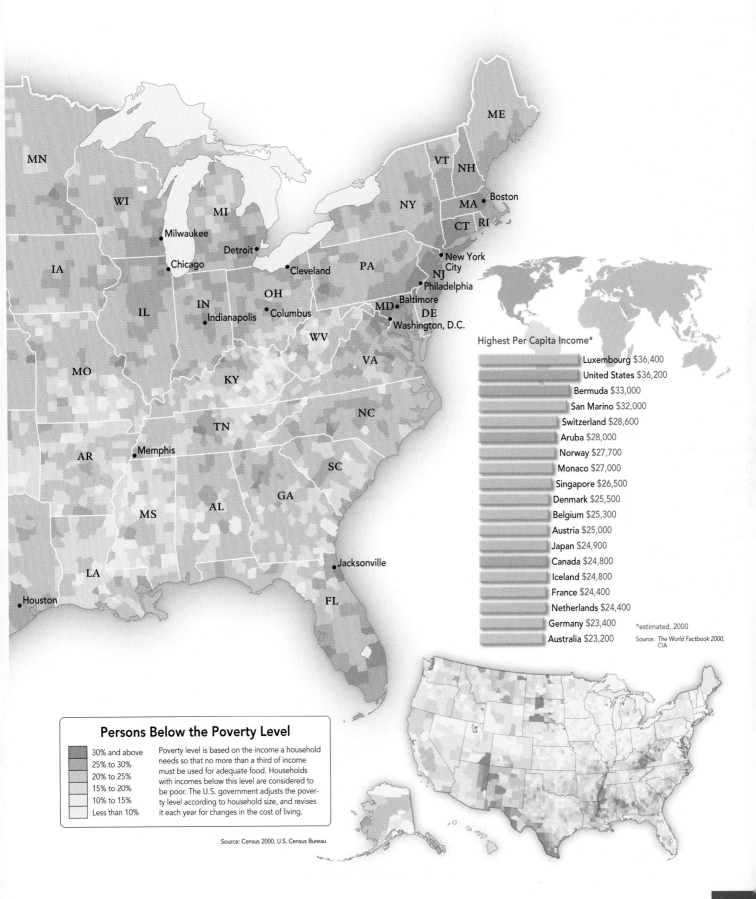

MN

WI

MI
Milwaukee
Detroit
Chicago
Cleveland

IA

IL

IN
Indianapolis

OH
Columbus

PA

ME

VT

NH

NY

MA
Boston

CT
RI

New York
City

NJ
Philadelphia

MD
Baltimore

DE
Washington, D.C.

WV

VA

MO

KY

TN
Memphis

NC

AR

SC

GA

MS

AL

LA

Houston

Jacksonville

FL

Highest Per Capita Income*

Luxembourg	$36,400
United States	$36,200
Bermuda	$33,000
San Marino	$32,000
Switzerland	$28,600
Aruba	$28,000
Norway	$27,700
Monaco	$27,000
Singapore	$26,500
Denmark	$25,500
Belgium	$25,300
Austria	$25,000
Japan	$24,900
Canada	$24,800
Iceland	$24,800
France	$24,400
Netherlands	$24,400
Germany	$23,400
Australia	$23,200

*estimated, 2000

Source: *The World Factbook 2000*, CIA

Persons Below the Poverty Level

▉	30% and above
▉	25% to 30%
▉	20% to 25%
▉	15% to 20%
▉	10% to 15%
▉	Less than 10%

Poverty level is based on the income a household needs so that no more than a third of income must be used for adequate food. Households with incomes below this level are considered to be poor. The U.S. government adjusts the poverty level according to household size, and revises it each year for changes in the cost of living.

Source: Census 2000, U.S. Census Bureau

Canada

- Area: 3,851,809 square miles (9,976,185 square kilometers)
- Highest Point: Mt. Logan, 19,551 ft. (5,959 m) [A]
- Lowest Point: sea level
- Longest River: Mackenzie-Slave-Peace-Finlay 2,635 mi. (4,240 km) [A]
- Largest Lake: Great Bear Lake, 12,275 sq. mi. (31,792 sq. km)
- Largest Urban Concentration: Toronto, Ontario 5,406,300 [B]

Sources:
[A] Natural Resources Canada
[B] Statistics Canada, metropolitan area, 2006 estimate

Legend

- International boundary
- Provincial boundary
- ⊛ National capital
- ★ Other capital

Symbol and label sizes indicate relative sizes of cities:
- **Toronto**
- Vancouver
- Sault Ste. Marie

Canada

Québec

Nunavut

Newfoundland and Labrador

Prince Edward Island

Nova Scotia

New Brunswick

Ontario

Manitoba

Saskatchewan

Alberta

British Columbia

Yukon Territory

Northwest Territories

All offshore islands in Hudson Bay, James Bay, Ungava Bay, and Hudson Strait are part of Nunavut

500 mi
500 km
250
250
0
0

ATLANTIC OCEAN

PACIFIC OCEAN

ARCTIC OCEAN

Beaufort Sea

Gulf of Alaska

Labrador Sea

Davis Strait

Baffin Bay

Foxe Basin

Hudson Strait

Ungava Bay

Hudson Bay

James Bay

Lancaster Sound

Gulf of Boothia

Viscount Melville Sound

Amundsen Gulf

ARCTIC CIRCLE

YUKON TERRITORY

NORTHWEST TERRITORIES

NUNAVUT

BRITISH COLUMBIA

ALBERTA

SASKATCHEWAN

MANITOBA

ONTARIO

QUÉBEC

NEWFOUNDLAND AND LABRADOR

NEW BRUNSWICK

NOVA SCOTIA

P.E.I.

CANADA

Cities and places:
Dawson, Whitehorse, Faro, Watson Lake, Inuvik, Fort McPherson, Holman, Kugluktuk, Cambridge Bay, Resolute, Pond Inlet, Arctic Bay, Pangnirtung, Iqaluit, Repulse Bay, Baker Lake, Rankin Inlet, Arviat, Churchill, Yellowknife, Déline, Fort Simpson, Hay River, Fort Smith, High Level, Fort Nelson, Fort St. John, Dawson Creek, Prince Rupert, Kitimat, Masset, Port Hardy, Nanaimo, Victoria, Vancouver, Kelowna, Kamloops, Williams Lake, Campbell River, Prince George, Mackenzie, Revelstoke, Trail, Cranbrook, Banff, Jasper, Grande Prairie, Peace River, La Loche, Fort McMurray, Edmonton, Red Deer, Lloydminster, Calgary, Medicine Hat, Lethbridge, La Ronge, Prince Albert, North Battleford, Saskatoon, Yorkton, Swift Current, Moose Jaw, Regina, Estevan, Brandon, Portage la Prairie, Dauphin, Flin Flon, The Pas, Thompson, Winnipeg, Kenora, Dryden, Fort Frances, Thunder Bay, Marathon, Wawa, Sault Ste. Marie, Sudbury, Timmins, Kapuskasing, Hearst, Moosonee, Owen Sound, North Bay, Elliot Lake, Barrie, Peterborough, Toronto, Kitchener, London, Hamilton, St. Catharines, Windsor, Sarnia, Kingston, Cornwall, Ottawa, Gatineau, Pembroke, Montréal, Trois-Rivières, Shawinigan, Val-d'Or, Rouyn-Noranda, Chibougamau, Chisasibi, Québec, Chicoutimi, Alma, Rivière-du-Loup, Baie-Comeau, Sept-Îles, Port-Cartier, Rimouski, Matane, Gaspé, Edmundston, Fredericton, Bathurst, Miramichi, Moncton, Saint John, St-Georges, Sherbrooke, Truro, New Glasgow, Sydney, Halifax, Yarmouth, Charlottetown, Channel-Port aux Basques, Corner Brook, Grand Falls, Windsor, Gander, St. Anthony, Cartwright, Nain, Happy Valley-Goose Bay, Labrador City, Havre-St-Pierre, St. John's, Marystown, St-Pierre & Miquelon (France), Kuujjuaq, Puvirnituq, Kuujjuarapik

Water features:
Yukon R., Mackenzie R., Great Slave Lake, Great Bear Lake, Lake Athabasca, Peace R., Fraser R., Columbia R., Reindeer Lake, Lake Winnipeg, Lake Winnipegosis, Lake Manitoba, Lake of the Woods, Lake Superior, Lake Nipigon, Nelson R., Churchill R., Back R., Smallwood Res., St. Lawrence R., Gulf of St. Lawrence, Bay of Fundy, Gulf of P.E.I.

60°W, 80°W, 100°W, 120°W, 110°W, 130°W, 140°W, 90°W, 70°W

50°N, 60°N, 70°N

N E S W (compass)

74

ATLANTIC OCEAN

PACIFIC OCEAN

ASIA

EUROPE

AFRICA

INDIAN OCEAN

AUSTRALIA

NORTH AMERICA

ATLANTIC OCEAN

SOUTH AMERICA

PACIFIC OCEAN

SOUTHERN OCEAN

ANTARCTICA

Equator

ARCTIC OCEAN

Robinson Projection

Denmark Strait

Greenland
(Kalaallit Nunaat)
(Denmark)

Davis Strait

Baffin
Bay

Labrador
Sea

Cape Chidley

ATLANTIC
OCEAN

Avalon
Cape Race
Newfoundland
Miquelon Islands
Cape Breton I.
Sable
Island
Nova
Scotia
Cape Sable

Strait of
Belle Isle
LONG RANGE MTS.
Anticosti
Island
Gaspé
Pen.
Gulf of St.
Lawrence
Prince
Edward
Island
St. John R.
Mt. Jacques-Cartier
4,160 ft.
(1,268 m)
LAURENTIAN MTS.
NOTRE DAME MTS.
St. Lawrence River

Labrador

Churchill R.
Smallwood
Reservoir
George R.
Caniapiscau R.
R. aux Feuilles
Ungava
Bay
Lac Bienville
La Grande
Reservoirs
Lac
Sakami
Lac
Mistassini
Saguenay R.
Lac St-Jean
Ottawa R.
Manicouagan
Rés.
L. Ontario
Lake Erie

Ungava
Peninsula

Hudson Strait

Resolution
Bay
Meta
Incognita
Pen.

Frobisher Bay
Hall
Pen.
Amadjuak
Lake
Nettilling
Lake

Cumberland Sound
Cumberland
Peninsula

Baffin
Island

Foxe
Pen.
Foxe
Basin

Prince
Charles
Island

Southampton
Island

Belcher
Islands

James
Bay
Akimiski
Island

Hudson
Bay

Cape Tatnam

Albany R.
Attawapiskat
R.

Manitoulin
Island

Lake
Nipigon

Lake Huron

Lake Michigan

Lake Superior

Devon
Island

Lancaster Sound

Brodeur
Pen.

Somerset
Island

Boothia
Pen.

Melville
Pen.

Gulf of Boothia

King
William
Island

Baker
Lake

Dubawnt
Lake

Southern
Indian
Lake

Winisk R.
Severn R.

Nelson River

Lake
Winnipeg

Lake of
the Woods

Red R.

UNITED STATES

Ellesmere
Island

Cape Columbia

Axel
Heiberg
Island

Parry Islands

Viscount Melville
Sound

Bathurst
Island

Prince
Patrick
Island

Melville Island

Prince of
Wales
Island

McClure Strait

Banks
Island

Victoria
Island

Back R.

Garry
Lake

Thelon R.

Dubawnt R.
Wholdaia L.
Kasba L.

Lake Athabasca

Wollaston
Lake

Reindeer
Lake

Cree
Lake

Churchill R.

Lac la Ronge

Saskatchewan R.

N. Saskatchewan R.

S. Saskatchewan R.

Lake
Winnipegosis

Lake
Manitoba

Qu'Appelle R.
Lake
Diefenbaker

GREAT PLAINS

Queen
Elizabeth
Islands

North
Magnetic
Pole

North
Pole

Source for elevation data:
Natural Resources Canada

ARCTIC
OCEAN

Amundsen
Gulf

Beaufort Sea

Cape
Bathurst

Mackenzie Bay

Anderson R.

Great
Bear
Lake

Lac la
Martre

Great
Slave Lake

Slave
R.

Hay R.
Peace River

Lesser
Slave
Lake

Athabasca
River

MACKENZIE
MOUNTAINS

Mackenzie River

Liard R.

Mt. Robson
12,972 ft.
(3,954 m)

ROCKY MOUNTAINS

COLUMBIA MTS.

Columbia R.

KLONDIKE
REGION

Pelly R.

Yukon R.

COAST MOUNTAINS

Williston
Lake

Fraser River

Skeena R.
Stikine R.

Hecate Strait

Queen
Charlotte
Islands

Queen
Charlotte
Sound

Vancouver
Island

Mt. Waddington
13,176 ft. (4,016 m)

Mt. Logan
19,551 ft.
(5,959 m)

ALASKA
(U.S.)

PACIFIC
OCEAN

Gulf of
Alaska

CANADA

N   E   W   S

500 mi

500 km

250

250

0

International boundary
Provincial boundary
▲ Mountain peak

Mexico

Mexico

- Area: 759,530 square miles (1,967,183 square kilometers)
- Highest Point: Pico de Orizaba, 18,700 ft. (5,700 m)
- Lowest Point: Laguna Salada, 33 ft. (10 m) below sea level [A]
- Longest River: Rio Bravo del Norte, 1,240 mi. (1,996 km), along U.S. border
- Largest Lake: Lake Chapala, 417 sq. mi. (1,080 sq. km)
- Largest Urban Concentration: Mexico City, 18,066,000

Source:
[A] World Factbook, CIA, 2007

400 mi

400 km

200

200

0

0

Legend

International boundary
State boundary
★ National capital
⊛ Other capital

Symbol and label sizes indicate relative sizes of cities:

Mexico City
● Veracruz
· Cancún

Yucatán Channel

Caribbean Sea

Gulf of Mexico

Bay of Campeche

Gulf of California

Gulf of Tehuantepec

PACIFIC OCEAN

Places

Cancún
Tizimín
Valladolid
QUINTANA ROO
Mérida
YUCATÁN
Campeche
CAMPECHE
Chetumal
Ciudad del Carmen
Villahermosa
TABASCO
CHIAPAS
San Cristóbal de las Casas
Comitán
Tuxtla Gutiérrez
Tonalá
Tapachula
COATZACOALCOS
VERACRUZ
Tehuacán
Tuxtepec
Huajuapan de León
OAXACA
Oaxaca
Salina Cruz
Juchitán
Puerto Escondido
Xalapa
Veracruz
Orizaba
PUEBLA
Puebla
TLAXCALA
Tlaxcala
Pachuca
Poza Rica
Tuxpan
Tampico
Ciudad Mante
Ciudad Victoria
TAMAULIPAS
Matamoros
Reynosa
Nuevo Laredo
Rio Grande
Rio Bravo del Norte
Anáhuac
NUEVO LEÓN
Monterrey
Linares
Ciudad Acuña
Piedras Negras
Nueva Rosita
COAHUILA
Monclova
San Pedro de las Colonias
Saltillo
Concepción del Oro
ZACATECAS
Fresnillo
Zacatecas
San Luis Potosí
SAN LUIS POTOSÍ
Matehuala
Ciudad de Valles
GUANAJUATO
León
Guanajuato
QUERÉTARO
Querétaro
Celaya
Acámbaro
HIDALGO
México
DISTRITO FEDERAL
Mexico City
MORELOS
Cuernavaca
Toluca
Taxco
Iguala
Chilpancingo
GUERRERO
Acapulco
Ixtapa
Lázaro Cárdenas
MICHOACÁN
Uruapan
Morelia
Ocotlán
JALISCO
Guadalajara
Ameca
Autlán
NAYARIT
Tepic
COLIMA
Colima
Manzanillo
Puerto Vallarta
Acaponeta
Lake Chapala
Lerma R.
Balsas R.
Mazatlán
Culiacán
SINALOA
Guasave
Los Mochis
Navojoa
Ciudad Obregón
Guaymas
SONORA
Hermosillo
Magdalena de Kino
Nogales
Caborca
Agua Prieta
Nuevo Casas Grandes
Ciudad Juárez
CHIHUAHUA
Chihuahua
Cuauhtémoc
Delicias
Ciudad Camargo
Hidalgo del Parral
Ojinaga
Conchos R.
Jiménez
DURANGO
Durango
Torreón
Villa Ahumada
Yaqui R.
Tijuana
Ensenada
Mexicali
San Luis Rio Colorado
Colorado R.
San Felipe
Puerto Peñasco
BAJA CALIFORNIA
Guerrero Negro
Santa Rosalía
Loreto
BAJA CALIFORNIA SUR
Ciudad Constitución
La Paz
San Lucas
TROPIC OF CANCER

30°N
25°N
20°N
15°N
20°N
15°N

115°W
110°W
105°W
100°W
95°W
90°W
85°W

N E W S

PACIFIC
OCEAN

ARCTIC OCEAN

EUROPE
ASIA

NORTH
AMERICA
ATLANTIC
OCEAN

AFRICA

INDIAN
OCEAN

AUSTRALIA

SOUTH
AMERICA

PACIFIC
OCEAN

Equator

SOUTHERN OCEAN

ANTARCTICA

Robinson Projection

UNITED STATES

Gulf of Mexico

CUBA

Yucatán Channel

Cape
Catoche

Cozumel I.

Point Allen
Point Herrero

Caribbean
Sea

Chetumal
Bay

HONDURAS

BELIZE

GUATEMALA

Yucatán Peninsula

Bay of
Campeche

Términos
Lagoon

Usumacinta R.

Angostura
Reservoir

SIERRA MADRE
DE CHIAPAS

Grijalva R.

Point
Zapotitlán

Gulf of
Tehuantepec

400 mi

400 km

200

200

0

0

Madre Lagoon

Tamiahua
Lagoon

Cape Rojo

Pánuco
R.

SIERRA
AZUL

Pico de Orizaba
18,700 ft.
(5,700 m)

Ixtacihuatl
17,343 ft.
(5,286 m)

Popocatépetl
17,930 ft.
(5,465 m)

Miguel Alemán
Reservoir

Nezahualcóyotl
Reservoir

OAXACA
PLATEAU

Isthmus of
Tehuantepec

SIERRA MADRE DEL SUR

Verde R.

Atoyac R.

Falcon
Reservoir

M.R. Gómez
Res.

SIERRA MADRE ORIENTAL

Río Grande

Río Bravo del Norte

Amistad
Reservoir

V. Carranza
Res.

MAPIMÍ
BASIN

Chihuahua
Desert

CABALLOS
MESTEÑOS
PLAIN

Balsas River

River

Lerma

Lake Chapala

Infiernillo
Reservoir

Petacalco
Bay

Point
Tejupan

SIERRA MADRE OCCIDENTAL

Conchos R.

Boquilla
Res.

Copper
Canyon

Bavispe R.

Álvaro
Obregón
Reservoir

M. Hidalgo
Res.

Fuerte R.

Yaqui R.

Río Grande
de Santiago

San Pedro R.

Point Mita
Banderas Bay

Cape
Corrientes

Marías Is.

Cerralvo I.

Cape
San Lucas

Sonora River

P.E. Gallés
Reservoir

Sonoran
Desert

Gulf of California

Tiburón I.

Angel de la
Guarda I.

Baja California

Cedros I.

Sebastián Vizcaíno
Bay

Eugenia
Point

Guadalupe I.

San Antonio
Point

Magdalena I.

Cape San Lázaro

Magdalena
Bay

Vizcaíno
Desert

SIERRA
SAN PEDRO
MÁRTIR

Colorado River

Altar
Desert

Laguna Salada
33 ft. (10 m) below sea level

Revillagigedo Islands

PACIFIC
OCEAN

N
E
S
W

International boundary

Mountain peak

Lowest point

Source for elevation data:
Merriam-Webster's Geographical Dictionary, 2007

15°N

20°N

TROPIC OF CANCER

25°N

30°N

85°W

90°W

95°W

100°W

105°W

110°W

115°W

115°W

110°W

105°W

100°W

95°W

90°W

15°N

20°N

25°N

TROPIC OF CANCER

30°N

South America

Caribbean Sea

International boundary
National capital
Other capital

Symbol and label sizes indicate relative sizes of cities:
- **Rio de Janeiro**
- Santos
- Jataí

PACIFIC OCEAN

ATLANTIC OCEAN

EQUATOR

TROPIC OF CAPRICORN

Galápagos Islands (Ecuador)

San Félix Island (Chile)
San Ambrosio Island (Chile)
Juan Fernández Islands (Chile)

VENEZUELA
GUYANA
SURINAME
FRENCH GUIANA (France)
COLOMBIA
ECUADOR
PERU
BRAZIL
BOLIVIA
PARAGUAY
CHILE
URUGUAY
ARGENTINA

Barranquilla, Cartagena, Sincelejo, Montería, Maracaibo, Valencia, **Caracas**, Cumaná, Barquisimeto, Maracay, El Tigre, Valera, Cúcuta, Mérida, San Cristóbal, Bucaramanga, Barrancabermeja, Ciudad Guayana, Medellín, Manizales, Pereira, Armenia, **Bogotá**, Ibagué, Georgetown, Paramaribo, Cayenne, Buenaventura, Cali, Neiva, Boa Vista, Pasto, Florencia, Macapá, Esmeraldas, **Quito**, Belém, São Luís, Parnaíba, Guayaquil, Cuenca, Iquitos, Manaus, Santarém, Imperatriz, Fortaleza, Machala, Tumbes, Benjamin Constant, Teresina, Floriano, Juàzeiro do Norte, Natal, Piura, Chiclayo, Cajamarca, Pucallpa, Cruzeiro do Sul, Rio Branco, Pôrto Velho, Campina Grande, João Pessoa, Trujillo, Chimbote, Huánuco, Riberalta, Guajará-Mirim, Petrolina, **Recife**, Maceió, Callao, **Lima**, Huancayo, Puerto Maldonado, Cuzco, Trinidad, Gurupi, Feira de Santana, Aracaju, Ayacucho, Ica, **La Paz**, Vitória da Conquista, **Salvador**, Arequipa, Juliaca, Cochabamba, Santa Cruz, Cuiabá, Goiânia, Jataí, **Brasília**, Ilhéus, Tacna, Oruro, Sucre, Corumbá, Uberlândia, Montes Claros, Arica, Lake Poopó, Potosí, Campo Grande, São José do Rio Prêto, Governador Valadares, Iquique, Tarija, Douradas, Bauru, Ribeirão Prêto, Campinas, Volta Redonda, Vitória, Calama, Concepción, **Belo Horizonte**, Niterói, Antofagasta, San Salvador de Jujuy, **Asunción**, Londrina, **São Paulo**, Santos, **Rio de Janeiro**, Salta, Curitiba, Copiapó, San Miguel de Tucumán, Resistencia, Encarnación, Corrientes, Reconquista, Passo Fundo, Florianópolis, Catamarca, Santiago del Estero, Santa Maria, La Serena, La Rioja, Córdoba, Santa Fe, Salto, Rivera, Porto Alegre, Pelotas, Valparaíso, Mendoza, Rosario, Paraná, Melo, Rancagua, **Santiago**, Rio Cuarto, **Buenos Aires**, Montevideo, Talca, La Plata, Chillán, Santa Rosa, Bahía Blanca, Mar del Plata, Concepción, Temuco, Neuquén, Necochea, Valdivia, San Carlos de Bariloche, Viedma, Puerto Montt, Rawson, Esquel, Comodoro Rivadavia, Rio Gallegos, Stanley, Falkland Islands (U.K.) (Islas Malvinas), Punta Arenas, Ushuaia

Orinoco R.
Amazon (Solimões) R.
Rio Negro
Madeira R.
Tapajós R.
Xingu R.
Tocantins R.
São Francisco R.
Araguaia R.
Paraguay R.
Paraná R.
Uruguay R.
Pilcomayo R.
Lake Titicaca
Magdalena R.
Putumayo R.
Marañón R.
Ucayali R.
Juruá R.
Purus R.
Guaporé R.
Mamoré R.
Beni R.
Grande R.

0 — 300 — 600 mi
0 — 300 — 600 km

N W E S

Source: [A] *World Factbook*, CIA, 2007

Facts

- Area: 6,765,422 square miles (17,522,371 square kilometers)
- Highest Point: Mt. Aconcagua, Argentina, 22,834 ft. (6,960 m)
- Lowest Point: Laguna del Carbón, Argentina, 344 ft. (105 m) below sea level [A]
- Longest River: Amazon-Ucayali-Apurimac, 4,000 mi. (6,436 km)
- Largest Lake: Lake Maracaibo, Venezuela, 5,217 sq. mi. (13,512 sq. km)
- Largest Country: Brazil, 3,284,426 sq. mi. (8,506,663 sq. km) (slightly smaller than the United States)
- Largest Urban Concentration: São Paulo, Brazil, 17,099,000

NORTH
AMERICA

Caribbean Sea

Gulf of
Panama

Galápagos
Islands

PACIFIC
OCEAN

Pariñas Pt.

Lake
Maracaibo

LLANOS

Orinoco River

GUIANA

Angel Falls ≈

HIGHLANDS

Orinoco River

Rio Negro

AMAZON

BASIN

Amazon (Solimões) River

Juruá River

Purus River

Madeira River

Amazon

River

Tapajós River

Teles Pires

River

Xingu

River

Tocantins

River

Parnaiba

River

São Francisco

River

BRAZILIAN

HIGHLANDS

Cape
São Roque

Cauca River

Magdalena River

Putumayo River

Marañón River

Ucayali River

ANDES

Mt. Huascarán
22,205 ft.
(6,768 m)

Paracas
Peninsula

Volcán Misti
19,101 ft.
(5,822 m)

Beni River

Lake
Titicaca

Mt. Illimani
21,122 ft.
(6,438 m)

Lake
Poopó

Guaporé River

Mamoré River

MATO GROSSO
PLATEAU

Paraguay River

ALTIPLANO

Atacama Desert

Pilcomayo River

GRAN
CHACO

Salado River

Paraná

Paraná River

Grande River

SERRA DO MAR

Iguazú
Falls

Uruguay River

San Félix I.

San Ambrosio I.

Juan
Fernández
Is.

Mt. Aconcagua
22,834 ft.
(6,960 m)

ANDES

PAMPAS

Río de la Plata

Colorado River

Negro River

Gulf of San Matías

Chiloé I.

Los Chonos
Archipelago

Patagonia

Gulf of
San Jorge

Laguna del Carbón
344 ft (105 m) below sea level

Santa Cruz
River

Strait of
Magellan

Falkland
Islands
(Islas Malvinas)

Tierra del
Fuego

Cape Horn

South
Georgia

ATLANTIC
OCEAN

ATLANTIC
OCEAN

0   300   600 mi
0   300   600 km

N
W   E
S

	International boundary
▲	Mountain peak
▽	Lowest point
≈	Falls

Sources for elevation data:
World Factbook, CIA, 2007
Smithsonian Global Volcanism Program

Elevation Profile

Paracas Peninsula   Lake Titicaca   Andes Mountains   Mato Grosso Plateau   Brazilian Highlands
20,000 ft.
10,000 ft.
5,000 ft.
Sea
level
A   B

Major Metropolitan Areas

Argentina
Buenos Aires	11,298,000
Córdoba	1,209,000
Rosario	1,119,000

Bolivia
La Paz	1,484,000
Santa Cruz	1,136,000
Cochabamba	517,000

Brazil
São Paulo	17,834,000
Rio de Janeiro	10,612,000
Belo Horizonte	4,800,000
Porto Alegre	3,655,000
Recife	3,332,000
Salvador	3,018,000
Fortaleza	2,975,000
Brasília	2,942,000
Curitiba	2,726,000
Belém	1,816,000
Manaus	1,011,000

Chile
Santiago	4,647,000
Viña del Mar	299,000

Colombia
Bogotá	6,422,000
Cali	2,129,000
Medellín	1,885,000
Barranquilla	1,549,000

Ecuador
Guayaquil	2,118,000
Quito	1,616,000

French Guiana
Cayenne	50,000

Guyana
Georgetown	187,000

Paraguay
Asunción	513,000

Peru
Lima	6,988,000
Arequipa	830,000
Chiclayo	766,000

Suriname
Paramaribo	291,000

Uruguay
Montevideo	1,303,000

Venezuela
Caracas	3,061,000
Maracaibo	1,220,000
Barquisimeto	896,000
Valencia	742,000

International comparability of population data is limited by varying census methods. Where metropolitan population is unavailable, core city population is shown.

Population

Persons per sq. mile	Persons per sq. km
Over 520	Over 200
260 to 519	100 to 199
130 to 259	50 to 99
25 to 129	10 to 49
1 to 24	1 to 9
0	0

Major metropolitan areas
- Over 2 million
- 1 million to 2 million
- Under 1 million

Estimated 2005 Population (in millions)

- Brazil 186
- Colombia 43
- Argentina 40
- Peru 28
- Venezuela 25
- Chile 16
- Ecuador 13
- Bolivia 9
- Paraguay 6
- All others 5

Source: U.S. Census Bureau

Gross Domestic Product

GDP per capita

	Over $20,000
	$10,000 to $20,000
	$5,000 to $9,999
	$2,500 to $4,999
	Less than $2,500
	No data

Source: *World Factbook*, CIA, 2005

Gross Domestic Product is a measure of the total goods and services generated by a country. Generally, manufacturing, high-tech services, and specialized agricultural products add more value than raw materials and basic food stuffs.

Electricity Use, 2002

United States 12,376
Ecuador 5,656
Suriname 4,211
Chile 2,616
Colombia 958
Paraguay 389

KWh (kilowatt hours) per person per year

Source: *World Factbook*, CIA, 2005

Non-manufacturing economic activity is generated primarily by commercial plantation agriculture, livestock raising, and the harvest of forest products, plus the extraction of oil and minerals. Manufacturing, like population, is concentrated in the continent's coastal areas.

Land Use and Resources

Predominant land use

	Commercial agriculture
	Livestock ranching
	Subsistence agriculture
	Primarily forestland
	Limited agricultural activity

Major resources

Coal		Uranium	
Natural gas		Bauxite	
Oil		Diamonds	
Forest products		Other minerals	
Gold		Fishing	
Silver		Major manufacturing and trade centers	
Iron ore			

81

Most of the continent is under the influence of wet and tropical air. Warm currents in the Atlantic Ocean as well as wet lowland elevations lying within the confines of the tropical latitudes directly affect the climate of the majority of the land area. The Andes Mountains and cold currents that hug the Pacific coast keep the Western and Southern regions of the continent temperate but dry.

See photographs taken in different kinds of climates on pages 24–25.

Rivadavia
Highest recorded temperature 120°F (49°C)

Sarmiento
Lowest recorded temperature -27°F (-33°C)

Climate

- Tropical wet
- Tropical wet and dry
- Arid
- Semiarid
- Mediterranean
- Humid subtropical
- Marine
- Subarctic
- Highland

Quibdo
Highest average annual precipitation: 354" (899 cm)

Arica
Lowest average annual precipitation: 0.03" (0.08 cm)

Moist and unstable air above the Equator—as well as highlands that wring out waterlogged clouds—produce heavy rainfall, but along the coast of Chile and elsewhere, cold ocean water and mountainous barriers keep rainfall at a minimum.

Annual Precipitation

Centimeters	Inches
Over 200	Over 80
150 to 200	60 to 80
100 to 150	40 to 60
50 to 100	20 to 40
25 to 50	10 to 20
Under 25	Under 10

Climate Graphs

Average daily temperature range (in °F)

Average monthly precipitation (in inches)

100° — High
65°
32° — Low
0°

20°
10°
0°

ASUNCIÓN, Paraguay

BOGOTÁ, Colombia

BUENOS AIRES, Argentina

CARACAS, Venezuela

CAYENNE, French Guiana

LA PAZ, Bolivia

LIMA, Peru

MANAUS, Brazil

PUNTA ARENAS, Chile

RECIFE, Brazil

RIO DE JANEIRO, Brazil

SANTIAGO, Chile

South America is dominated by tropical vegetation, including Earth's most extensive rain forest. Farther south, a vast grassland, the Pampa, fades gradually into the dry and meager vegetation of Patagonia.

See photographs of the different kinds of vegetation on pages 26–27.

Vegetation

- Unclassified highlands or ice cap
- Midlatitude deciduous forest
- Mixed forest
- Midlatitude scrubland
- Midlatitude grassland
- Desert
- Tropical seasonal and scrub
- Tropical rain forest
- Tropical savanna

The destruction of forest areas—especially in the Amazon Basin—is one of the leading environmental issues in South America. In Brazil, it is estimated that an average of 15,000 acres of forest are lost each day as people clear land for timber and to grow crops. Human activities have impacted other types of vegetation, as well. For example, overgrazing has caused damage to grasslands in many areas, putting them at risk of becoming infertile deserts. Poor urban air quality is another serious concern in the region, with nearly 80 percent of the population living in cities.

Environmental Issues

- Current forest
- Cleared forest
- Area at highest risk of desertification
- ● Poor air quality*

*Cities exceeding at least one of the World Health Organization's (WHO) annual mean guidelines for air quality

Sources: *Global Distribution of Original and Remaining Forests*, UNEP-WCMC, 2002
World Soil Resources Map Index, USDA/NRCS, 2002
World Development Indicators, World Bank, 1999

Europe

Facts

- Area: 3,749,322 square mi. (9,710,705 square km)
- Highest Point: Mt. Elbrus, Russia, 18,510 ft. (5,642 m)
- Lowest Point: Caspian Sea 92 ft. (28 m) below sea level
- Longest River: Volga, 2,293 mi. (3,689 km)
- Largest Lake: Lake Ladoga, 6,826 sq. mi. (17,679 sq. km)
- Largest Country: Russia (European), 1,528,964 sq. mi. (3,960,017 sq. km)
- Largest Urban Concentration: Moscow, Russia 10,500,000

International boundary
⊛ National capital
★ Other capital

Symbol and label sizes
indicate relative sizes of cities:
● **London**
• Helsinki
· Varna

ARCTIC OCEAN

ATLANTIC OCEAN

Norwegian Sea

North Sea

Barents Sea

White Sea

Baltic Sea

Mediterranean Sea

Black Sea

Caspian Sea

Sea of Azov

Aegean Sea

Ionian Sea

Adriatic Sea

Tyrrhenian Sea

Bay of Biscay

English Channel

Gulf of Bothnia

Gulf of Finland

ICELAND
Reykjavík
Akureyri

IRELAND
Dublin
Cork

UNITED KINGDOM
Scotland
Glasgow
Edinburgh
Aberdeen
Newcastle upon Tyne
England
Leeds
Manchester
Liverpool
Sheffield
Birmingham
Wales
Cardiff
London
Bristol
Portsmouth
Northern Ireland
Belfast
Faroe Is. (Denmark)
Shetland Is. (U.K.)
Orkney Is.
Channel Is. (U.K.)

NORWAY
Oslo
Bergen
Stavanger
Trondheim
Hammerfest
Tromsø
Bodø

SWEDEN
Stockholm
Göteborg
Malmö
Uppsala
Linköping
Sundsvall
Umeå
Luleå
Kiruna
Gotland
Öland

FINLAND
Helsinki
Tampere
Turku
Oulu
Vaasa
Lahti
Åland

DENMARK
Copenhagen
Århus
Odense
Ålborg

ESTONIA
Tallinn
Tartu

LATVIA
Riga
Daugavpils

LITHUANIA
Vilnius
Kaunas
Klaipeda

RUSSIA
Moscow
St. Petersburg
Murmansk
Arkhangel'sk
Perm'
Izhevsk
Kazan
Samara
Ul'yanovsk
Naberezhnyye Chelny
Penza
Saratov
Volgograd
Rostov-na-Donu
Krasnodar
Astrakhan'
Grozny
Voronezh
Lipetsk
Tambov
Ryazan'
Tula
Kaluga
Bryansk
Kursk
Smolensk
Tver
Yaroslavl'
Ivanovo
Nizhnij Novgorod
Kirov
Syktyvkar
Ukhta
Pechora
Orenburg
Veliky Novgorod
Petrozavodsk
Kandalaksha
Vicebsk
Kaliningrad
Novaya Zemlya
L. Onega
L. Ladoga
Pechora R.
Kama R.
Volga R.
Don R.
S. Dvina R.
N. Dvina R.
Vistula R.

BELARUS
Minsk
Hrodna
Homel'
Brest

UKRAINE
Kyiv (Kiev)
Kharkiv
Dnipropetrovs'k
Donets'k
Odesa
Luhans'k
Mariupol'
Zaporizhzhia
Kryvyy Rih
Mykolaiv
Lviv
Simferopol'
Sevastopol'
Chernivtsi
Dnieper R.
Dniester R.

MOLDOVA
Chişinău
Iaşi

POLAND
Warsaw
Łódź
Kraków
Wrocław
Poznań
Gdańsk
Szczecin
Katowice
Oder R.
Bug R.

GERMANY
Berlin
Hamburg
Munich
Cologne
Frankfurt
Essen
Dortmund
Stuttgart
Düsseldorf
Bremen
Hannover
Leipzig
Dresden
Mannheim
Bonn
Elbe R.
Rhine R.

CZECH REP.
Prague
Brno
Ostrava

SLOVAKIA
Bratislava
Košice

AUSTRIA
Vienna
Graz
Linz

HUNGARY
Budapest
Debrecen
Pécs

ROMANIA
Bucharest
Timişoara
Constanţa
Ploieşti

BULGARIA
Sofia
Plovdiv
Varna
Burgas

GREECE
Athens
Thessaloniki
Larisa
Patras
Corfu
Crete
Iraklio
Rhodes
Cyclades

TURKEY
Istanbul

GEORGIA
Tbilisi

ARMENIA
Yerevan

AZERBAIJAN
Baku

MACEDONIA
Skopje

KOSOVO
Pristina

ALBANIA
Tirana

SERBIA
Belgrade
Novi Sad

MONTENEGRO
Podgorica

BOSNIA & HERZEGOVINA
Sarajevo

CROATIA
Zagreb
Split
Dubrovnik

SLOVENIA
Ljubljana

ITALY
Rome
Milan
Naples
Turin
Genoa
Florence
Bologna
Venice
Verona
Palermo
Catania
Bari
Taranto
Salerno
Sicily
Sardinia (Italy)
Corsica (France)
Elba
Pantelleria (Italy)
VATICAN CITY
SAN MARINO
MONACO

MALTA
Valletta

FRANCE
Paris
Marseille
Lyon
Toulouse
Nice
Nantes
Strasbourg
Bordeaux
Le Havre
Rennes
Dijon
Toulon
Brest
Rouen
Tours
Rhône R.
Loire R.
Seine R.

SWITZERLAND
Zürich
Geneva
Bern

LIECHTENSTEIN

LUXEMBOURG
Luxembourg

BELGIUM
Brussels
Antwerp
Liège

NETH.
Amsterdam
Rotterdam

ANDORRA

SPAIN
Madrid
Barcelona
Valencia
Seville
Zaragoza
Málaga
Bilbao
Alicante
Córdoba
Valladolid
Vigo
Gijón
Granada
Cádiz
Balearic Is. (Spain)
Majorca
Minorca
Palma de Mallorca
Ibiza
Ebro R.
Tagus R.

PORTUGAL
Lisbon
Porto
Badajoz

GIBRALTAR (U.K.)
Strait of Gibraltar

500 mi
500 km
250
250
0
0

ARCTIC CIRCLE

N E S W

Major Metropolitan Areas

Albania
Tirana — 244,000

Andorra
Andorra la Vella — 21,000

Armenia
Yerevan — 1,247,000

Austria
Vienna — 1,562,000

Azerbaijan
Baku — 1,792,000

Belarus
Minsk — 1,681,000

Belgium
Brussels — 978,000

Bosnia & Herzegovina
Sarajevo — 529,000

Bulgaria
Sofia — 1,191,000

Croatia
Zagreb — 692,000

Czech Republic
Prague — 1,179,000

Denmark
Copenhagen — 1,085,000

Estonia
Tallinn — 398,000

Finland
Helsinki — 965,000

France
Paris — 9,645,000
Marseille — 1,350,000
Lyon — 1,349,000
Lille — 1,001,000

Georgia
Tbilisi — 1,399,000

Germany (core city only)
Berlin — 3,382,000
Hamburg — 1,715,000
Munich — 1,210,000
Cologne — 963,000
Frankfurt — 647,000
Essen — 595,000

Greece
Athens — 3,073,000

Hungary
Budapest — 1,825,000

Iceland
Reykjavík — 175,000

Ireland
Dublin — 1,123,000

Italy
Rome — 2,460,000
Milan — 1,183,000
Naples — 993,000
Turin — 857,000
Palermo — 653,000
Genoa — 604,000

Kosovo
Pristina — 155,499

Latvia
Riga — 793,000

Liechtenstein
Vaduz — 5,000

Lithuania
Vilnius — 578,000

Luxembourg
Luxembourg — 77,000

Macedonia
Skopje — 545,000

Malta
Valletta — 8,000

Moldova
Chişinău — 658,000

Monaco
Monaco — 27,000

Montenegro
Podgorica — 152,242

Netherlands
Amsterdam — 1,207,000
Rotterdam — 1,161,000

Norway
Oslo — 513,000

Poland
Warsaw — 1,610,000
Łódź — 787,000
Kraków — 741,000
Wrocław — 634,000

Portugal
Lisbon — 1,947,000

Romania
Bucharest — 2,009,000

Russia (European)
Moscow — 8,538,000
St. Petersburg — 4,678,000
Niżnij Novgorod — 1,366,000
Samara — 1,183,000
Kazan' — 1,092,000
Ufa — 1,094,000
Volgograd — 1,025,000
Perm' — 1,024,000
Rostov-na-Donu — 1,004,000

San Marino
San Marino — 5,000

Serbia
Belgrade — 1,619,000

Slovakia
Bratislava — 429,000

Slovenia
Ljubljana — 264,000

Spain
Madrid — 2,939,000
Barcelona — 1,504,000
Valencia — 738,000
Seville — 685,000

Sweden
Stockholm — 1,665,000

Switzerland
Zürich — 933,000
Geneva — 451,000

Turkey (European)
Istanbul — 8,803,000

Ukraine
Kyiv (Kiev) — 2,590,000
Kharkiv — 1,494,000
Dnipropetrovs'k — 1,109,000
Donets'k — 1,050,000
Odesa — 1,002,000

United Kingdom
London — 7,652,000
Birmingham — 2,296,000
Manchester — 2,277,000
Leeds-Bradford — 1,446,000
Newcastle — 886,000
Glasgow — 867,000
Liverpool — 838,000
Sheffield — 633,000

International comparability of population data is limited by varying census methods. Where metropolitan population is unavailable, core city population is shown.

Population

Persons per sq. mile	Persons per sq. km	Major metropolitan areas
Over 520	Over 200	● Over 2 million
260 to 519	100 to 199	● 1 million to 2 million
130 to 259	50 to 99	• Under 1 million
25 to 129	10 to 49	
1 to 24	1 to 9	
0	0	

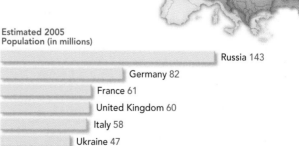

Estimated 2005 Population (in millions)

Russia 143
Germany 82
France 61
United Kingdom 60
Italy 58
Ukraine 47
Spain 40
Poland 39
Romania 22
All others 177

Source: U.S. Census Bureau

Gross Domestic Product

GDP per capita

- Over $20,000
- $10,000 to $20,000
- $5,000 to $9,999
- $2,500 to $4,999
- Under $2,500
- No data

Source: *World Factbook*, CIA, 2005

Gross Domestic Product is a measure of the total goods and services generated by a country. Generally, manufacturing, high-tech services, and specialized agricultural products add more value than raw materials and basic food stuffs.

Electricity Use, 2002

- Iceland 25,922
- Finland 15,044
- United States 12,376
- France 6,837
- Russia 6,236*
- United Kingdom 5,582*
- Moldova 1,034

KWh (kilowatt hours) per person per year
*2003 data

Source: *World Factbook*, CIA, 2005

Land Use and Resources

Predominant land use

- Commercial agriculture
- Dairying
- Livestock ranching
- Nomadic herding
- Subsistence agriculture
- Primarily forestland
- Limited agricultural activity

Major resources

- Coal
- Natural gas
- Oil
- Au Gold
- Fe Iron ore
- Ag Silver
- U Uranium
- Al Bauxite
- Other minerals
- Fishing
- ● Major manufacturing and trade centers

Europe, particularly Western Europe, is a consolidation of high-tech, market-driven, globally connected economies, where manufacturing and commercial agriculture predominate. Crucial to continental economic integration is the European Union, a partnership of 25 member nations whose combined economic clout rivals the U.S. Russia and former Soviet-satellite nations are, in large part, reaching harmony with the rest of Europe after an initial and unsettling period of adjustment. Despite centuries of exploration and exploitation, commercially-valuable mineral resources continue to be mined, notably in Russia, the Ukraine, and Scandinavia. The bountiful oil and gas fields of the North Sea are one of the most important and most recent discoveries.

Climate

- Semiarid
- Mediterranean
- Humid subtropical
- Marine
- Humid continental
- Subarctic
- Tundra
- Ice cap
- Highland

The far-reaching influence and effects of warm ocean currents cannot be overstated. The ceaseless torrent distributed by the Gulf Stream along the coasts of Western Europe, even to the shores of Iceland and Norway, produces much milder weather than would be expected at its latitudes and provides a ready source of moisture. Along the Mediterranean margin of Europe the typical weather—mild, wet winters and hot, dry summers—has been defined as a climate category that is now used worldwide.

See photographs taken in different kinds of climates on pages 24–25.

Ust'Shchugor Lowest recorded temperature, -67°F (-55°C), date unknown

Seville Highest recorded temperature, 122°F (50°C), 1881

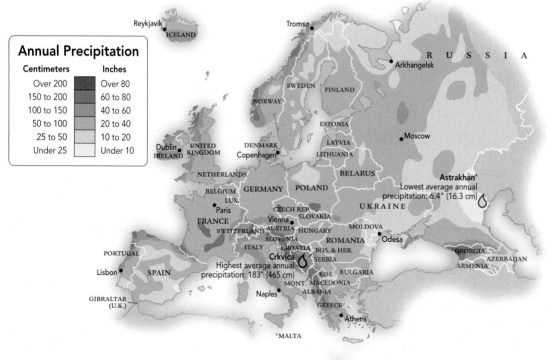

Annual Precipitation

Centimeters	Inches
Over 200	Over 80
150 to 200	60 to 80
100 to 150	40 to 60
50 to 100	20 to 40
25 to 50	10 to 20
Under 25	Under 10

Astrakhan' Lowest average annual precipitation: 6.4" (16.3 cm)

Crkvica Highest average annual precipitation: 183" (465 cm)

Though regionally formidable mountains rise to extract snow and rain, no continental-scale alpine barrier exists—thereby permitting moisture-laden, westerly winds springing from warm oceanic waters to distribute precipitation uniformly across Europe. However, by the time these currents of air reach the landlocked heart of Eastern Europe, northeast of the Black Sea, much of the moisture has already been spent.

Climate Graphs

Average daily temperature range (in °F)   Average monthly precipitation (in inches)

100° High
65° Low
32°
0°
20"
10"
0"

ARKHANGELSK, Russia

ATHENS, Greece

COPENHAGEN, Denmark

DUBLIN, Ireland

LISBON, Portugal

MOSCOW, Russia

NAPLES, Italy

ODESA, Ukraine

PARIS, France

REYKJAVÍK, Iceland

TROMSØ, Norway

VIENNA, Austria

Vegetation

- Unclassified highlands or ice cap
- Tundra and alpine tundra
- Coniferous forest
- Midlatitude deciduous forest
- Mixed forest
- Midlatitude scrubland
- Midlatitude grassland

Forests, nourished by plentiful precipitation, dominate in Europe, but grassland and scrubland thrive where rainfall becomes sparse or is seasonal. Deciduous trees disappear as the winters grow harsh, replaced by vast and hardy stands of coniferous forest that are merely the western end of an immense belt stretching across Russia to the Pacific Ocean.

See photographs of the different kinds of vegetation on pages 26–27.

Environmental Issues

- Current forest
- Cleared forest
- Area at highest risk of desertification
- Areas most affected by acid rain
- • Poor air quality*

*Cities exceeding at least one of the World Health Organization's (WHO) annual mean guidelines for air quality

Sources: *Global Distribution of Original and Remaining Forests,* UNEP-WCMC, 2002
World Soil Resources Map Index, USDA/NRCS, 2002
World Development Indicators, World Bank, 1999

Emissions from the many cars, trucks, and factories in Europe have led to problems with air pollution and acid rain over a large part of the continent. Land and water pollution (from fertilizers, pesticides, and industrial waste) is also widespread. Since the 1960's, the amount of forest area in Western and Central Europe has actually increased, but many forests (nearly 60%) are damaged due to acidification, pollution, drought, or fires. Overfishing—especially in the North Sea—is a serious problem for marine ecosystems.

Africa

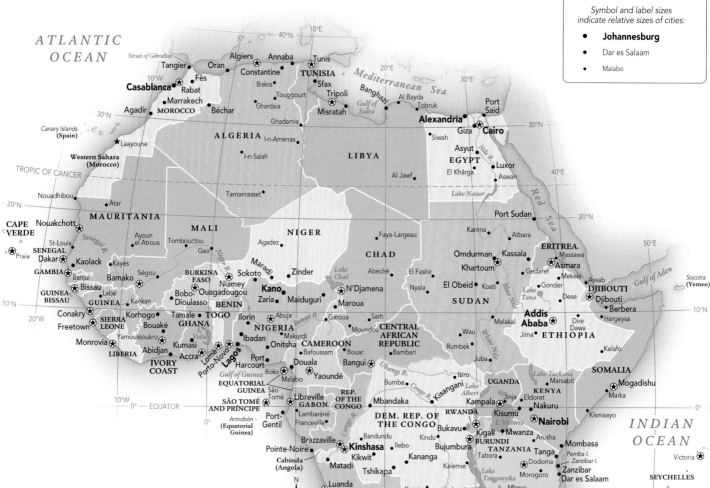

ATLANTIC
OCEAN

Strait of Gibraltar

Tangier
Algiers
Annaba
Tunis
Oran
Constantine
TUNISIA
Mediterranean Sea
Biskra
Sfax
Fès
Casablanca
Rabat
Tripoli
Banghazi
Al Bayda
Port Said
Marrakech
Touggourt
Misratah
Gulf of Sidra
Tobruk
Agadir
MOROCCO
Béchar
Ghardaia
Alexandria
Ghadamis
Giza ⊛ **Cairo**
30°N

Canary Islands
(Spain)
ALGERIA
I-n-Amenas
LIBYA
Siwah
EGYPT
Asyut
Luxor

★ Laayoune

Western Sahara
(Morocco)
I-n-Salah
Al Jawf
El Khârga
Aswan

TROPIC OF CANCER

Tamanrasset
Lake Nasser
Red Sea

Nouadhibou
Atar
Port Sudan

CAPE
VERDE
Nouakchott ⊛
MAURITANIA
MALI
NIGER
Faya-Largeau
CHAD
Karima
Atbara
ERITREA
Massawa

St-Louis
Ayoun el Atrous
Tombouctou
Agadez
Omdurman
Kassala
Asmara ⊛
Gedaref
Mekele

Praia
SENEGAL
Dakar ⊛
Kaolack
Kayes
Gao
Maradi
Zinder
Lake Chad
Abéché
El Fashir
Khartoum
DJIBOUTI
Berbera

GAMBIA
Banjul
Bamako ⊛
Ségou
BURKINA FASO
Sokoto
N'Djamena ⊛
Nyala
El Obeid
Kosti
SUDAN
Gonder
Lake Tana
Djibouti ⊛
Dese

GUINEA-BISSAU
Bissau
Labé
Kankan
Bobo-Dioulasso
Niamey ⊛ Ouagadougou
Kano
Zaria
Maiduguri
Maroua
Blue Nile
Addis Ababa
Dire Dawa

Conakry
GUINEA
Korhogo
Tamale
BENIN
Ilorin
Abuja
Garoua
Sarh
Moundou
Wau
Malakal
Jima
ETHIOPIA
Hargeysa

Freetown
SIERRA LEONE
Bouaké
GHANA
TOGO
NIGERIA
Ibadan
Onitsha
Makurdi
CAMEROON
Bafoussam
CENTRAL AFRICAN REPUBLIC
Bambari
Rumbek
White Nile
Juba
Kelafo

Monrovia
Yamoussoukro
Kumasi
Accra
Lomé
Porto-Novo
Lagos
Port Harcourt
Douala
Bouar
Bangui
Bumba
Isiro
SOMALIA
Mogadishu

LIBERIA
Abidjan
IVORY COAST
Volta
Bioko
Malabo
Yaoundé
Ubangi R.
Congo R.
Kisangani
Lake Albert
UGANDA
Marsabit
Marka

EQUATORIAL GUINEA
São Tomé
Libreville ⊛
REP. OF THE CONGO
Mbandaka
KENYA
Eldoret
Nakuru
Kismaayo

SÃO TOMÉ AND PRÍNCIPE
GABON
Lambaréné
Franceville
DEM. REP. OF THE CONGO
Bandundu
Kindu
Bukavu
RWANDA
Kigali ⊛
Mwanza
Arusha
Mombasa
INDIAN OCEAN

Annobón
(Equatorial Guinea)
Port-Gentil
Brazzaville
Kikwit
Ilebo
Bujumbura
BURUNDI
Tabora
TANZANIA
Tanga
Pemba I.
Victoria ⊛
SEYCHELLES

Pointe-Noire
Kinshasa
Matadi
Tshikapa
Kananga
Kalemie
Dodoma
Morogoro
Zanzibar
Dar es Salaam

Cabinda
(Angola)
Luanda ⊛
Malanje
Kamina
Lake Tanganyika
Mbeya
Songea
Mtwara

Benguela
ANGOLA
Huambo
Luena
Kolwezi
Lubumbashi
MALAWI
COMOROS
Moroni
Mayotte
(France)
Antsiranana

Lubango
Menongue
Chingola
Ndola
Kabwe
ZAMBIA
Lusaka ⊛
Lilongwe ⊛
Blantyre
Nampula
Mahajanga
Toamasina

Tsumeb
Livingstone
Tete
MOZAMBIQUE
Quelimane
Antananarivo ⊛
MAURITIUS

NAMIBIA
BOTSWANA
Francistown
ZIMBABWE
Bulawayo
Gweru
Harare ⊛
Mutare
Beira
MADAGASCAR
Fianarantsoa
Reunion
(France)
Port Louis

Windhoek ⊛
Serowe
Thohoyandou
Toliara
Tolanaro

Walvis Bay
Gaborone ⊛
Pretoria
(Tshwane)
Xai-Xai
Maputo

Lüderitz
Johannesburg
Klerksdorp
SWAZILAND
Mbabane
Keetmanshoop
Kimberley
Bloemfontein
Pietermaritzburg

Springbok
SOUTH AFRICA
Maseru
Durban
(eThekwini)

Middelburg
LESOTHO
Umtata

East London

Cape Town ⊛
Port Elizabeth (Nelson Mandela Bay)

ATLANTIC
OCEAN

Facts

- Area: 11,507,789 square miles (29,805,048 square kilometers)

- Highest Point: Mt. Kilimanjaro, Tanzania 19,341 ft. (5,895 m)

- Lowest Point: Lake Assal, Djibouti 500 ft. (152 m) below sea level

- Longest River: Nile 4,160 mi. (6,693 km)

- Largest Lake: Lake Victoria, Uganda/Kenya/Tanzania 26,828 sq. mi. (69,484 sq. km)

- Largest Country: Sudan 967,500 sq. mi. (2,505,825 sq. km) [A]

- Largest Urban Concentration: Cairo, Egypt 10,398,000

Source:
[A] *World Factbook*, CIA, 2007

International boundary
▲ Mountain peak
▽ Lowest point
≈ Falls

Sources for elevation data:
World Factbook, CIA, 2007
Shuttle Radar Topography

EUROPE

ASIA

Mediterranean Sea

S A H A R A

S A H E L

ATLANTIC OCEAN

CONGO BASIN

INDIAN OCEAN

Kalahari Desert

Madagascar

Elevation Profile

0   500   1,000 mi
0   500   1,000 km

Jebel Toubkal   Ahaggar Mountains   Sahara   Sahel   Lake Victoria   Mt. Kilimanjaro

Nile River

Great Rift Valley

20,000 ft.
10,000 ft.
5,000 ft.
Sea level A

Great Rift Valley, Lake Albert

B

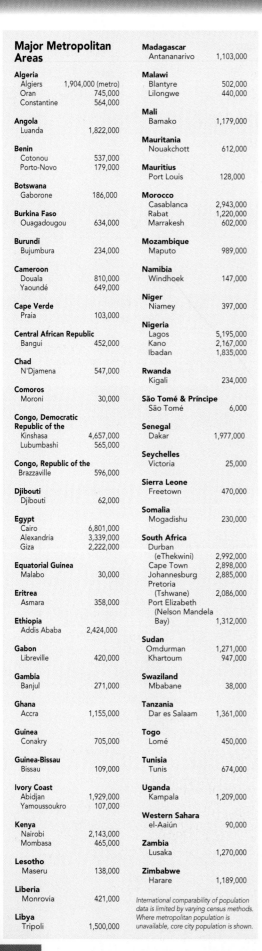

Major Metropolitan Areas

Algeria
Algiers 1,904,000 (metro)
Oran 745,000
Constantine 564,000

Angola
Luanda 1,822,000

Benin
Cotonou 537,000
Porto-Novo 179,000

Botswana
Gaborone 186,000

Burkina Faso
Ouagadougou 634,000

Burundi
Bujumbura 234,000

Cameroon
Douala 810,000
Yaoundé 649,000

Cape Verde
Praia 103,000

Central African Republic
Bangui 452,000

Chad
N'Djamena 547,000

Comoros
Moroni 30,000

Congo, Democratic Republic of the
Kinshasa 4,657,000
Lubumbashi 565,000

Congo, Republic of the
Brazzaville 596,000

Djibouti
Djibouti 62,000

Egypt
Cairo 6,801,000
Alexandria 3,339,000
Giza 2,222,000

Equatorial Guinea
Malabo 30,000

Eritrea
Asmara 358,000

Ethiopia
Addis Ababa 2,424,000

Gabon
Libreville 420,000

Gambia
Banjul 271,000

Ghana
Accra 1,155,000

Guinea
Conakry 705,000

Guinea-Bissau
Bissau 109,000

Ivory Coast
Abidjan 1,929,000
Yamoussoukro 107,000

Kenya
Nairobi 2,143,000
Mombasa 465,000

Lesotho
Maseru 138,000

Liberia
Monrovia 421,000

Libya
Tripoli 1,500,000

Madagascar
Antananarivo 1,103,000

Malawi
Blantyre 502,000
Lilongwe 440,000

Mali
Bamako 1,179,000

Mauritania
Nouakchott 612,000

Mauritius
Port Louis 128,000

Morocco
Casablanca 2,943,000
Rabat 1,220,000
Marrakesh 602,000

Mozambique
Maputo 989,000

Namibia
Windhoek 147,000

Niger
Niamey 397,000

Nigeria
Lagos 5,195,000
Kano 2,167,000
Ibadan 1,835,000

Rwanda
Kigali 234,000

São Tomé & Príncipe
São Tomé 6,000

Senegal
Dakar 1,977,000

Seychelles
Victoria 25,000

Sierra Leone
Freetown 470,000

Somalia
Mogadishu 230,000

South Africa
Durban (eThekwini) 2,992,000
Cape Town 2,898,000
Johannesburg 2,885,000
Pretoria (Tshwane) 2,086,000
Port Elizabeth (Nelson Mandela Bay) 1,312,000

Sudan
Omdurman 1,271,000
Khartoum 947,000

Swaziland
Mbabane 38,000

Tanzania
Dar es Salaam 1,361,000

Togo
Lomé 450,000

Tunisia
Tunis 674,000

Uganda
Kampala 1,209,000

Western Sahara
el-Aaiún 90,000

Zambia
Lusaka 1,270,000

Zimbabwe
Harare 1,189,000

International comparability of population data is limited by varying census methods. Where metropolitan population is unavailable, core city population is shown.

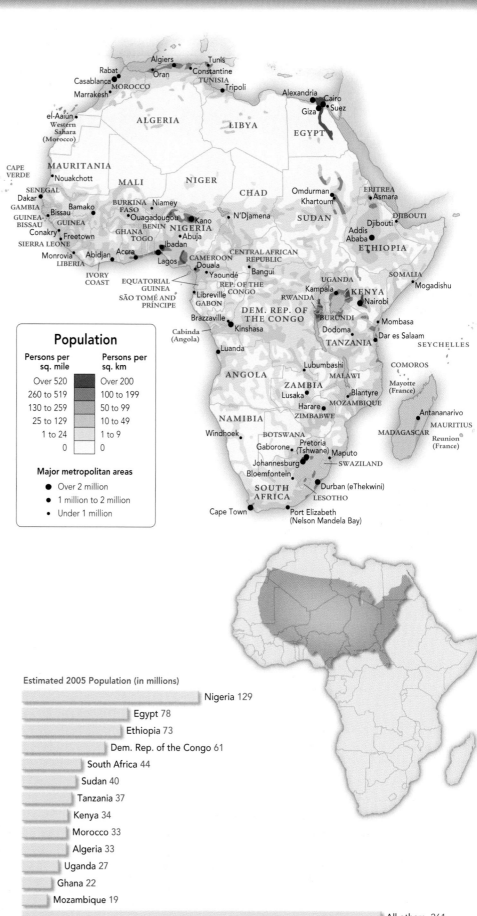

Population

Persons per sq. mile	Persons per sq. km
Over 520	Over 200
260 to 519	100 to 199
130 to 259	50 to 99
25 to 129	10 to 49
1 to 24	1 to 9
0	0

Major metropolitan areas
● Over 2 million
● 1 million to 2 million
• Under 1 million

Estimated 2005 Population (in millions)

Nigeria 129
Egypt 78
Ethiopia 73
Dem. Rep. of the Congo 61
South Africa 44
Sudan 40
Tanzania 37
Kenya 34
Morocco 33
Algeria 33
Uganda 27
Ghana 22
Mozambique 19
All others 261

Source: U.S. Census Bureau

Gross Domestic Product is a measure of the total goods and services generated by a country. Generally, manufacturing, high-tech services, and specialized agricultural products add more value than raw materials and basic food stuffs.

South Africa is the only African nation considered to have a developed economy, even though their GDP is less then half that of the United States.

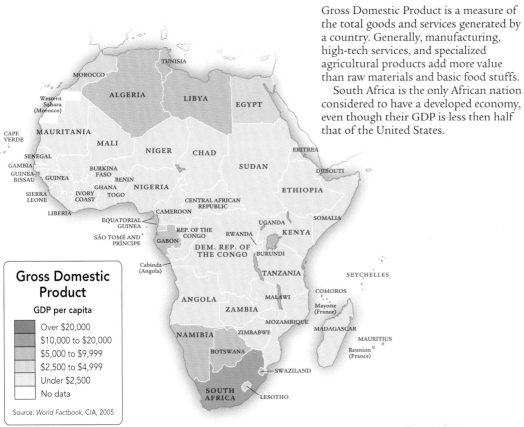

Gross Domestic Product

GDP per capita

- Over $20,000
- $10,000 to $20,000
- $5,000 to $9,999
- $2,500 to $4,999
- Under $2,500
- No data

Source: *World Factbook*, CIA, 2005

Electricity Use, 2002

- United States 12,376
- South Africa 4,271
- Libya 3,370
- Botswana 1,152
- Zambia 475
- Nigeria 143

KWh (kilowatt hours) per person per year

Source: *World Factbook*, CIA, 2005

Agriculture supplies the livelihood for the vast majority of Africans. Agricultural exports include coffee, cocoa beans, peanuts, palm oil, and spices. These important export crops are mainly cultivated on plantations and large farms. Areas of subsistence farming supply the needs of local communities.

Unfortunately, poor soils and unfavorable climate conditions, as well as political unrest and unstable economies, all have an adverse impact on agricultural activity and therefore the standard of living.

Minerals account for more then one half of Africa's exports. Oil, diamonds, gold, cobalt, and several other minerals are leading exports. However, important mineral deposits are limited to a handful of countries.

Manufacturing has been slow to develop on the continent. Lack of money and skilled labor are the main deterrents.

Land Use and Resources

Predominant land use

- Commercial agriculture
- Livestock ranching
- Subsistence agriculture
- Nomadic herding
- Primarily forestland
- Limited agricultural activity

Major resources

- Coal
- Natural gas
- Oil
- Au Gold
- Fe Iron ore
- Pt Platinum
- U Uranium
- Al Bauxite
- Diamonds
- Other minerals
- Fishing
- ● Major manufacturing and trade centers

The climate of Africa is clearly a study in geographic contrasts. Perpetually wet and tropical areas surrounding the Equator quickly acquire seasonal variety as you move north and south. Roaming even farther leads to the vast, hot and arid zones of northern and southern Africa. The influence of neighboring water bodies is limited to small regions of northern Africa, namely Morocco, Algeria, and Libya, where the mild currents of the Mediterranean Sea temper the climate, and eastern South Africa, where the mixture of warm currents flowing close to shore and the seasonal onshore winds striking the Drakensberg uplands provide for a moist and temperate marine coast climate.

See photographs taken in different kinds of climates on pages 24–25.

Climate

- Tropical wet
- Tropical wet and dry
- Arid
- Semiarid
- Mediterranean
- Humid subtropical
- Marine
- Highland

Ifrane
Lowest recorded temperature, -11°F (-24°C)

El Azizia
Highest recorded temperature, 136°F (58°C)

Wadi Halfa
Lowest average annual precipitation: 0.1" (0.254 cm)

Debundscha
Highest average annual precipitation: 405" (1,029 cm)

Africa's precipitation pattern is determined by its position on Earth's grid. Heavy precipitation near the Equator dwindles both to north, home of the immense Sahara, and to the south, realm of the Namib and Kalahari Deserts. Moist conditions exist on Madagascar as a result of the tropical influences of winds and currents from the Indian Ocean.

Annual Precipitation

Centimeters	Inches
Over 203	Over 80
152 to 203	60 to 80
102 to 152	40 to 60
51 to 102	20 to 40
25 to 51	10 to 20
Under 25	Under 10

Climate Graphs

Average daily temperature range (in °F)	Average monthly precipitation (in inches)
100° — High 65° — Low 32° 0°	20" 10" 0"

ADDIS ABABA, Ethiopia

ANTANANARIVO, Madagascar

CAIRO, Egypt

CAPE TOWN, South Africa

CASABLANCA, Morocco

CONAKRY, Guinea

DAKAR, Senegal

DAR ES SALAAM, Tanzania

FAYA-LARGEAU, Chad

KINSHASA, Dem. Rep. of the Congo

LAGOS, Nigeria

LUSAKA, Zambia

The dense, tropical rain forest surrounding the Equator is offset by the contrastingly sparse vegetation on the rest of the continent. Vast areas consist of grassland and scrub vegetation with trees only occasionally dotting the landscape. Evergreen and mixed forests of more temperate climates are limited to the Mediterranean areas of Morocco and Algeria, the Ethiopian Highlands, and Kenya.

See photographs of the different kinds of vegetation on pages 26–27.

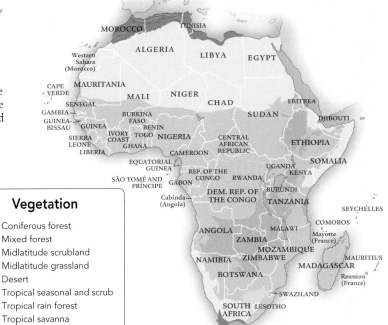

Vegetation

- Coniferous forest
- Mixed forest
- Midlatitude scrubland
- Midlatitude grassland
- Desert
- Tropical seasonal and scrub
- Tropical rain forest
- Tropical savanna

Environmental Issues

- Current forest
- Cleared forest
- Area at highest risk of desertification
- • Poor air quality*

*Cities exceeding at least one of the World Health Organization's (WHO) annual mean guidelines for air quality

Sources: *Global Distribution of Original and Remaining Forests,* UNEP-WCMC, 2002
World Soil Resources Map Index, USDA/NRCS, 2002
World Development Indicators, World Bank, 1999

Desertification (land turning into desert) is one of the leading environmental issues in Africa. Two leading causes of desertification are the removal of vegetation (often for cooking fuel) and overgrazing, especially in semiarid and drought-prone areas. Other environmental problems include deforestation, soil loss, declining biodiversity, and decreasing air and water quality. Water scarcity is also a concern in many African countries, such as Egypt, Libya, Algeria, Tunisia, and Morocco.

Asia

Source:
[A] Israel Marine Data Center

Facts

- Area: 17,043,481 square miles (44,142,430 square kilometers)
- Highest Point: Mt. Everest, China/Nepal 29,035 ft. (8,850 m)
- Lowest Point: Dead Sea, Israel/Jordan 1,371 ft. (418 m) below sea level [A]
- Longest River: Chang (Yangtze), China 3,965 mi. (6,380 km)
- Largest Lake: Lake Baikal, 11,780 sq. mi. (30,510 sq. km)
- Largest Country: Russia (Asian) 5,063,805 sq. mi. (13,115,255 sq. km)
- Largest Urban Concentration: Tokyo, Japan 34,450,000

PACIFIC OCEAN

ARCTIC OCEAN

INDIAN OCEAN

R U S S I A

C H I N A

MONGOLIA

KAZAKHSTAN

INDIA

IRAN

SAUDI ARABIA

INDONESIA

MALAYSIA

PHILIPPINES

JAPAN

N. KOREA

S. KOREA

TAIWAN (Taiwan administered separately from China)

VIETNAM

THAILAND

CAMBODIA

LAOS

MYANMAR (BURMA)

BANGLADESH

BHUTAN

NEPAL

PAKISTAN

AFGHANISTAN

TAJIKISTAN

KYRGYZSTAN

UZBEKISTAN

TURKMENISTAN

SRI LANKA

MALDIVES

BRUNEI

SINGAPORE

TIMOR-LESTE (EAST TIMOR)

TURKEY

CYPRUS

LEBANON

ISRAEL

JORDAN

SYRIA

IRAQ

KUWAIT

BAHRAIN

QATAR

UNITED ARAB EMIRATES

OMAN

YEMEN

Tokyo
Yokohama
Osaka
Kyoto
Kitakyushu
Sendai
Sapporo
Beijing
Tianjin
Shanghai
Shenyang
Harbin
Changchun
Wuhan
Chongqing
Guangzhou
Hong Kong
Taipei
Seoul
Busan
Pyeongyang
N. KOREA
Manila
Quezon City
Cebu
Davao
Manado
Makassar
Surabaya
Bandung
Jakarta
Palembang
Medan
Padang
Banjarmasin
Kuching
Bandar Seri Begawan
Kota Kinabalu
Kuala Lumpur
Singapore
Bangkok
Phnom Penh
Ho Chi Minh City
Da Nang
Hanoi
Vientiane
Naypyidaw
Yangon (Rangoon)
Mandalay
Dhaka
Kolkata (Calcutta)
Thimphu
Kathmandu
Lhasa
Chengdu
Kunming
Nanning
Guiyang
Changsha
Nanchang
Fuzhou
Nanjing
Zhengzhou
Jinan
Qingdao
Taiyuan
Xi'an
Lanzhou
Baotou
Yumen
Ürümqi
Hotan
Kashi
Almaty
Bishkek
Tashkent
Samarqand
Dushanbe
Ashgabat
Mashhad
Tehran
Esfahan
Shiraz
Tabriz
Baghdad
Basra
Kuwait
Riyadh
Mecca
Jeddah
Sanaa
Aden
Muscat
Abu Dhabi
Doha
Manama
Damascus
Amman
Jerusalem
Beirut
Nicosia
Ankara
Bursa
Izmir
Mumbai (Bombay)
Pune
Ahmadabad
Karachi
Hyderabad
Bengaluru (Bangalore)
Chennai (Madras)
Madurai
Colombo
Male
Hyderabad
Nagpur
Kanpur
Lucknow
Delhi
New Delhi
Jaipur
Faisalabad
Lahore
Islamabad
Srinagar
Kabul
Astana
Qaraghandy
Pavlodar
Semey
Novosibirsk
Omsk
Tomsk
Kemerovo
Novokuznetsk
Kyzyl
Krasnoyarsk
Bratsk
Irkutsk
Ulan-Ude
Ulaanbaatar
Dund-Us
Chita
Blagoveshchensk
Skovorodino
Komsomol'sk-na-Amure
Khabarovsk
Vladivostok
Yakutsk
Mirnyy
Noril'sk
Surgut
Yekaterinburg
Chelyabinsk
Yenisey River
Nadym
North Pole
Magadan
Anadyr
Petropavlovsk-Kamchatskiy
Aleutian Islands (U.S.)
Kuril Islands (Russia)
Sakhalin
Jayapura
Dili
Andaman Islands (India)
Nicobar Islands (India)
Socotra (Yemen)
Lakshadweep (India)

Bering Sea
Chukchi Sea
East Siberian Sea
Laptev Sea
Kara Sea
Barents Sea
Sea of Okhotsk
Sea of Japan (East Sea)
Yellow Sea
East China Sea
South China Sea
Philippine Sea
Celebes Sea
Java Sea
Banda Sea
Arafura Sea
Luzon Strait
Bay of Bengal
Arabian Sea
Persian Gulf
Gulf of Oman
Gulf of Aden
Red Sea
Mediterranean Sea
Black Sea
Caspian Sea
Aral Sea
Lake Balkhash
Lake Baikal
Gulf of Thailand
Andaman Sea
Macau
Hainan

TROPIC OF CANCER
EQUATOR
ARCTIC CIRCLE

Ob River
Irtysh River
Ural River
Lena River
Angara River
Tigris River
Euphrates River
Huang (Yellow) River
Chang (Yangtze) River
Mekong River
Ganges River
Brahmaputra River
Indus River
Irrawaddy R.

North Pole

1,000 mi
500
0
1,000 km
500
0

N
W E
S

PACIFIC OCEAN

ARCTIC OCEAN

North Pole

EUROPE

AFRICA

INDIAN OCEAN

AUSTRALIA

Legend

International boundary
▲ Mountain peak
▽ Lowest point

Sources for elevation data:
Merriam-Webster's Geographical Dictionary, 2007
World Factbook, CIA, 2007
Israel Marine Data Center

1,000 mi
1,000 km
500
500
0
0

Robinson Projection

Mt. Fuji
12,388 ft. (3,776 m)

Honshu
Hokkaido
Kuril Islands
Sakhalin
Kamchatka Peninsula
Bering Sea
Sea of Okhotsk
Chukchi Peninsula
Wrangel Island
Chukchi Sea
East Siberian Sea
New Siberian Islands
Laptev Sea
Severnaya Zemlya
Taymyr Peninsula
Kara Sea
Novaya Zemlya
Franz Josef Land
Barents Sea

CENTRAL RANGE
KORYAK RANGE
KOLYMA RANGE
CHERSKY RANGE
VERKHOYANSK RANGE
STANOVOY RANGE
YABLONOVYY RANGE
GREATER KHINGAN RANGE

Amur River
Aldan River
Shilka River
Lena River
Angara River
Tunguska River
Lower Tunguska River
Yenisey
Ob River
Irtysh River
Ishim River
Ural River

S I B E R I A
CENTRAL SIBERIAN PLATEAU
WEST SIBERIAN PLAIN
SAYAN MOUNTAINS
ALTAY MTS.
MONGOLIAN PLATEAU
G O B I
Lake Baikal

MANCHURIAN PLAIN
NORTH CHINA PLAIN
Huang (Yellow) River
Chang (Yangtze) River
Xi River
Hong River

Korean Pen.
Sea of Japan (East Sea)
Yellow Sea
East China Sea
Korea Strait
Okinawa
Ryukyu Islands
Taiwan
Luzon Strait
Luzon
Philippine Islands
Mindanao
Palawan
Celebes Sea
Sulawesi (Celebes)
Moluccas
Banda Sea
New Guinea
MAOKE MTS.
Arafura Sea
Timor Sea
Timor
Lesser Sunda Is.
Bali
Java
Java Sea
Borneo
Greater Sunda Islands
South China Sea
Philippine Sea
Hainan
Gulf of Thailand
Malay Peninsula
Mekong River
Salween River
Irrawaddy River
Andaman Sea
Sumatra
Strait of Malacca
Mentawai Islands
Nicobar Islands
Andaman Islands

TIAN SHAN
KUNLUN SHAN
PLATEAU OF TIBET
TARIM BASIN
Taklimakan Desert
DZUNGARIAN BASIN
KAZAKH UPLANDS
Lake Balkhash
Syr Darya
Kyzyl Kum
Amu Darya
Karakum
USTYURT PLATEAU
TURAN LOWLAND
Aral Sea
Caspian Sea

K2
28,250 ft. (8,611 m)

H I M A L A Y A S
Mt. Everest 29,035 ft. (8,850 m)
Brahmaputra River
GANGETIC PLAIN
Ganges R.
Sutlej R.
Indus River
HINDU KUSH
PAMIRS
Thar Desert
DECCAN PLATEAU
Godavari River
EASTERN GHATS
WESTERN GHATS

Bay of Bengal
Sri Lanka
Cape Comorin
Lakshadweep
Maldives
A r a b i a n   S e a
Socotra
Gulf of Aden
Gulf of Oman

URAL MOUNTAINS

Mt. Ararat 16,945 ft. (5,165 m)
Anatolia
Black Sea
Bosporus
Cyprus
Mediterranean Sea
Dead Sea 1,371 ft. (418 m) below sea level
Tigris River
Euphrates River
Mesopotamia
Syrian Desert
An Nafud
ELBURZ MTS.
ZAGROS MTS.
Dasht-e Kavir
Persian Gulf
Arabian Peninsula
Rub' al-Khali
Red Sea

ARCTIC CIRCLE

Elevation Profile

30,000 ft.		Japan
25,000 ft.		South Korea
20,000 ft.		Yellow Sea
15,000 ft.		Himalayas
10,000 ft.		Mount Everest
5,000 ft.		Indus Valley
Sea level		Zagros Mts.

Dead Sea
Syrian Desert
Zagros Mts.
Indus Valley
Mount Everest
Himalayas
Yellow Sea
South Korea
Japan

A
B

Major Metropolitan Areas

Afghanistan
Kabul 2,029,000

Bahrain
Manama 151,000

Bangladesh
Dhaka 6,487,000

Bhutan
Thimphu 8,900

Brunei
Bandar Seri Begawan 50,000

Cambodia
Phnom Penh 1,000,000

China
Shanghai 12,910,000
Beijing 10,820,000
Tianjin 8,970,000
Hong Kong 6,708,000
Shenyang 4,740,000
Wuhan 4,450,000
Chongqing 4,070,000
Guangzhou 3,910,000
Chengdu 3,120,000
Xi'an 2,990,000
Harbin 2,960,000
Nanjing 2,670,000

Cyprus
Nicosia 273,000

East Timor
Dili 140,000

India
Mumbai (Bombay) 16,368,000
Kolkata (Calcutta) 13,217,000
Delhi 12,791,000
Chennai (Madras) 6,425,000
Bengaluru (Bangalore) 5,687,000
Hyderabad 5,534,000

Indonesia
Jakarta 9,374,000
Bandung 5,919,000
Bogor 5,000,000
Malang 3,174,000

Iran
Tehran 6,759,000
Mashhad 1,887,000

Iraq
Baghdad 4,336,000

Israel
Tel Aviv-Jaffa 2,595,000
Jerusalem 628,000

Japan
Tokyo 12,059,000
Yokohama 3,427,000
Osaka 2,599,000
Nagoya 2,171,000
Sapporo 1,822,000
Kobe 1,494,000
Kyoto 1,468,000
Fukuoka 1,341,000
Kawasaki 1,250,000
Hiroshima 1,126,000

Jordan
Amman 1,147,000

Kazakhstan
Almaty 1,129,000

North Korea
Pyeongyang 2,741,000

South Korea (core city only)
Seoul 9,854,000
Busan 3,655,000
Daegu 2,474,000

Kuwait
Kuwait 193,000

Kyrgyzstan
Bishkek 753,000

Laos
Vientiane 331,000

Lebanon
Beirut 1,500,000

Malaysia
Kuala Lumpur 1,379,000

Maldives
Male 74,000

Mongolia
Ulaanbaatar 760,000

Myanmar (Burma)
Yangon (Rangoon) 4,101,000

Nepal
Kathmandu 421,000

Oman
Muscat 477,000

Pakistan
Karachi 9,339,000
Lahore 5,143,000
Faisalabad 2,009,000
Islamabad 529,000

Philippines
Manila 9,933,000

Qatar
Doha 264,000

Russia (Asian)
Novosibirsk 1,400,000
Yekaterinburg 1,314,000
Omsk 1,177,000
Chelyabinsk 1,111,000

Saudi Arabia
Riyadh 2,776,000
Jeddah 2,046,000

Singapore
Singapore 4,131,000

Sri Lanka
Colombo 642,000

Syria
Halab (Aleppo) 1,813,000
Damascus 1,394,000

Taiwan
Taipei 2,720,000

Tajikistan
Dushanbe 529,000

Thailand
Bangkok 6,320,000

Turkey (Asian)
Ankara 3,203,000
Izmir 2,232,000

Turkmenistan
Ashgabat 407,000

United Arab Emirates
Abu Dhabi 904,000

Uzbekistan
Tashkent 2,142,000

Vietnam
Ho Chi Minh City 4,990,000
Hanoi 2,464,000

Yemen
Sanaa 927,000

International comparability of population data is limited by varying census methods. Where metropolitan population is unavailable, core city population is shown.

Population

Persons per sq. mile
- Over 520
- 260 to 519
- 130 to 259
- 25 to 129
- 1 to 24
- 0

Persons per sq. km
- Over 200
- 100 to 199
- 50 to 99
- 10 to 49
- 1 to 9
- 0

Major metropolitan areas
- ● Over 2 million
- ● 1 million to 2 million
- • Under 1 million

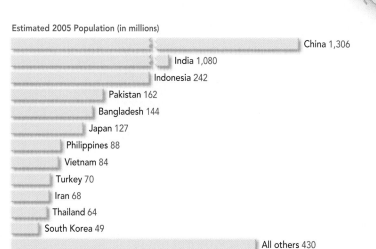

Estimated 2005 Population (in millions)

- China 1,306
- India 1,080
- Indonesia 242
- Pakistan 162
- Bangladesh 144
- Japan 127
- Philippines 88
- Vietnam 84
- Turkey 70
- Iran 68
- Thailand 64
- South Korea 49
- All others 430

Source: U.S. Census Bueau

98

Gross Domestic Product is a measure of the total goods and services generated by a country. Generally, manufacturing, high-tech services, and specialized agricultural products add more value than raw materials and basic food stuffs. The high-tech and oil producing countries on the fringes of Asia are the exceptions in this generally poor continent.

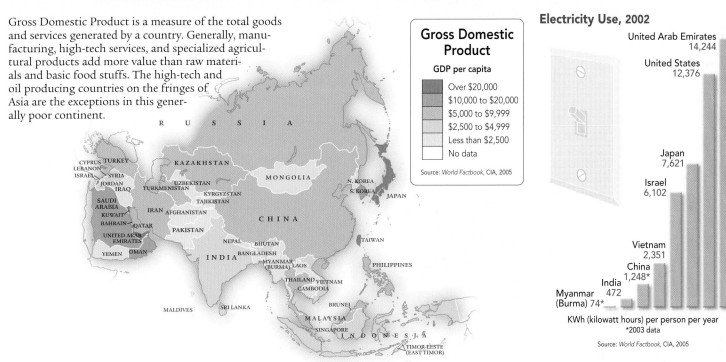

Gross Domestic Product

GDP per capita

- Over $20,000
- $10,000 to $20,000
- $5,000 to $9,999
- $2,500 to $4,999
- Less than $2,500
- No data

Source: *World Factbook*, CIA, 2005

Electricity Use, 2002

United Arab Emirates 14,244
United States 12,376
Japan 7,621
Israel 6,102
Vietnam 2,351
China 1,248*
India 472
Myanmar (Burma) 74*

KWh (kilowatt hours) per person per year
*2003 data

Source: *World Factbook*, CIA, 2005

Agriculture is the predominant land use in Asia, though only one-sixth of the land is arable. Wet grains, such as rice, are the principal crops of China and Southeast Asian countries. Dry grains, such as wheat, are grown in limited areas of Russia and China. A lack of modern farming methods, except in Japan, Russia, and Israel, has historically limited food production. However, production is increasing in some countries as governments supply the needed technology. The rugged land and climate in Northern, Central and Southwest Asia limits land use to nomadic herding. Here, animals supply food, shelter, clothing, and transportation.

Land Use and Resources

Predominant land use

- Commercial agriculture
- Nomadic herding
- Subsistence agriculture
- Primarily forestland
- Limited agricultural activity

Major resources

- Coal
- Natural gas
- Oil
- Forest products
- Au Gold
- Ag Silver
- Fe Iron ore
- U Uranium
- Al Bauxite
- Diamonds
- Other minerals
- Fishing
- Major manufacturing and trade centers

Most Asian countries have an insignificant number of manufacturing jobs relative to other occupations. Japan, South Korea, Taiwan, China, and Singapore are exceptions.

Natural resources are Asia's most important export. The oil fields of Southwest Asia supply much of the World's energy needs. Southeast Asia supplies the World with its tin, and coal is plentiful in areas of Russia, China and India. The lack of processing facilities limits many Asian countries in the use of their resources.

99

Asia has many climates. This can be expected on a landmass that covers an area from below the Equator to the Arctic Ocean and from the Mediterranean Sea to the Pacific Ocean. Weather conditions fluctuate from the sub-freezing temperatures and snow of the tundra climate in Northern Russia, through the more temperate humid continental climate, past the arid conditions of Southwest and Central Asia, and finally to the warm and wet zones of South and Southeast Asia.

See photographs taken in different kinds of climates on pages 24–25.

Verkhoyansk
Lowest recorded temperature, -90°F (-68°C), 1892

Tirat Tsvi
Highest recorded temperature,129°F (54°C)

Climate

- Tropical wet
- Tropical wet and dry
- Arid
- Semiarid
- Mediterranean
- Humid subtropical
- Humid continental
- Subarctic
- Tundra
- Highland

Annual Precipitation

Centimeters	Inches
Over 203	Over 80
152 to 203	60 to 80
102 to 152	40 to 60
51 to 102	20 to 40
25 to 51	10 to 20
Under 25	Under 10

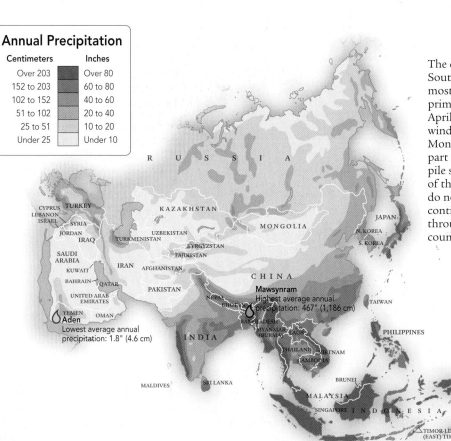

Mawsynram
Highest average annual precipitation: 467" (1,186 cm)

Aden
Lowest average annual precipitation: 1.8" (4.6 cm)

The countries of South and Southeast Asia experience the most rainfall. This rainfall occurs primarily between the months of April and October. Warm, moist winds from the south, called Monsoons, bring the rain to this part of the continent and also pile snow deeply upon the peaks of the Himalayas. The Monsoons do not reach the interior of the continent, which remains dry throughout the year. The driest countries are in the southwest.

Climate Graphs

Average daily temperature range (in °F)   Average monthly precipitation (in inches)

ALMATY, Kazakhstan

BEIRUT, Lebanon

COLOMBO, Sri Lanka

DHAKA, Bangladesh

HONG KONG, China

JAKARTA, Indonesia

NEW DELHI, India

RIYADH, Saudi Arabia

TEHRAN, Iran

TIANJIN, China

TOKYO, Japan

YAKUTSK, Russia

Vegetation

- Unclassified highlands or ice cap
- Tundra and alpine tundra
- Coniferous forest
- Midlatitude deciduous forest
- Subtropical broadleaf evergreen forest
- Mixed forest
- Midlatitude scrub
- Midlatitude grassland
- Desert
- Tropical seasonal and scrub
- Tropical rain forest
- Tropical savanna

The continent's vegetation is as varied as its climate, ranging from the lush tropical vegetation of the South, Southeast, and East Asian countries to the sparse vegetation of Russia's vast arctic tundra.

See photographs of the different kinds of vegetation on pages 26–27.

Environmental Issues

- Current forest
- Cleared forest
- Area at highest risk of desertification
- Areas most affected by acid rain
- • Poor air quality*

*Cities exceeding at least one of the World Health Organization's (WHO) annual mean guidelines for air quality

Sources: *Global Distribution of Original and Remaining Forests,* UNEP-WCMC, 2002
World Soil Resources Map Index, USDA/NRCS, 2002
World Development Indicators, World Bank, 1999

Asia's high population densities have led to a multitude of environmental problems, including pollution, deforestation, overfishing, and water shortages. With rapid population growth, pressures on land and water resources will only continue to increase. In western Asia, desertification and groundwater issues are the most pressing concerns. Most land in the region is either currently desert or is vulnerable to becoming desert in the future, and water is being withdrawn more quickly than it can be replaced.

Australia/Oceania

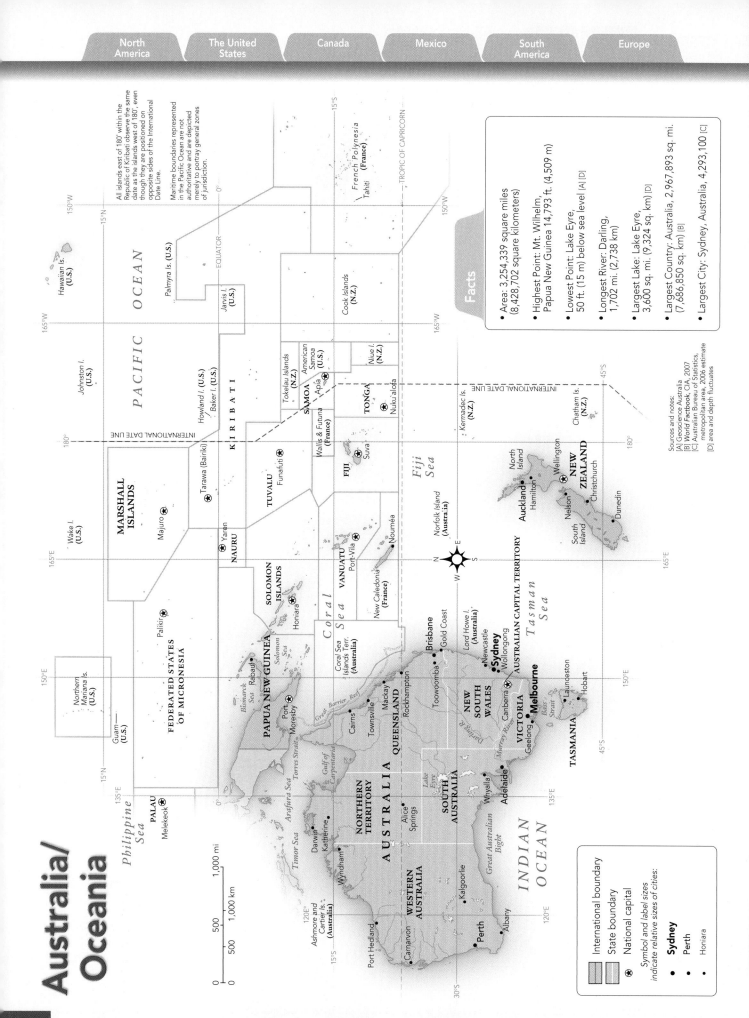

All islands east of 180° within the same date as the islands west of 180°, even though they are positioned on opposite sides of the International Date Line.

Maritime boundaries represented in the Pacific Ocean are not authoritative and are depicted merely to portray general zones of jurisdiction.

Legend:

International boundary
State boundary
⊛ National capital

Symbol and label sizes indicate relative sizes of cities:

Sydney
• Perth
• Honiara

PACIFIC OCEAN

TROPIC OF CAPRICORN

EQUATOR

INTERNATIONAL DATE LINE

Hawaiian Is. (U.S.)

Palmyra Is. (U.S.)

Jarvis I. (U.S.)

French Polynesia (France)
— Tahiti

Cook Islands (N.Z.)

Johnston I. (U.S.)

Howland I. (U.S.)
Baker I. (U.S.)

Tokelau Islands (N.Z.)

American Samoa (U.S.)
Apia — SAMOA

Niue I. (N.Z.)

TONGA
Nuku'alofa

Kermadec Is. (N.Z.)

Chatham Is. (N.Z.)

Wallis & Futuna (France)

FIJI
Suva

Fiji Sea

NEW ZEALAND
North Island
Auckland
Hamilton
Wellington
Nelson
South Island
Christchurch
Dunedin

Wake I. (U.S.)

MARSHALL ISLANDS
Majuro ⊛

Yaren ⊛
NAURU

TUVALU
Funafuti

KIRIBATI
Tarawa (Bairiki) ⊛

Norfolk Island (Australia)

Palikir ⊛
FEDERATED STATES OF MICRONESIA

SOLOMON ISLANDS
Honiara ⊛

VANUATU
Port-Vila ⊛

New Caledonia (France)
Nouméa

Coral Sea

Northern Mariana Is. (U.S.)

Guam (U.S.)

PALAU
Melekeok ⊛

PAPUA NEW GUINEA
Port Moresby ⊛
Rabaul

Bismarck Sea
Solomon Sea

Coral Sea Islands Terr. (Australia)

Lord Howe I. (Australia)

Philippine Sea

Tasman Sea

Timor Sea

Arafura Sea

Torres Strait

Gulf of Carpentaria

Great Barrier Reef

AUSTRALIA

NORTHERN TERRITORY
Darwin
Katherine
Alice Springs

WESTERN AUSTRALIA
Wyndham
Port Hedland
Carnarvon
Kalgoorlie
Perth
Albany

Ashmore and Cartier Is. (Australia)

Great Australian Bight

INDIAN OCEAN

SOUTH AUSTRALIA
Lake Eyre
Whyalla
Adelaide

QUEENSLAND
Cairns
Townsville
Mackay
Rockhampton
Toowoomba
Brisbane
Gold Coast

NEW SOUTH WALES
Newcastle
Sydney ⊛
Wollongong

AUSTRALIAN CAPITAL TERRITORY
Canberra ⊛

VICTORIA
Geelong
Melbourne
Murray River
Darling River

TASMANIA
Launceston
Hobart
Bass Strait

N
E
S
W

1,000 mi
1,000 km
500
500
0
0

PACIFIC OCEAN

TROPIC OF CAPRICORN

EQUATOR

Marquesas
Islands

Tuamotu Archipelago

French
Polynesia

Society Islands Tahiti

Austral Is.

Line Islands

Kiritimati I.

Starbuck I.

Flint I.

Palmyra Is.

Jarvis I.

Tongareva Is.

Manihiki I.

Cook Islands

Rarotonga I.

Chatham Is.

Johnston I.

Phoenix Is.

Tokelau Islands

Samoa Islands

Niue I.

Tonga

Kermadec Is.

Howland I.

Baker I.

Wallis &
Futuna

Kauaʻi
Oʻahu
Maui
Hawaiʻi
Hawaiian Is.

Wake I.

Marshall
Islands

Tarawa

Gilbert Is.

Tuvalu

Vanua
Levu

Viti
Levu

Fiji
Sea

Norfolk Island

North
Island

Ruapehu
9,176 ft.
(2,797 m)

Mt. Cook
12,316 ft.
(3,754 m)

SOUTHERN ALPS

South
Island

Stewart I.

Cook Strait

Great Barrier
I. Bay of
Plenty L. Taupo

Cape
Reinga

Nauru

Micronesia

Caroline Islands

Guam

Northern
Mariana Is.

Babelthuap

Solomon Islands

Santa Isabel I.

Malaita I.

Guadalcanal I.

Espiritu
Santo

New Caledonia

Lord Howe I.

Tasman
Sea

Melanesia

New
Ireland

Bougainville

New Britain

Louisiade
Arch.

Bismarck
Sea

Solomon
Sea

Mt. Wilhelm 14,793 ft.
(4,509 m)

CENTRAL
RANGE

Admiralty Is.

New Guinea

Cape York

Coral
Sea

Fraser I.

Great Barrier
Reef

Redcliffe Bay

Halifax Bay

GREAT DIVIDING RANGE

AUSTRALIAN ALPS

Mt. Kosciuszko
7,310 ft.
(2,228 m)

Flinders I.

Bass
Strait

King I.

Tasmania

South East
Cape

South
Cape

Flinders R.

Great
Artesian
Basin

Warrego R.

Lachlan R.

Murray River

Darling R.

FLINDERS
RANGES

Encounter
Bay

Kangaroo I.

Eyre
Pen.

Spencer Gulf

Torres Strait

Gulf
of
Carpentaria

Groote I.

Wellesley
Is.

Barkly
Tableland

Mt. Zeil
5,023 ft.
(1,531 m)

MACDONNELL
RANGES

MUSGRAVE
RANGES

Lake
Eyre

Lake Eyre
50 ft. (15 m)
below sea level

Arnhem
Land

Gibson
Desert

Great
Victoria Desert

Great Australian
Bight

Cape
Pasley

NULLARBOR PLAIN

Cape
Catastrophe

Arafura Sea

Timor Sea

Melville I.

Bathurst I.

KIMBERLEY
PLATEAU

L. Argyle

Fitzroy R.

Great Sandy
Desert

WESTERN
PLATEAU

Joseph
Bonaparte
Gulf

Ashmore and
Cartier Is.

HAMERSLEY
RANGE

Barrow I.

INDIAN
OCEAN

Dirk Hartog I.

Steep Point

Geographe Bay

Cape Naturaliste
Cape Leeuwin

West Cape
Howe

Philippine
Sea

Celebes
Sea

South
China
Sea

ASIA

PACIFIC
OCEAN

ASIA

AUSTRALIA

INDIAN
OCEAN

ANTARCTICA

NORTH
AMERICA

SOUTH
AMERICA

EUROPE

AFRICA

ATLANTIC
OCEAN

ARCTIC OCEAN

SOUTHERN OCEAN

Equator

Robinson Projection

N
E
W
S

1,000 mi

1,000 km

500

500   1,000 km

0

0

International boundary

State boundary

Mountain peak

Lowest point

Sources for elevation data:
World Factbook, CIA, 2007
Geoscience Australia
Smithsonian Global Volcanism Program

Elevation Profile

6,000 ft.
4,500 ft.
3,000 ft.
1,500 ft.
Sea level

A

B

Kimberley
Plateau

Mount Zeil

MacDonnell
Ranges

Lake
Eyre

Flinders
Ranges

Mount
Kosciuszko

A

B

165°W

165°W

180°

180°

15°N

0°

15°S

30°S

45°S

15°S

30°S

45°S

120°E

135°E

150°E

165°E

Major Metropolitan Areas

Australia
Sydney	3,997,000
Melbourne	3,367,000
Brisbane	1,628,000
Perth	1,340,000
Adelaide	1,073,000
Newcastle	471,000
Gold Coast (Southport)	397,000
Canberra	312,000

Fiji
Suva	167,000
Lautoka	29,000

Kiribati
Tarawa (Bairiki)	25,000

Marshall Islands
Majuro	18,000

Micronesia
Weno	15,000
Colonia	3,000

Nauru
Yaren	4,000

New Zealand
Auckland	1,075,000
Wellington	340,000
Christchurch	334,000

Palau
Melekeok	400

Papua New Guinea
Port Moresby	332,000
Lae	81,000
Madang	27,000
Wewak	23,000

Samoa
Apia	34,000

Solomon Islands
Honiara	61,000

Tonga
Nuku'alofa	30,000

Tuvalu
Funafuti	4,000

Vanuatu
Port-Vila	30,000

International comparability of population data is limited by varying census methods. Where metropolitan population is unavailable, core city population is shown.

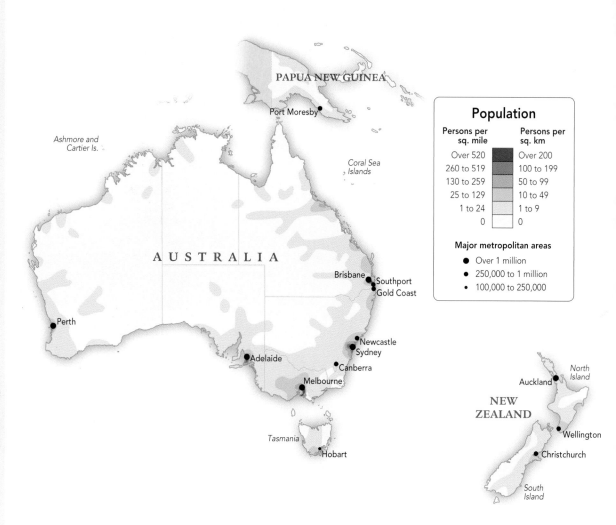

Population

Persons per sq. mile	Persons per sq. km
Over 520	Over 200
260 to 519	100 to 199
130 to 259	50 to 99
25 to 129	10 to 49
1 to 24	1 to 9
0	0

Major metropolitan areas
- ● Over 1 million
- ● 250,000 to 1 million
- • 100,000 to 250,000

Estimated 2005 Population (in millions)
- Australia 20
- Papua New Guinea 6
- New Zealand 4
- All others 3

Source: U.S. Census Bureau

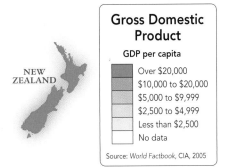

PAPUA NEW GUINEA

AUSTRALIA

Gross Domestic Product is a measure of the total goods and services generated by a country. Generally, manufacturing, high-tech services, and specialized agricultural products add more value than raw materials and basic food stuffs.

Australia derives its wealth and high standard of living from service industries and mineral extraction and processing. New Zealand's economy is oriented towards the export of animal products. Papua New Guinea's subsistence economy generates little excess wealth.

Electricity Use, 2002

United States 12,376

Australia 9,736

New Zealand 8,849

Fiji 781

Papua New Guinea 282

KWh (kilowatt hours) per person per year

Gross Domestic Product

GDP per capita

	Over $20,000
	$10,000 to $20,000
	$5,000 to $9,999
	$2,500 to $4,999
	Less than $2,500
	No data

NEW ZEALAND

GDP of Island Nations

Fiji	Samoa
Kiribati	Solomon Islands
Marshall Islands	Tonga
Micronesia	Tuvalu
Nauru	Vanuatu
Palau	

GDP of Island Territories

American Samoa (U.S.)	
Cook Is. (N.Z.)	
French Polynesia (Fr.)	
Guam (U.S.)	
New Caledonia (Fr.)	
Niue (N.Z.)	
Northern Mariana Is. (U.S.)	
Tokelau (N.Z.)	
Wallis & Futuna (Fr.)	

Land Use and Resources

Predominant land use

	Commercial agriculture
	Dairying
	Livestock ranching
	Primarily forestland
	Limited agricultural activity

Major resources

Coal	
Natural gas	
Oil	
Forest products	
Au	Gold
Ag	Silver
Fe	Iron ore
U	Uranium
Al	Bauxite
	Diamonds
	Other minerals
	Fishing
●	Major manufacturing and trade centers

PAPUA NEW GUINEA

Ashmore and Cartier Is.

Coral Sea Islands

AUSTRALIA

Brisbane

Perth

Adelaide

Sydney

Melbourne

Tasmania

Auckland

North Island

South Island

NEW ZEALAND

Australia is rich in mineral resources. It ranks first in the mining of bauxite, diamonds, lead, and zinc while being a leading producer of coal, gold, and iron ore. Its uranium deposits are the largest in the world, though largely undeveloped. Modern methods of farming and irrigation allow a very limited area of commercial agriculture to be highly productive. Despite arid conditions, vast areas of the interior support sheep and cattle grazing.

The New Zealand economy is built on livestock, raising more animals per person then any other country in the world. Meat and dairy products are important exports.

The economies of Papua New Guinea and the other island nations in the region rely primarily on subsistence agriculture and tourism.

Australia's climate is predominately warm and dry. The northern half of the country lies within the tropics and has very warm conditions year round. The southern half of the country lies below the tropics and experiences a warm summer and a cool winter.

New Zealand's climate is like that of the U.S. Pacific Northwest—mild and moist. Papua New Guinea and other island nations surrounding the equator have climates that are mainly very warm and moist year round.

See photographs taken in different kinds of climates on pages 24–25.

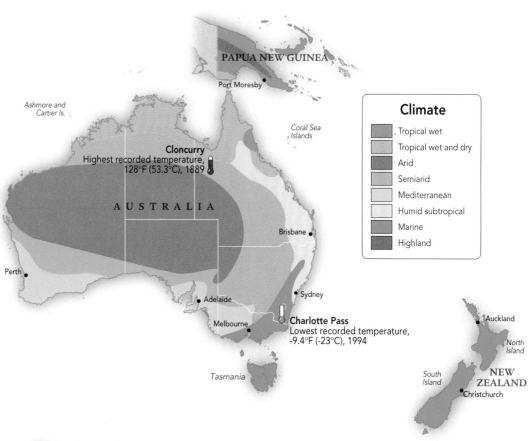

PAPUA NEW GUINEA
Port Moresby

Coral Sea Islands

Ashmore and Cartier Is.

Cloncurry
Highest recorded temperature, 128°F (53.3°C), 1889

A U S T R A L I A

Brisbane

Perth

Adelaide
Sydney

Melbourne
Charlotte Pass
Lowest recorded temperature, -9.4°F (-23°C), 1994

Tasmania

Climate

- Tropical wet
- Tropical wet and dry
- Arid
- Semiarid
- Mediterranean
- Humid subtropical
- Marine
- Highland

Auckland

North Island

South Island

NEW ZEALAND
Christchurch

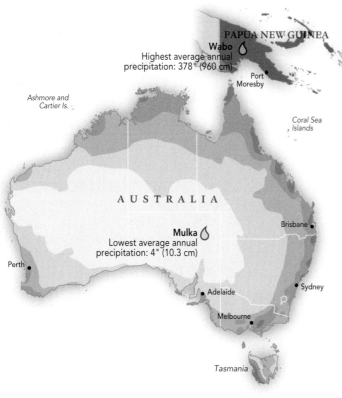

PAPUA NEW GUINEA

Wabo
Highest average annual precipitation: 378" (960 cm)

Port Moresby

Coral Sea Islands

Ashmore and Cartier Is.

A U S T R A L I A

Mulka
Lowest average annual precipitation: 4" (10.3 cm)

Brisbane

Perth

Adelaide
Sydney

Melbourne

Tasmania

Annual Precipitation

Centimeters	Inches
Over 200	Over 80
150 to 200	60 to 80
100 to 150	40 to 60
50 to 100	20 to 40
25 to 50	10 to 20
Under 25	Under 10

While Papua New Guinea and other island nations within the tropics receive plentiful and reliable rainfall, rain can be a problem in Australia—typically a case of feast or famine or bad timing. Westerly winds off of the Tasman Sea deposit precipitation on the mountain ranges of New Zealand, often in the form of snow that can be seen on some peaks year round.

Auckland

North Island

South Island

NEW ZEALAND
Christchurch

Climate Graphs

Average daily temperature range (in °F)

Average monthly precipitation (in inches)

BRISBANE, Australia

PERTH, Australia

AUCKLAND, New Zealand

PORT MORESBY, Papua New Guinea

ADELAIDE, Australia

MELBOURNE, Australia

SYDNEY, Australia

CHRISTCHURCH, New Zealand

Abundant Australian forestlands are limited to relatively narrow coastal regions where moisture, even if seasonal, is adequate. Most of the rest of the continent is covered by species of trees, bush, and grasses adapted to arid conditions. Eucalyptus are the most common trees in Australia.

Papua New Guinea has dense tropical rain forests, and New Zealand has mixed forests and grasslands arising from its temperate climate.

See photographs of different kinds of vegetation on pages 26–27.

Vegetation

- Subtropical broadleaf evergreen forest
- Mixed forest
- Midlatitude scrubland
- Midlatitude grassland
- Desert
- Tropical seasonal and scrub
- Tropical rain forest
- Tropical savanna

Environmental Issues

- Current forest
- Cleared forest
- Area at highest risk of desertification
- • Poor air quality*

*Cities exceeding at least one of the World Health Organization's (WHO) annual mean guidelines for air quality

Sources: Global Distribution of Original and Remaining Forests, UNEP-WCMC, 2002
World Soil Resources Map Index, USDA/NRCS, 2002
World Development Indicators, World Bank, 1999

Biodiversity loss (a decrease in the variety of life forms and ecosystems) is a leading environmental problem in both Australia and New Zealand. Over the past two hundred years, vast areas have been cleared for settlements and farmland. This land clearing, along with the introduction of non-native plant and animal species, has permanently altered the ecological balance. In New Zealand, it is estimated that eighty-five percent of the original lowland forests and wetlands have been lost due to human influences. Desertification, often brought on by overgrazing, is another serious environmental threat in many parts of Australia.

Name	Page	Latitude	Longitude
Columbia, C., cape	75	86°00'N	70°00'W
Columbia Mts., mountains	75	51°00'N	119°00'W
Columbia Plat., plateau	54	45°00'N	118°00'W
Columbus, GA	51	32°28'N	84°59'W
Columbus, OH	51	39°58'N	83°00'W
Comitán, Mexico	76	16°15'N	92°07'W
Comodoro Rivadavia, Argentina	78	45°51'S	67°29'W
Comorin, C., cape	97	8°00'N	78°00'E
Comoros, country	90	12°00'S	43°00'E
Comoros Is., islands	91	11°00'S	43°00'E
Conakry, Guinea	90	9°31'N	13°42'W
Concepción, Chile	78	36°48'S	73°02'W
Concepción, Paraguay	78	23°23'S	57°25'W
Concepción del Oro, Mexico	76	24°36'N	101°26'W
Conception, Pt., cape	54	34°00'N	120°00'W
Conchos, river	77	29°00'N	105°00'W
Concord, NH	51	43°12'N	71°32'W
Congo, river	91	2°00'N	23°00'E
Congo Basin, basin	91	1°00'S	23°00'E
Connecticut, river	55	42°00'N	73°00'W
Connecticut, state, U.S.	51	42°00'N	73°00'W
Constance, L., lake	85	48°00'N	9°00'E
Constanta, Romania	84	44°11'N	28°39'E
Constantine, Algeria	90	36°22'N	6°36'E
Cook Is., dependency, N.Z.	102	20°00'S	158°00'W
Cook Is., islands	103	20°00'S	158°00'W
Cook, Mt., peak	103	44°00'S	170°00'E
Cook Str., strait	103	41°00'S	174°00'E
Copenhagen, Denmark	84	55°41'N	12°35'E
Copiapó, Chile	78	27°23'S	70°18'W
Copper Canyon, canyon	77	27°00'N	108°00'W
Coral Sea, sea	103	15°00'S	155°00'E
Coral Sea Islands Terr., dependency, Austl.	102	17°00'S	150°00'E
Córdoba, Argentina	78	31°23'S	64°11'W
Córdoba, Spain	84	37°53'N	4°47'W
Cork, Ireland	84	51°54'N	8°28'W
Corner Brook, Canada	74	48°57'N	57°57'W
Cornwall, Canada	74	45°02'N	74°45'W
Corpus Christi, TX	50	27°48'N	97°24'W
Corrientes, Argentina	78	27°30'S	58°49'W
Corrientes, C., cape	77	20°00'N	106°00'W
Corsica, island	85	43°00'N	9°00'E
Corumbá, Brazil	78	19°01'S	57°38'W
Costa Rica, country	44	10°00'N	85°00'W
Cozumel, I., island	77	20°00'N	87°00'W
Cranbrook, Canada	74	49°31'N	115°46'W
Cree L., lake	75	57°00'N	108°00'W
Crete, island	85	35°00'N	25°00'E
Crete, Sea of, sea	85	36°00'N	25°00'E
Crimea, peninsula	85	45°00'N	34°00'E
Croatia, country	84	45°00'N	15°00'E
Cruzeiro do Sul, Brazil	78	7°38'S	72°40'W
Cuando, river	91	15°00'S	22°00'E
Cuauhtémoc, Mexico	76	28°25'N	106°51'W
Cuba, country	44	22°00'N	80°00'W
Cuba, island	45	22°00'N	80°00'W
Cubango, river	91	15°00'S	18°00'E
Cúcuta, Colombia	78	7°53'N	72°29'W
Cuenca, Ecuador	78	2°54'S	79°01'W
Cuernavaca, Mexico	76	18°55'N	99°14'W
Cuiabá, Brazil	78	15°35'S	56°07'W
Culiacán, Mexico	76	24°47'N	107°23'W
Cumaná, Venezuela	78	10°27'N	64°11'W
Cumberland, river	55	37°00'N	88°00'W
Cumberland Pen., peninsula	75	66°00'N	65°00'W
Cumberland Plat., plateau	55	35°00'N	85°00'W
Cumberland Sound, bay	45	12°10'N	69°00'W
Curaçao, island	45	12°10'N	69°00'W
Curitiba, Brazil	78	25°27'S	49°16'W
Cuzco, Peru	78	13°32'S	71°56'W
Cyclades, islands	85	37°00'N	25°00'E
Cyprus, country	96	35°00'N	33°00'E
Cyprus, island	85	35°00'N	33°00'E
Cyrenaica, region	91	25°00'N	24°00'E
Czech Rep., country	84	49°00'N	15°00'E

D

Name	Page	Latitude	Longitude
Dakar, Senegal	90	14°42'N	17°27'W
Dallas, TX	50	32°47'N	96°48'W
Dalmatia, region	85	44°00'N	16°00'E
Damaraland, region	91	21°00'S	19°00'E
Damascus, Syria	96	33°31'N	36°18'E
d'Ambre, Cap, cape	91	12°00'S	48°00'E
Da Nang, Vietnam	96	16°03'N	108°12'E
Danube, river	85	49°00'N	10°00'E
Danube Delta, delta	85	45°00'N	29°00'E
Dardanelles, strait	85	40°00'N	27°00'E
Dar es Salaam, Tanzania	90	6°49'S	39°17'E
Darling, river	103	31°00'S	144°00'E
Darwin, Australia	102	12°25'S	130°52'E
Dasht-e-Kavir, desert	97	35°00'N	54°00'E
Daugavpils, Latvia	84	55°53'N	26°32'E
Dauphin, Canada	74	51°10'N	100°04'W
Davao, Philippines	96	7°04'N	125°36'E
Davenport, IA	51	41°31'N	90°35'W
Davis, sea	15	65°00'S	95°00'E
Davis Str., strait	45	66°00'N	58°00'W
Dawson, Canada	74	64°04'N	139°24'W
Dawson Creek, Canada	74	55°45'N	120°15'W
Dayton, OH	51	39°46'N	84°12'W
Dead Sea, depression	97	31°00'N	35°00'E
Death Val., depression	54	36°00'N	117°00'W
Debrecen, Hungary	84	47°32'N	21°39'E
Decatur, IL	51	39°50'N	88°57'W
Deccan Plat., plateau	97	23°00'N	79°00'E
Delaware, river	55	41°00'N	75°00'W
Delaware, state, U.S.	51	39°00'N	74°00'W
Delaware Bay, bay	55	39°00'N	75°00'W
Delgado, C., cape	91	10°00'S	41°00'E
Delhi, India	96	28°41'N	77°12'E
Delicias, Mexico	76	28°12'N	105°28'W
Déline, Canada	74	65°12'N	123°27'W
Democratic Rep. of the Congo, country	90	1°00'S	21°00'E
Denakil, region	91	13°00'N	41°00'E
Denmark, country	84	56°00'N	10°00'E
Denmark Str., strait	45	65°00'N	31°00'W
Denver, CO	50	39°44'N	104°59'W
Dese, Ethiopia	90	11°10'N	39°37'E
Des Moines, IA	51	41°36'N	93°37'W
Des Moines, river	55	43°00'N	94°00'W
Desna, river	85	52°00'N	32°00'E
Detroit, MI	51	42°20'N	83°03'W
Devon I., island	75	76°00'N	85°00'W
Dhaka, Bangladesh	96	23°43'N	90°26'E
Diefenbaker, L., lake	75	50°00'N	107°00'W
Dijon, France	84	47°19'N	5°02'E
Dili, East Timor	96	8°35'S	125°36'E
Dinaric Alps, mountains	85	44°00'N	17°00'E
Dire Dawa, Ethiopia	90	9°36'N	41°52'E
Dirk Hartog I., island	103	26°00'S	113°00'E
Distrito Federal, fed. dist., Mex.	76	19°00'N	101°00'W
Djibouti, country	90	11°00'N	41°00'E
Djibouti, Djibouti	90	11°34'N	43°08'E
Dnieper, river	85	47°00'N	33°00'E
Dnieper Upland, highlands	85	49°00'N	32°00'E
Dniester, river	85	49°00'N	26°00'E
Dnipropetrovs'k, Ukraine	84	48°27'N	34°59'E
Dodoma, Tanzania	90	6°09'S	35°42'E
Doha, Qatar	96	25°15'N	51°26'E
Dominica, country	44	16°00'N	61°00'W
Dominican Rep., country	44	20°00'N	70°00'W
Don, river	85	48°00'N	40°00'E
Donets, river	85	49°00'N	38°00'E
Donets Basin, basin	85	48°00'N	38°00'E
Donets'k, Ukraine	84	48°00'N	37°48'E
Douala, Cameroon	90	4°03'N	9°43'E
Dourados, Brazil	78	22°14'S	54°48'W
Douro, river	85	43°00'N	7°00'W
Dover, DE	51	39°09'N	75°31'W
Dover, Str. of, strait	85	51°00'N	1°00'E
Drakensberg, mountains	91	30°00'S	30°00'E
Drake Passage, strait	14	59°00'S	70°00'W
Dresden, Germany	84	51°03'N	13°44'E
Dryden, Canada	74	49°47'N	92°49'W
Dubawnt, river	75	63°00'N	104°00'W
Dubawnt L., lake	75	63°00'N	100°00'W
Dublin, Ireland	84	53°21'N	6°16'W
Dubrovnik, Croatia	84	42°39'N	18°05'E
Duluth, MN	51	46°47'N	92°06'W
Dund-Us, Mongolia	96	47°59'N	91°39'E
Dunedin, New Zealand	102	45°52'S	170°28'E
Durango, Mexico	76	24°02'N	104°39'W
Durango, state, Mex.	76	24°00'N	104°00'W
Durban, S. Africa	90	29°51'S	31°01'E
Dushanbe, Tajikistan	96	38°34'N	68°48'E
Dzungarian Basin, basin	97	45°00'N	88°00'E

E

Name	Page	Latitude	Longitude
East China Sea, sea	97	29°00'N	124°00'E
Easter I., dependency	16	27°07'S	109°22'W
Easter I., island	14	27°07'S	109°22'W
Eastern Desert, desert	91	26°00'N	32°00'E
Eastern Ghats, mountains	97	15°00'N	82°00'E
East London, S. Africa	90	33°00'S	27°54'E
East Siberian Sea, sea	97	73°00'N	165°00'E
East Timor, country	96	9°00'S	125°00'E
Ebro, river	85	42°00'N	2°00'W
Ecuador, country	78	2°00'S	80°00'W
Edinburgh, United Kingdom	84	55°57'N	3°11'W
Edmonton, Canada	74	53°35'N	113°31'W
Edwards Plat., plateau	54	31°00'N	101°00'W
Egypt, country	90	26°00'N	29°00'E
Elba, island	85	43°00'N	10°00'E
Elbe, river	85	54°00'N	11°00'E
Elbert, Mt., peak	54	39°00'N	106°00'W
Elbrus, Mt., peak	85	43°00'N	42°00'E
Elburz Mts., mountains	97	36°00'N	53°00'E
Eldoret, Kenya	90	0°32'N	35°16'E
El Fashir, Sudan	90	13°38'N	25°21'E
El Khârga, Egypt	90	25°27'N	30°33'E
Ellesmere I., island	75	83°00'N	76°00'W
Elliot Lake, Canada	74	46°23'N	82°39'W
Ellsworth Land, region	15	76°00'S	90°00'W
Ellsworth Mts., mountains	15	80°00'S	85°00'W
El Obeid, Sudan	90	13°11'N	30°13'E
El Paso, TX	50	31°46'N	106°29'W
El Salvador, country	44	14°00'N	89°00'W
El Tigre, Venezuela	78	8°53'N	64°16'W
Emi Koussi, peak	91	19°00'N	21°00'E
Encarnación, Paraguay	78	27°20'S	55°52'W
Encounter Bay, bay	103	37°00'S	139°00'E
Enderby Land, region	15	70°00'S	40°00'E
England, division, U.K.	84	52°00'N	2°00'W
English Channel, strait	85	50°00'N	4°00'W
Ensenada, Mexico	76	31°52'N	116°37'W
Equatorial Guinea, country	90	2°00'N	11°00'E
Erg Chech, desert	91	24°00'N	3°00'W
Erie, PA.	51	42°08'N	80°05'W
Erie, L., lake	45	43°00'N	83°00'W
Eritrea, country	90	18°00'N	38°00'E
Esfahan, Iran	96	32°39'N	51°39'E
Esmeraldas, Ecuador	78	0°57'N	79°40'W
Espíritu Santo, island	103	15°00'S	167°00'E
Esquel, Argentina	78	42°55'S	71°20'W
Essen, Germany	84	51°27'N	7°03'E
Estevan, Canada	74	49°08'N	103°00'W
Estonia, country	84	59°00'N	26°00'E
Ethiopia, country	90	8°00'N	40°00'E
Ethiopian Highlands, plateau	91	9°00'N	39°00'E
Etna, Mt., peak	85	38°00'N	15°00'E
Eugene, OR	50	44°03'N	123°05'W
Eugenia Pt., cape	77	28°00'N	115°00'W
Euphrates, river	97	33°00'N	42°00'E
Europe, continent	84	50°00'N	15°00'E
Evansville, IN	51	37°58'N	87°33'W
Everest, Mt., peak	97	28°00'N	87°00'E
Eyre, L., lake	103	29°00'S	137°00'E
Eyre Pen., peninsula	103	33°00'S	136°00'E

F

Name	Page	Latitude	Longitude
Fairbanks, AK	50	64°50'N	147°43'W
Faisalabad, Pakistan	96	31°24'N	73°04'E
Falcon Res., lake	77	27°00'N	99°00'W
Falkland Is., dependency, U.K.	78	52°00'S	59°00'W
Falkland Is., islands	79	52°00'S	59°00'W
Farewell, C., cape	45	60°00'N	44°00'W
Fargo, ND	50	46°53'N	96°47'W
Faro, Canada	74	62°16'N	133°24'W
Faroe Is., dependency, Den.	84	62°00'N	7°00'W
Faroe Is., islands	85	62°00'N	7°00'W
Faya-Largeau, Chad	90	17°56'N	19°07'E
Fear, C., cape	55	34°00'N	78°00'W
Federated States of Micronesia, country	102	6°00'N	150°00'E
Feira de Santana, Brazil	78	12°15'S	38°58'W
Fès, Morocco	90	34°04'N	4°58'W
Feuilles, R. aux, river	75	58°00'N	73°00'W
Fianarantsoa, Madagascar	90	21°27'S	47°04'E
Fiji, country	102	19°00'S	178°00'E
Fiji Sea, sea	103	27°00'S	177°00'E
Filchner Ice Shelf, ice shelf	15	80°00'S	40°00'W
Fimbul Ice Shelf, ice shelf	15	70°00'S	5°00'W
Finisterre, C., cape	85	43°00'N	9°00'W
Finland, country	84	66°00'N	26°00'E
Finland, G. of, gulf	85	60°00'N	26°00'E
Fitzroy, river	103	18°00'S	125°00'E
Flagstaff, AZ	50	35°12'N	111°39'W
Flattery, C., cape	54	48°00'N	125°00'W
Flinders, river	103	19°00'S	141°00'E
Flinders I., island	103	40°00'S	148°00'E
Flinders Ranges, mountains	103	32°00'S	139°00'E
Flin Flon, Canada	74	54°48'N	101°52'W
Flint, MI	51	43°01'N	83°41'W
Flint, river	55	31°00'N	84°00'W
Flint Hills, hills	55	38°00'N	97°00'W
Flint I., island	103	11°00'S	152°00'W
Florence, Italy	84	43°46'N	11°15'E
Florencia, Colombia	78	1°36'N	75°35'W
Floriano, Brazil	78	6°47'S	43°00'W
Florianópolis, Brazil	78	27°36'S	48°34'W
Florida, state, U.S.	51	29°00'N	82°00'W
Florida Keys, islands	55	25°00'N	82°00'W
Florida, Straits of, strait	45	24°00'N	82°00'W
Fortaleza, Brazil	78	3°45'S	38°33'W
Fort Collins, CO	50	40°35'N	105°05'W
Fort Frances, Canada	74	48°38'N	93°23'W
Fort Lauderdale, FL	51	26°07'N	80°09'W
Fort McMurray, Canada	74	56°41'N	111°22'W
Fort McPherson, Canada	74	67°26'N	134°52'W
Fort Nelson, Canada	74	58°47'N	122°42'W
Fort Peck L., lake	54	48°00'N	107°00'W
Fort St. John, Canada	74	56°13'N	120°51'W
Fort Simpson, Canada	74	61°50'N	121°21'W
Fort Smith, AR	51	35°23'N	94°24'W
Fort Smith, Canada	74	60°00'N	111°57'W
Fort Worth, TX	50	32°44'N	97°19'W
Foxe Basin, bay	75	66°00'N	79°00'W
Foxe Pen., peninsula	75	65°00'N	78°00'W
France, country	84	47°00'N	2°00'E
Franceville, Gabon	90	1°39'S	13°34'E
Francistown, Botswana	90	21°12'S	27°32'E
Frankfort, KY	51	38°12'N	84°52'W
Frankfurt, Germany	84	50°07'N	8°41'E
Franz Josef Land, islands	97	81°00'N	55°00'E
Fraser, river	75	52°00'N	123°00'W
Fraser I., island	103	25°00'S	153°00'E
Fredericton, Canada	74	45°57'N	66°40'W
Freetown, Sierra Leone	90	8°27'N	13°13'W
French Guiana, dependency, Fr.	78	4°00'N	52°00'W
French Polynesia, dependency, Fr.	102	15°00'S	140°00'W
French Polynesia, islands	103	15°00'S	140°00'W
Fresnillo, Mexico	76	23°10'N	102°53'W
Fresno, CA	50	36°45'N	119°46'W
Fria, C., cape	91	18°00'S	12°00'E
Frisian Is., islands	85	54°00'N	6°00'E
Frobisher Bay, bay	75	64°00'N	66°00'W
Front Range, mountains	54	40°00'N	105°00'W
Fuerte, river	77	26°00'N	109°00'W
Fuji, Mt., peak	97	35°22'N	138°44'E
Funafuti, Tuvalu	102	8°37'S	179°07'E
Fundy, Bay of, bay	75	45°00'N	67°00'W
Fuzhou, China	96	26°04'N	119°18'E

G

Name	Page	Latitude	Longitude
Gabes, G. of, gulf	91	34°00'N	12°00'E
Gabon, country	90	0°00'	12°00'E
Gaborone, Botswana	90	24°38'S	25°55'E
Galápagos Is., islands	79	1°00'S	91°00'W
Galdhøpiggen, peak	85	62°00'N	8°00'E
Galveston Bay, bay	55	29°00'N	95°00'W
Gambia, country	90	12°00'N	16°00'W
Gander, Canada	74	48°57'N	54°36'W
Ganges, river	97	25°00'N	80°00'E
Gangetic Plain, plain	97	28°00'N	81°00'E
Gao, Mali	90	16°16'N	0°00'
Garonne, river	85	45°00'N	0°00'
Garoua, Cameroon	90	9°18'N	13°23'E
Garry L., lake	75	66°00'N	100°00'W
Gary, IN	51	41°36'N	87°21'W
Gaspé, Canada	74	48°50'N	64°30'W
Gaspé Pen., peninsula	75	49°00'N	63°00'W
Gdansk, Poland	84	54°22'N	18°38'E
Gedaref, Sudan	90	14°02'N	35°23'E
Geelong, Australia	102	38°11'S	144°23'E
Genesee, river	55	43°00'N	78°00'W
Geneva, Switzerland	84	46°12'N	6°09'E
Geneva, L., lake	85	46°00'N	6°00'E
Genoa, Italy	84	44°25'N	8°56'E
Geographe Bay, bay	103	33°00'S	115°00'E
George, river	75	57°00'N	77°00'W
Georgetown, Guyana	78	6°47'N	58°07'W
Georgia, country	84	43°00'N	43°00'E
Georgia, state, U.S.	51	33°00'N	83°00'W
Germany, country	84	52°00'N	11°00'E
Ghadamis, Libya	90	30°08'N	9°30'E
Ghana, country	90	9°00'N	2°00'W
Ghardaia, Algeria	90	32°30'N	3°40'E
Gibraltar, dependency, U.K.	84	37°00'N	5°00'W
Gibraltar, Str. of, strait	85	36°00'N	6°00'W
Gibson Desert, desert	103	25°00'S	127°00'E
Gijón, Spain	84	43°32'N	5°41'W
Gila, river	54	33°00'N	112°00'W
Gilbert Is., islands	103	0°00'	173°00'E
Giza, Egypt	90	30°01'N	31°13'E
Glasgow, United Kingdom	84	55°51'N	4°16'W
Gobi, desert	97	43°00'N	105°00'E
Godavari, river	97	19°00'N	78°00'E
Goiânia, Brazil	78	16°42'S	49°15'W
Gold Coast, Australia	102	27°57'S	153°23'E
Gold Coast, region	91	5°00'N	1°00'W
Gonder, Ethiopia	90	12°34'N	37°26'E
Good Hope, C. of, cape	91	35°00'S	18°00'E
Göteborg, Sweden	84	57°42'N	11°56'E
Gotland, island	85	57°00'N	18°00'E
Governador Valadares, Brazil	78	18°51'S	41°59'W
Grain Coast, region	91	6°00'N	10°00'W
Granada, Spain	84	37°11'N	3°36'W
Gran Chaco, plain	79	23°00'S	62°00'W
Grand, river	55	43°00'N	86°00'W
Grand Canyon, canyon	54	36°00'N	113°00'W
Grande, river	79	20°00'S	48°00'W
Grande Prairie, Canada	74	55°11'N	118°48'W
Grand Erg Occidental, desert	91	31°00'N	2°00'E
Grand Erg Oriental, desert	91	31°00'N	8°00'E
Grand Falls-Windsor, Canada	74	49°00'N	55°35'W
Grand Forks, ND	50	47°56'N	97°02'W
Grand Rapids, MI	51	42°58'N	85°40'W
Granite Peak, peak	54	45°00'N	110°00'W
Graz, Austria	84	47°05'N	15°27'E
Great Artesian Basin, basin	103	22°00'S	141°00'E
Great Australian Bight, bay	103	34°00'S	130°00'E
Great Barrier I., island	103	36°00'S	175°00'E
Great Barrier Reef, reef	103	14°00'S	146°00'E
Great Basin, basin	54	40°00'N	117°00'W
Great Bear L., lake	75	65°00'N	120°00'W
Great Dividing Range, mountains	103	20°00'S	149°00'E
Greater Antilles, islands	45	18°00'N	75°00'W
Greater Khingan Range, mountains	97	45°00'N	118°00'E
Greater Sunda Is., islands	97	5°00'S	110°00'E
Great Falls, MT	50	47°30'N	111°18'W
Great Plains, plain	54	45°00'N	104°00'W
Great Salt L., lake	54	41°00'N	113°00'W
Great Salt Lake Desert, desert	54	41°00'N	114°00'W
Great Sandy Desert, desert	103	21°00'S	125°00'E
Great Slave L., lake	75	61°00'N	114°00'W
Great Victoria Desert, desert	103	28°00'S	128°00'E
Greece, country	84	39°00'N	22°00'E
Green, river	54	38°00'N	87°00'W
Green, river	54	42°00'N	110°00'W
Green Bay, WI	51	44°31'N	88°01'W
Greenland, island	45	75°00'N	40°00'W
Greenland (Kalaallit Nunaat), dependency, Den.	44	75°00'N	40°00'W
Greenland Sea, sea	45	78°00'N	0°00'
Green Mts., mountains	55	44°00'N	73°00'W
Greensboro, NC	51	36°04'N	79°48'W
Grenada, country	44	12°00'N	62°00'W
Grijalva, river	77	17°00'N	93°00'W
Groote I., island	103	14°00'S	137°00'E
Groznyy, Russia	84	43°24'N	45°47'E
Guadalajara, Mexico	76	20°40'N	103°21'W
Guadalcanal I., island	103	10°00'S	160°00'E
Guadalupe I., island	44	29°00'N	118°00'W
Guadalupe Peak, peak	54	32°00'N	104°00'W
Guadeloupe, dependency, Fr.	44	18°00'N	62°00'W
Guadiana, river	85	39°00'N	8°00'W
Guajará-Mirim, Brazil	78	10°48'S	65°22'W
Guam, dependency, U.S.	102	13°00'N	145°00'E
Guam, island	103	13°00'N	145°00'E
Guanajuato, Mexico	76	21°00'N	101°17'W
Guanajuato, state, Mex.	76	22°00'N	101°00'W
Guangzhou, China	96	23°08'N	113°18'E
Guaporé, river	79	13°00'S	63°00'W
Guasave, Mexico	76	25°34'N	108°29'W
Guatemala, country	44	16°00'N	91°00'W
Guatemala City, Guatemala	44	14°37'N	90°31'W
Guayaquil, Ecuador	78	2°12'S	79°54'W
Guayaquil, G. of, gulf	79	3°00'S	80°00'W
Guaymas, Mexico	76	27°55'N	110°53'W
Guernsey, Island	85	49°00'N	2°00'W
Guerrero, state, Mex.	76	17°00'N	101°00'W
Guerrero Negro, Mexico	76	27°58'N	114°03'W
Guiana Highlands, plateau	79	5°00'N	62°00'W
Guinea, country	90	11°00'N	12°00'W
Guinea-Bissau, country	90	11°00'N	16°00'W
Guinea, G. of, gulf	91	2°00'N	3°00'E
Guiyang, China	96	26°36'N	106°41'E
Gulf Coastal Plain, plain	55	30°00'N	93°00'W
Gurupi, Brazil	78	11°46'S	49°05'W
Guyana, country	78	7°00'N	59°00'W
Gwardafuy, C., cape	91	12°00'N	51°00'E
Gweru, Zimbabwe	90	19°28'S	29°49'E

H

Name	Page	Latitude	Longitude
Hainan, island	97	19°00'N	110°00'E
Haiti, country	44	19°00'N	73°00'W
Halifax, Canada	74	44°38'N	63°36'W
Halifax Bay, bay	103	19°00'S	147°00'E
Hall Pen., peninsula	75	65°00'N	66°00'W
Hamburg, Germany	84	53°33'N	10°01'E
Hamersley Range, mountains	103	23°00'S	118°00'E
Hamilton, Canada	74	43°16'N	79°51'W
Hamilton, New Zealand	102	37°47'S	175°18'E
Hammerfest, Norway	84	70°40'N	23°42'E
Hannover, Germany	84	52°22'N	9°45'E
Hanoi, Vietnam	96	21°02'N	105°49'E
Happy Valley-Goose Bay, Canada	74	53°20'N	60°23'W
Harare, Zimbabwe	90	17°49'S	31°03'E
Harbin, China	96	45°43'N	126°43'E
Hargeisa, Somalia	90	9°31'N	44°03'E
Harrisburg, PA	51	40°16'N	76°53'W
Hartford, CT	51	41°46'N	72°41'W
Hatteras, C., cape	55	35°00'N	75°00'W
Havana, Cuba	44	23°09'N	82°23'W
Havre-St-Pierre, Canada	74	50°15'N	63°36'W
Hawaii, island	54	20°00'N	155°00'W
Hawaii, state, U.S.	50	21°00'N	158°00'W
Hawaiian Is., islands	54	21°00'N	157°00'W
Hay, river	75	58°00'N	118°00'W
Hay River, Canada	74	60°49'N	115°46'W
Hearst, Canada	74	49°42'N	83°40'W
Hecate Str., strait	75	53°00'N	131°00'W
Helena, MT	50	46°36'N	112°02'W
Helsinki, Finland	84	60°11'N	24°56'E
Hermosillo, Mexico	76	29°04'N	110°55'W
Herrero, Pt., cape	77	19°00'N	87°00'W
Hidalgo, state, Mex.	76	21°00'N	99°00'W
Hidalgo del Parral, Mexico	76	26°56'N	105°41'W
Highlands, mountains	85	57°00'N	5°00'W
High Level, Canada	74	58°31'N	117°06'W
Hiiumaa I., island	85	59°00'N	22°00'E
Hilo, HI	50	19°44'N	155°05'W
Himalayas, mountains	97	27°00'N	86°00'E
Hindu Kush, mountains	97	35°00'N	71°00'E
Hispaniola, island	45	18°00'N	69°00'W
Hobart, Australia	102	42°48'S	147°18'E
Ho Chi Minh City, Vietnam	96	10°43'N	106°43'E
Hokkaido, island	97	44°00'N	143°00'E
Holman, Canada	74	70°43'N	117°41'W
Homel', Belarus	84	52°29'N	31°00'E
Honduras, country	44	17°00'N	85°00'W
Hong, river	97	23°00'N	104°00'E
Hong Kong, China	96	22°15'N	114°11'E
Honiara, Solomon Islands	102	9°19'S	159°44'E
Honolulu, HI	50	21°18'N	157°51'W
Honshu, island	97	37°00'N	140°00'E
Hood, Mt., peak	54	45°00'N	122°00'W
Hormuz, Str. of, strait	97	26°00'N	56°00'E
Horn, C., cape	79	56°00'S	68°00'W
Horn of Africa, region	91	9°00'N	47°00'E
Hotan, China	96	37°08'N	79°54'E
Houston, TX	50	29°46'N	95°22'W
Howland I., dependency, U.S.	102	1°00'N	177°00'W
Howland I., island	103	1°00'N	177°00'W
Hrodna, Belarus	84	53°41'N	23°51'E
Huajuapan de León, Mexico	76	17°48'N	97°47'W
Huambo, Angola	90	12°46'S	15°44'E
Huancayo, Peru	78	12°05'S	75°13'W
Huang (Yellow), river	97	37°00'N	111°00'E
Huánuco, Peru	78	9°54'S	76°16'W
Huascarán, Mt., peak	79	9°00'S	78°00'W
Hudson, river	55	42°00'N	74°00'W
Hudson Bay, bay	75	59°00'N	85°00'W
Hudson Str., strait	75	63°00'N	73°00'W
Hull, Canada	74	45°26'N	75°44'W
Humphreys Peak, peak	54	35°00'N	111°00'W
Hungary, country	84	47°00'N	19°00'E
Huntsville, AL	51	34°44'N	86°35'W
Huron, L., lake	45	45°00'N	82°00'W
Hyderabad, India	96	17°20'N	78°31'E

I

Name	Page	Latitude	Longitude
Iasi, Romania	84	47°10'N	27°36'E
Ibadan, Nigeria	90	7°24'N	3°53'E
Ibagué, Colombia	78	4°24'N	75°15'W
Iberian Pen., peninsula	85	41°00'N	4°00'W
Ibiza, island	85	39°00'N	1°00'E
Ica, Peru	78	14°03'S	75°45'W
Iceland, country	84	65°00'N	18°00'W
Iceland, island	85	65°00'N	18°00'W
Idaho, state, U.S.	50	44°00'N	114°00'W
Iguala, Mexico	76	18°21'N	99°32'W
Iguaçu Falls, falls	79	26°00'S	55°00'W
Ilebo, Dem. Rep. of Congo	90	4°20'S	20°38'E
Ilhéus, Brazil	78	14°47'S	39°03'W
Illimani, Mt., peak	79	17°00'S	68°00'W
Illinois, river	55	41°00'N	90°00'W
Illinois, state, U.S.	51	40°00'N	89°00'W
Ilorin, Nigeria	90	8°29'N	4°33'E
Imperatriz, Brazil	78	5°29'S	47°30'W
I-n-Amenas, Algeria	90	28°03'N	9°34'E
India, country	96	23°00'N	79°00'E
Indiana, state, U.S.	51	41°00'N	86°00'W
Indianapolis, IN	51	39°46'N	86°09'W
Indian Ocean, ocean	15	10°00'S	80°00'E
Indochina Pen., peninsula	97	16°00'N	105°00'E
Indonesia, country	96	2°00'S	119°00'E
Indus, river	97	31°00'N	71°00'E
Infiernillo, Res., lake	77	19°00'N	102°00'W
In-Salah, Algeria	90	27°12'N	2°31'E
Inuvik, Canada	74	68°22'N	133°42'W
Ionian Sea, sea	85	37°00'N	19°00'E
Iowa, river	55	42°00'N	92°00'W
Iowa, state, U.S.	51	42°00'N	94°00'W
Iqaluit, Canada	74	63°45'N	68°27'W
Iquique, Chile	78	20°14'S	70°07'W
Iquitos, Peru	78	3°45'S	73°11'W
Iraklio, Greece	84	35°20'N	25°08'E
Iran, country	96	31°00'N	57°00'E
Irapuato, Mexico	76	20°39'N	101°22'W
Iraq, country	96	32°00'N	41°00'E
Ireland, country	84	54°00'N	9°00'W
Irish Sea, sea	85	54°00'N	5°00'W

Name	Page	Latitude	Longitude
Irkutsk, Russia	96	52°21'N	104°19'E
Irrawaddy, river	97	24°00'N	96°00'E
Irtysh, river	97	57°00'N	74°00'E
Ishim, river	97	55°00'N	68°00'E
Isiro, Dem. Rep. of Congo	90	2°47'N	27°37'E
Islamabad, Pakistan	96	33°40'N	73°06'E
Isle Royale, island	55	48°00'N	89°00'W
Israel, country	96	31°00'N	34°00'E
Istanbul, Turkey	84	41°01'N	28°59'E
Italy, country	84	43°00'N	12°00'E
Ivanovo, Russia	84	57°02'N	41°00'E
Ivory Coast, country	90	5°00'N	5°00'W
Ixtacihuatl, peak	77	20°00'N	99°00'W
Ixtapa, Mexico	76	17°40'N	101°36'W
Izhevsk, Russia	84	56°47'N	53°17'E
Izmir, Turkey	96	38°26'N	27°09'E

J

Name	Page	Latitude	Longitude
Jackson, MS	51	32°18'N	90°11'W
Jacksonville, FL	51	30°20'N	81°39'W
Jacques-Cartier, Mt., peak	75	48°00'N	65°00'W
Jaipur, India	96	26°55'N	75°48'E
Jakarta, Indonesia	96	6°08'S	106°51'E
Jalisco, state, Mex.	76	20°00'N	104°00'W
Jamaica, country	44	18°00'N	77°00'W
Jamaica, island	44	18°00'N	77°00'W
James, river	55	45°00'N	98°00'W
James, river	55	38°00'N	79°00'W
James Bay, bay	75	54°00'N	81°00'W
Japan, country	96	38°00'N	140°00'E
Japan, Sea of, sea	97	41°00'N	135°00'E
Jarvis I., dependency, U.S.	102	0°00'	160°00'W
Jarvis I., island	103	0°00'	160°00'W
Jasper, Canada	74	52°53'N	118°05'W
Jataí, Brazil	78	17°54'S	51°44'W
Java, island	97	7°00'S	110°00'E
Java Sea, sea	97	5°00'S	110°00'E
Jayapura, Indonesia	96	2°30'S	140°40'E
Jebel Toubkal, peak	91	31°00'N	6°00'W
Jeddah, Saudi Arabia	96	21°29'N	39°14'E
Jefferson City, MO	51	38°35'N	92°10'W
Jersey, island	85	49°00'N	2°00'W
Jerusalem, Israel	96	31°47'N	35°14'E
Jima, Ethiopia	90	7°40'N	36°50'E
Jiménez, Mexico	76	27°09'N	104°54'W
Jinan, China	96	36°39'N	117°02'E
Jinja, Uganda	90	0°26'N	33°12'E
João Pessoa, Brazil	78	7°07'S	34°53'W
Johannesburg, S. Africa	90	26°11'S	28°04'E
Johnston I., dependency, U.S.	102	17°00'N	170°00'W
Johnston I., island	103	17°00'N	170°00'W
Jordan, country	96	31°00'N	39°00'E
Joseph Bonaparte G., gulf	103	14°00'S	129°00'E
Jos Plat., plateau	91	10°00'N	10°00'E
Juan de Fuca, Str. of, strait	54	48°00'N	124°00'W
Juan Fernández Is., islands	78	33°00'S	79°00'W
Juàzeiro do Norte, Brazil	78	7°14'S	39°20'W
Juba, Sudan	90	4°51'N	31°36'E
Juchitán, Mexico	76	16°25'N	95°04'W
Juliaca, Peru	78	15°29'S	70°07'W
Juneau, AK	50	58°18'N	134°25'W
Juruá, river	79	7°00'S	68°00'W
Jutland, peninsula	85	57°00'N	9°00'E

K

Name	Page	Latitude	Longitude
K2, peak	97	35°53'N	76°30'E
Kabul, Afghanistan	96	34°31'N	69°11'E
Kabwe, Zambia	90	14°26'S	28°26'E
Kahoolawe, island	54	21°00'N	157°00'W
Kakhovka Res., lake	85	47°00'N	34°00'E
Kalahari Desert, desert	91	23°00'S	22°00'E
Kalemie, Dem. Rep. of Congo	90	5°56'S	29°10'E
Kalgoorlie, Australia	102	30°44'S	121°28'E
Kaliningrad, Russia	84	54°43'N	20°30'E
Kaluga, Russia	84	54°37'N	36°16'E
Kama, river	85	60°00'N	57°00'E
Kamchatka Pen., peninsula	97	54°00'N	160°00'E
Kamina, Dem. Rep. of Congo	90	8°44'S	24°59'E
Kamloops, Canada	74	50°40'N	120°20'W
Kampala, Uganda	90	0°17'N	32°31'E
Kananga, Dem. Rep. of Congo	90	5°53'S	22°23'E
Kandalaksha, Russia	84	67°09'N	32°25'E
Kangaroo I., island	103	36°00'S	137°00'E
Kanin Pen., peninsula	85	68°00'N	44°00'E
Kankan, Guinea	90	10°24'N	9°18'W
Kano, Nigeria	90	12°00'N	8°32'E
Kanpur, India	96	26°24'N	80°21'E
Kansas, river	55	39°00'N	97°00'W
Kansas, state, U.S.	50	39°00'N	99°00'W
Kansas City, KS	51	39°07'N	94°38'W
Kansas City, MO	51	39°06'N	94°35'W
Kaolack, Senegal	90	14°09'N	16°05'W
Kapuskasing, Canada	74	49°25'N	82°25'W
Karachi, Pakistan	96	24°51'N	67°04'E
Karakum, desert	97	39°00'N	60°00'E
Kara Sea, sea	97	74°00'N	70°00'E
Kariba, L., lake	91	18°00'S	28°00'E
Karima, Sudan	90	18°31'N	31°50'E
Kasai, river	91	4°00'S	20°00'E
Kasba L., lake	75	61°00'N	102°00'W
Kashi, China	96	39°28'N	76°00'E
Kaskaskia, river	55	39°00'N	89°00'W
Kassala, Sudan	90	15°26'N	36°23'E
Katanga Plat., plateau	91	10°00'S	26°00'E
Katherine, Australia	102	14°31'S	132°15'E
Kathmandu, Nepal	96	27°43'N	85°19'E
Katowice, Poland	84	50°16'N	19°01'E
Kattegat, strait	85	57°00'N	11°00'E
Kauai, island	54	22°00'N	160°00'W
Kaunas, Lithuania	84	54°54'N	23°56'E
Kayes, Mali	90	14°26'N	11°26'W
Kazakhstan, country	96	49°00'N	71°00'E
Kazakh Uplands, mountains	97	48°00'N	76°00'E
Kazan, Russia	84	55°45'N	49°15'E
Keetmanshoop, Namibia	90	26°35'S	18°09'E
Kefallinía I., island	85	38°00'N	20°00'E
Kelafo, Ethiopia	90	5°36'N	44°13'E
Kelowna, Canada	74	49°53'N	119°27'W
Kemerovo, Russia	96	55°21'N	86°02'E
Kenai Pen., peninsula	54	60°00'N	150°00'W
Kenora, Canada	74	49°46'N	94°29'W
Kentucky, river	55	38°00'N	84°00'W
Kentucky, state, U.S.	51	37°00'N	86°00'W
Kenya, country	90	2°00'N	38°00'E
Kenya, Mt., peak	91	1°00'S	37°00'E
Kerguelen Is., islands	15	49°00'S	69°00'E
Kermadec Is., islands	103	30°00'S	179°00'W
Ketchikan, AK	50	55°21'N	131°39'W
Khabarovsk, Russia	96	48°31'N	135°09'E
Kharkiv, Ukraine	84	50°00'N	36°16'E
Khartoum, Sudan	90	15°29'N	32°30'E
Kiel Canal, canal	85	54°00'N	9°00'E
Kiev (Kyiv), Ukraine	84	50°30'N	30°31'E
Kigali, Rwanda	90	1°56'S	30°02'E
Kikwit, Dem. Rep. of Congo	90	5°02'S	18°50'E
Kilimanjaro, Mt., peak	91	3°00'S	37°00'E
Kimberley, S. Africa	90	28°44'S	24°46'E
Kimberley Plat., plateau	103	16°00'S	126°00'E
Kindu, Dem. Rep. of Congo	90	2°57'S	25°53'E
King I., island	103	40°00'S	144°00'E
King Peak, peak	74	61°00'N	110°00'W
Kingston, Canada	74	44°17'N	76°32'W
Kingston, Jamaica	44	18°00'N	76°48'W
King William I., island	75	69°00'N	99°00'W
Kinshasa, Dem. Rep. of Congo	90	4°20'S	15°19'E
Kiribati, country	102	2°00'S	177°00'W
Kiritimati I., island	103	2°00'N	157°00'W
Kirov, Russia	84	58°34'N	49°41'E
Kiruna, Sweden	84	67°52'N	20°18'E
Kisangani, Dem. Rep. of Congo	90	0°32'N	25°14'E
Kismaayo, Somalia	90	0°21'S	42°33'E
Kisumu, Kenya	90	0°06'S	34°46'E
Kitakyushu, Japan	96	33°52'N	130°54'E
Kitchener, Canada	74	43°26'N	80°31'W
Kitimat, Canada	74	54°07'N	128°40'W
Kivu, L., lake	91	3°00'S	29°00'E
Klerksdorp, S. Africa	90	26°51'S	26°41'E
Klondike Region, region	75	64°00'N	138°00'W
Knoxville, TN	51	35°58'N	83°55'W
Kodiak I., island	54	57°00'N	154°00'W
Kola Pen., peninsula	85	67°00'N	37°00'E
Kolguyev I., island	85	69°00'N	49°00'E
Kolkata (Calcutta), India	96	22°34'N	88°23'E
Kolwezi, Dem. Rep. of Congo	90	10°43'S	25°27'E
Kolyma Range, mountains	97	62°00'N	155°00'E
Komsomol'sk-na-Amure, Russia	96	50°37'N	136°57'E
Korean Pen., peninsula	97	39°00'N	127°00'E
Korea Str., strait	97	34°00'N	129°00'E
Korhogo, Ivory Coast	90	9°27'N	5°38'W
Koryak Range, mountains	97	62°00'N	170°00'E
Kosciuszko, Mt., peak	103	37°00'S	148°00'E
Kosice, Slovakia	84	48°43'N	21°16'E
Kosovo, country	84	42°35'N	21°00'E
Kosti, Sudan	90	13°07'N	32°37'E
Kota Kinabalu, Malaysia	96	5°58'N	116°05'E
Kraków, Poland	84	50°04'N	19°57'E
Krasnodar, Russia	84	45°02'N	39°01'E
Krasnoyarsk, Russia	96	56°02'N	92°51'E
Kremenchuk Res., lake	85	49°00'N	32°00'E
Kryvyi Rih, Ukraine	84	47°55'N	33°22'E
Kuala Lumpur, Malaysia	96	3°09'N	101°41'E
Kuching, Malaysia	96	1°32'N	110°20'E
Kugluktuk, Canada	74	67°48'N	115°09'W
Kumasi, Ghana	90	6°42'N	1°38'W
Kunlun Shan, mountains	97	37°00'N	89°00'E
Kunming, China	96	25°01'N	102°45'E
Kuril Is., islands	97	46°00'N	152°00'E
Kursk, Russia	84	51°49'N	36°11'E
Kuujjuaq, Canada	74	58°05'N	68°29'W
Kuwait, country	96	29°00'N	48°00'E
Kuwait, Kuwait	96	29°22'N	47°59'E
Kuybyshev Res., lake	85	54°00'N	49°00'E
Kyoto, Japan	96	34°59'N	135°45'E
Kyrgyzstan, country	96	41°00'N	78°00'E
Kyushu, island	97	33°00'N	131°00'E
Kyzyl, Russia	96	51°42'N	94°32'E
Kyzyl Kum, desert	97	42°00'N	64°00'E

L

Name	Page	Latitude	Longitude
Laayoune, Morocco	90	27°07'N	13°09'W
Labé, Guinea	90	11°19'N	12°15'W
Labrador, region	75	55°00'N	61°00'W
Labrador City, Canada	74	52°56'N	66°54'W
Labrador Sea, sea	45	57°00'N	56°00'W
Lachlan, river	103	33°00'S	147°00'E
Ladoga, L., lake	85	61°00'N	31°00'E
Lagos, Nigeria	90	6°29'N	3°23'E
La Grande Reservoirs, lakes	75	54°00'N	75°00'W
Laguna Salada, depression	77	33°00'N	116°00'W
Lahore, Pakistan	96	31°31'N	74°21'E
Lahti, Finland	84	60°59'N	25°40'E
Lakshadweep, islands	97	11°00'N	73°00'E
La Loche, Canada	74	56°29'N	109°24'W
La Martre, Lac, lake	75	63°00'N	120°00'W
Lambaréné, Gabon	90	0°41'S	10°13'E
Lanai, island	54	21°00'N	157°00'W
Lancaster Sound, strait	75	75°00'N	85°00'W
Land's End, cape	85	50°00'N	5°00'W
Lansing, MI	51	42°44'N	84°33'W
Lanzhou, China	96	36°03'N	103°53'E
Laos, country	96	21°00'N	101°00'E
La Paz, Bolivia	78	16°30'S	68°09'W
La Paz, Mexico	76	24°10'N	110°19'W
Lapland, region	85	67°00'N	26°00'E
La Plata, Argentina	78	34°55'S	57°57'W
Laptev Sea, sea	97	75°00'N	125°00'E
Laredo, TX	50	27°31'N	99°30'W
La Rioja, Argentina	78	29°24'S	66°49'W
Larisa, Greece	84	39°38'N	22°25'E
La Ronge, Canada	74	55°07'N	105°16'W
La Ronge, Lac, lake	75	55°00'N	105°00'W
Las Cruces, NM	50	32°19'N	106°47'W
La Serena, Chile	78	29°55'S	71°13'W
Las Vegas, NV	50	36°10'N	115°08'W
Latvia, country	84	57°00'N	26°00'E
Launceston, Australia	102	41°19'S	147°09'E
Laurentian Mts., mountains	75	48°00'N	72°00'W
Lawton, OK	50	34°37'N	98°23'W
Lázaro Cárdenas, Mexico	76	17°58'N	102°12'W
Lebanon, country	96	34°00'N	36°00'E
Leeds, United Kingdom	84	53°48'N	1°33'W
Leeuwin, C., cape	103	34°00'S	115°00'E
Leeward Is., islands	45	18°00'N	61°00'W
Le Havre, France	84	49°30'N	0°07'E
Leipzig, Germany	84	51°20'N	12°23'E
Lena, river	97	65°00'N	124°00'E
León, Mexico	76	21°06'N	101°42'W
Lerma, river	77	20°00'N	101°00'W
Lesotho, country	90	29°00'S	29°00'E
Lesser Antilles, islands	45	16°00'N	62°00'W
Lesser Caucasus, mountains	85	41°00'N	45°00'E
Lesser Slave L., lake	75	56°00'N	117°00'W
Lesser Sunda Is., islands	97	8°00'S	121°00'E
Lethbridge, Canada	74	49°41'N	112°50'W
Lexington, KY	51	38°03'N	84°30'W
Lhasa, China	96	29°41'N	91°07'E
Liard, river	75	61°00'N	122°00'W
Liberia, country	90	6°00'N	10°00'W
Libreville, Gabon	90	0°24'N	9°28'E
Libya, country	90	26°00'N	18°00'E
Libyan Desert, desert	91	23°00'N	25°00'E
Liechtenstein, country	84	47°00'N	9°00'E
Liège, Belgium	84	50°39'N	5°34'E
Ligurian Sea, sea	85	44°00'N	9°00'E
Lille, France	84	50°38'N	3°00'E
Lilongwe, Malawi	90	13°58'S	33°46'E
Lima, Peru	78	12°06'S	77°02'W
Limpopo, river	91	23°00'S	28°00'E
Linares, Mexico	76	24°51'N	99°35'W
Lincoln, NE	50	40°48'N	96°40'W
Line Is., islands	103	3°00'S	152°00'W
Linköping, Sweden	84	58°24'N	15°37'E
Linz, Austria	84	48°17'N	14°18'E
Lions, G. of, gulf	85	43°00'N	4°00'E
Lipetsk, Russia	84	52°39'N	39°35'E
Lisbon, Portugal	84	38°43'N	9°10'W
Lithuania, country	84	56°00'N	24°00'E
Little Missouri, river	54	47°00'N	104°00'W
Little Rock, AR	51	34°45'N	92°17'W
Liverpool, United Kingdom	84	53°25'N	3°00'W
Livingstone, Zambia	90	17°51'S	25°51'E
Ljubljana, Slovenia	84	46°04'N	14°31'E
Llano Estacado, plain	54	34°00'N	103°00'W
Llanos, plain	79	8°00'N	69°00'W
Lloydminster, Canada	74	53°17'N	109°59'W
Łódź, Poland	84	51°45'N	19°28'E
Logan, Mt., peak	75	61°00'N	141°00'W
Loire, river	85	47°00'N	0°00'
Lomé, Togo	90	6°08'N	1°13'E
London, Canada	74	42°59'N	81°15'W
London, United Kingdom	84	51°31'N	0°07'W
Londrina, Brazil	78	23°18'S	51°08'W
Long I., island	55	41°00'N	73°00'W
Long Island Sound, bay	55	42°00'N	73°00'W
Long Range Mts., mountains	75	50°00'N	58°00'W
Lopez, C., cape	91	1°00'S	9°00'E
Lord Howe I., island	103	32°00'S	159°00'E
Loreto, Mexico	76	22°16'N	101°57'W
Los Angeles, CA	50	34°03'N	118°15'W
Los Chonos Arch., islands	79	45°00'S	75°00'W
Los Mochis, Mexico	76	25°46'N	109°00'W
Louisiade Arch., islands	103	10°00'S	154°00'E
Louisiana, state, U.S.	51	31°00'N	93°00'W
Louisville, KY	51	38°15'N	85°46'W
Loup, river	55	42°00'N	98°00'W
Lower Pen., peninsula	55	44°00'N	85°00'W
Lower Tunguska, river	97	65°00'N	104°00'E
Lualaba, river	91	5°00'S	26°00'E
Luanda, Angola	90	8°49'S	13°15'E
Lubango, Angola	90	14°54'S	13°31'E
Lubbock, TX	50	33°35'N	101°51'W
Lubumbashi, Dem. Rep. of Congo	90	11°40'S	27°29'E
Lucknow, India	96	26°48'N	80°56'E
Lüderitz, Namibia	90	26°40'S	15°10'E
Luena, Angola	90	11°47'S	19°55'E
Luhans'k, Ukraine	84	48°34'N	39°15'E
Luleå, Sweden	84	65°36'N	22°09'E
Lusaka, Zambia	90	15°25'S	28°17'E
Luxembourg, country	84	49°00'N	5°00'E
Luxembourg, Luxembourg	84	49°37'N	6°07'E
Luxor, Egypt	90	25°40'N	32°39'E
Luzon, island	96	16°00'N	121°00'E
Luzon Str., strait	97	20°00'N	122°00'E
L'viv, Ukraine	84	49°51'N	24°02'E
Lyon, France	84	45°44'N	4°50'E

M

Name	Page	Latitude	Longitude
Macau, China	96	22°14'N	113°32'E
Macapá, Brazil	78	0°05'N	51°06'W
MacDonnell Ranges, mountains	103	25°00'S	134°00'E
Macedonia, country	84	41°00'N	22°00'E
Maceió, Brazil	78	9°35'S	35°43'W
Machala, Ecuador	78	3°18'S	79°52'W
Mackay, Australia	102	21°10'S	149°11'E
Mackenzie, Canada	74	55°21'N	123°03'W
Mackenzie, river	75	65°00'N	125°00'W
Mackenzie Bay, bay	75	70°00'N	135°00'W
Mackenzie Mts., mountains	75	64°00'N	130°00'W
Macon, GA	51	32°50'N	83°38'W
Madagascar, country	90	20°00'S	47°00'E
Madagascar, island	91	20°00'S	47°00'E
Madeira, river	79	6°00'S	63°00'W
Madeira Is., islands	91	33°00'N	17°00'W
Madison, WI	51	43°04'N	89°24'W
Madre Lagoon, bay	77	25°00'N	97°00'W
Madrid, Spain	84	40°25'N	3°42'W
Madurai, India	96	9°52'N	78°06'E
Magadalena de Kino, Mexico	76	30°38'N	110°57'W
Magadan, Russia	96	59°35'N	150°50'E
Magdalena, river	79	8°00'N	75°00'W
Magdalena Bay, bay	77	25°00'N	112°00'W
Magdalena I., island	77	25°00'N	112°00'W
Magellan, Str. of, strait	79	53°00'S	70°00'W
Mahajanga, Madagascar	90	15°43'S	46°21'E
Maiduguri, Nigeria	90	11°51'N	13°10'E
Maine, state, U.S.	51	45°00'N	69°00'W
Maine, G. of, gulf	55	44°00'N	70°00'W
Majorca, island	85	39°00'N	3°00'E
Majuro, Marshall Islands	102	7°09'N	171°03'E
Makassar, Indonesia	96	5°08'S	119°25'E
Makurdi, Nigeria	90	7°43'N	8°34'E
Malabo, Equatorial Guinea	90	3°45'N	8°47'E
Malacca, Str. of, strait	97	4°00'N	99°00'E
Málaga, Spain	84	36°43'N	4°25'W
Malaita I., island	103	9°00'S	161°00'E
Malakal, Sudan	90	9°36'N	31°42'E
Malange, Angola	90	9°36'S	16°21'E
Malawi, country	90	12°00'S	34°00'E
Malay Pen., peninsula	97	5°00'N	101°00'E
Malaysia, country	96	5°00'N	107°00'E
Maldives, country	96	3°00'N	73°00'E
Maldives, islands	97	3°00'N	73°00'E
Male, Maldives	96	4°26'N	73°30'E
Mali, country	90	19°00'N	1°00'W
Malmö, Sweden	84	55°37'N	13°00'E
Malta, country	84	36°00'N	14°00'E
Malta, island	85	36°00'N	14°00'E
Mamoré, river	79	17°00'S	63°00'W
Manado, Indonesia	96	1°29'N	124°52'E
Managua, Nicaragua	44	12°08'N	86°16'W
Manama, Bahrain	96	26°10'N	50°29'E
Manaus, Brazil	78	3°06'S	60°03'W
Manchester, NH	51	43°00'N	71°27'W
Manchester, United Kingdom	84	53°29'N	2°15'W
Manchurian Plain, plateau	97	45°00'N	124°00'E
Mandalay, Myanmar	96	21°59'N	96°05'E
Manicouagan, Rés., lake	75	52°00'N	69°00'W
Manihiki I., island	103	10°00'S	161°00'W
Manila, Philippines	96	14°34'N	121°00'E
Manitoba, province, Can.	74	55°00'N	98°00'W
Manitoba, L., lake	75	51°00'N	99°00'W
Manitoulin I., island	55	46°00'N	83°00'W
Manizales, Colombia	78	5°03'N	75°29'W
Mannheim, Germany	84	49°29'N	8°28'E
Manzanillo, Mexico	76	19°03'N	104°20'W
Maoke Mts., mountains	97	5°00'S	149°00'E
Mapimí Basin, depression	77	27°00'N	103°00'W
Maputo, Mozambique	90	25°55'S	32°37'E
Maracaibo, Venezuela	78	10°39'N	71°38'W
Maracaibo, L., lake	79	10°00'N	72°00'W
Maracay, Venezuela	78	10°16'N	67°38'W
Maradi, Niger	90	13°30'N	7°06'E
Marañón, river	79	5°00'S	78°00'W
Marathon, Canada	74	48°43'N	86°23'W
Mar del Plata, Argentina	78	37°59'S	57°35'W
Margherita Peak, peak	91	1°00'N	30°00'E
Marías Is., islands	77	22°00'N	107°00'W
Marie Byrd Land, region	15	80°00'S	120°00'W
Mariupol', Ukraine	84	47°07'N	37°32'E
Marka, Somalia	90	1°43'N	44°45'E
Marmara, Sea of, sea	85	41°00'N	28°00'E
Marne, river	85	49°00'N	3°00'E
Maroua, Cameroon	90	10°36'N	14°20'E
Marquesas Is., islands	103	10°00'S	140°00'W
Marrakech, Morocco	90	31°39'N	8°00'W
Marra Mts., mountains	91	14°00'N	24°00'E
Marsabit, Kenya	90	2°20'N	37°59'E
Marseille, France	84	43°18'N	5°23'E
Marshall Islands, country	102	10°00'N	170°00'E
Marshall Islands, islands	103	8°00'N	171°00'E
Martinique, dependency, Fr.	44	15°00'N	61°00'W
Maryland, state, U.S.	51	38°00'N	76°00'W
Marystown, Canada	74	47°10'N	55°09'W
Maseru, Lesotho	90	29°18'S	27°31'E
Mashhad, Iran	96	36°18'N	59°36'E
Massachusetts, state, U.S.	51	43°00'N	71°00'W
Massawa, Eritrea	90	15°37'N	39°24'E
Masset, Canada	74	54°01'N	132°08'W
Massif Central, highlands	85	46°00'N	2°00'E
Matadi, Dem. Rep. of Congo	90	5°49'S	13°29'E
Matamoros, Mexico	76	25°52'N	97°31'W
Matane, Canada	74	48°50'N	67°33'W
Matehuala, Mexico	76	23°40'N	100°38'W
Mato Grosso Plat., plateau	79	15°00'S	56°00'W
Maui, island	54	21°00'N	156°00'W
Mauna Kea, peak	54	20°00'N	155°00'W
Mauritania, country	90	19°00'N	10°00'W
Mauritius, country	90	20°00'S	58°00'E
Mauritius, island	91	20°00'S	58°00'E
Mayotte, dependency, Fr.	90	12°00'S	44°00'E
Mazatlán, Mexico	76	23°12'N	106°23'W
Mbabane, Swaziland	90	26°18'S	31°08'E
Mbandaka, Dem. Rep. of Congo	90	0°04'N	18°22'E
Mbeya, Tanzania	90	8°54'S	33°26'E
McClure Str., strait	75	75°00'N	120°00'W
McKinley, Mt., peak	54	63°00'N	151°00'W
McMurdo Sound, bay	15	77°00'S	165°00'E
Mead, L., lake	54	36°00'N	115°00'W
Mecca, Saudi Arabia	96	21°26'N	39°49'E
Medan, Indonesia	96	3°35'N	98°40'E
Medellín, Colombia	78	6°12'N	75°34'W
Medford, OR	50	42°20'N	122°52'W
Medicine Hat, Canada	74	50°02'N	110°42'W
Mediterranean Sea, sea	85	38°00'N	6°00'E
Mekele, Ethiopia	90	13°28'N	39°24'E
Mekong, river	97	19°00'N	104°00'E
Melanesia, region	103	4°00'S	163°00'E
Melbourne, Australia	102	37°47'S	144°56'E
Melekeok, Palau	102	7°30'N	134°38'E
Melo, Uruguay	78	32°22'S	54°11'W
Melville I., island	103	11°00'S	131°00'E
Melville I., island	75	76°00'N	110°00'W
Melville Pen., peninsula	75	69°00'N	84°00'W
Memphis, TN	51	35°09'N	90°03'W
Mendocino, C., cape	54	40°00'N	124°00'W
Mendoza, Argentina	78	32°55'S	68°50'W
Menongue, Angola	90	14°39'S	17°39'E
Mentawai Is., islands	97	1°00'S	98°00'E
Mérida, Mexico	76	20°58'N	89°37'W
Mérida, Venezuela	78	8°36'N	71°10'W
Meridian, MS	51	32°22'N	88°42'W
Merrimack, river	55	44°00'N	72°00'W
Mesabi Range, hills	55	47°00'N	92°00'W
Messina, Str. of, strait	85	38°00'N	16°00'E
Meta Incognita Pen., peninsula	75	64°00'N	68°00'W
Mexicali, Mexico	76	32°39'N	115°29'W
Mexico, country	44	24°00'N	101°00'W
México, state, Mex.	76	19°27'N	99°09'W
Mexico City, Mexico	76	19°27'N	99°09'W
Mexico, G. of, gulf	45	26°00'N	90°00'W
Miami, FL	51	25°46'N	80°12'W
Michigan, state, U.S.	51	45°00'N	85°00'W
Michigan, L., lake	55	44°00'N	87°00'W
Michoacán, state, Mex.	76	18°00'N	103°00'W
Micronesia, region	103	8°00'N	150°00'E
Middelburg, S. Africa	90	25°46'S	29°28'E
Miguel Alemán Res., lake	77	18°00'N	96°00'W
Milan, Italy	84	45°28'N	9°11'E
Milk, river	54	48°00'N	109°00'W
Milwaukee, WI	51	43°02'N	87°54'W
Mindanao, island	97	8°00'N	125°00'E
Mindoro, island	97	13°00'N	121°00'E
Minneapolis, MN	51	44°59'N	93°16'W
Minnesota, river	55	45°00'N	96°00'W
Minnesota, state, U.S.	51	46°00'N	94°00'W
Minorca, island	85	40°00'N	4°00'E
Minsk, Belarus	84	53°54'N	27°32'E
Miquelon Is., islands	75	47°00'N	57°00'W
Miramichi, Canada	74	46°58'N	65°33'W
Mirnyy, Russia	96	62°35'N	113°54'E
Misratah, Libya	90	32°23'N	15°06'E
Mississippi, river	55	45°00'N	92°00'W
Mississippi, state, U.S.	51	33°00'N	90°00'W
Mississippi Delta, delta	55	29°00'N	89°00'W
Missouri, river	55	41°00'N	96°00'W
Missouri, state, U.S.	51	37°00'N	93°00'W
Mistassini, Lac, lake	75	52°00'N	74°00'W
Mita, Pt., cape	77	21°00'N	106°00'W
Mitchell, Mt., peak	55	36°00'N	82°00'W
Mitumba Mts., mountains	91	7°00'S	28°00'E
Mobile, AL	51	30°42'N	88°03'W
Mobile Bay, bay	55	31°00'N	88°00'W
Mogadishu, Somalia	90	2°04'N	45°21'E
Mojave Desert, desert	54	35°00'N	117°00'W
Moldova, country	84	48°00'N	28°00'E
Moldoveanu, peak	85	46°00'N	25°00'E
Molokai, island	54	21°00'N	157°00'W
Moluccas, islands	97	2°00'S	128°00'E
Mombasa, Kenya	90	4°05'S	39°39'E
Monaco, country	84	44°00'N	7°00'E
Monclova, Mexico	76	26°51'N	101°26'W
Moncton, Canada	74	46°06'N	64°47'W
Mongolia, country	96	47°00'N	103°00'E
Mongolian Plat., plateau	97	48°00'N	104°00'E
Monrovia, Liberia	90	6°20'N	10°44'W
Montana, state, U.S.	50	47°00'N	112°00'W
Monterey Bay, bay	54	37°00'N	122°00'W
Monteria, Colombia	78	8°46'N	75°52'W
Monterrey, Mexico	76	25°40'N	100°19'W
Montes Claros, Brazil	78	16°44'S	43°50'W
Montevideo, Uruguay	78	34°52'S	56°13'W
Montgomery, AL	51	32°22'N	86°18'W
Montpelier, VT	51	44°16'N	72°35'W
Montréal, Canada	74	45°30'N	73°35'W
Montserrat, dependency, U.K.	44	16°00'N	62°00'W
Moose Jaw, Canada	74	50°24'N	105°31'W
Moosonee, Canada	74	51°17'N	80°39'W
Morelia, Mexico	76	19°42'N	101°12'W
Morelos, state, Mex.	76	18°00'N	99°00'W
Morocco, country	90	31°00'N	8°00'W
Morogoro, Tanzania	90	6°49'S	37°40'E
Moroni, Comoros	90	11°34'S	43°16'E
Morris Jesup, C., cape	45	83°00'N	34°00'W
Moscow, Russia	84	55°46'N	37°36'E
Moundou, Chad	90	8°36'N	16°05'E
Mozambique, country	90	18°00'S	37°00'E
Mozambique Channel, strait	91	18°00'S	42°00'E
Mtwara, Tanzania	90	10°18'S	40°12'E
Muchinga Mts., mountains	91	11°00'S	31°00'E
Mulhacén, peak	85	37°00'N	3°00'W
Mumbai (Bombay), India	96	18°58'N	72°52'E
Munich, Germany	84	48°08'N	11°34'E
Muonio, river	85	68°00'N	23°00'E
Murmansk, Russia	84	68°59'N	33°05'E
Murray, river	103	35°00'S	143°00'E
Musala Peak, peak	85	42°00'N	24°00'E
Muscat, Oman	96	23°32'N	58°39'E
Musgrave Ranges, mountains	103	27°00'S	132°00'E
Mutare, Zimbabwe	90	18°57'S	32°38'E
Mwanza, Tanzania	90	2°31'S	32°54'E
Mweru, L., lake	91	9°00'S	29°00'E
Myanmar (Burma), country	96	21°00'N	95°00'E
Mykolaiv, Ukraine	84	47°00'N	32°01'E

N

Name	Page	Latitude	Longitude
Naberezhnyye Chelny, Russia	84	55°41'N	52°28'E
Nacala, Mozambique	90	14°29'S	40°42'E
Nagpur, India	96	21°09'N	79°06'E
Nain, Canada	74	56°31'N	61°43'W
Nairobi, Kenya	90	1°18'S	36°50'E
Nakuru, Kenya	90	0°16'S	36°04'E
Namib Desert, desert	91	23°00'S	14°00'E
Namibia, country	90	22°00'S	17°00'E
Nampula, Mozambique	90	15°07'S	39°15'E
Nanaimo, Canada	74	49°10'N	123°57'W
Nanchang, China	96	28°40'N	115°56'E
Nanjing, China	96	32°08'N	118°48'E
Nanning, China	96	22°50'N	108°19'E
Nantes, France	84	47°13'N	1°34'W
Naples, Italy	84	40°51'N	14°17'E
Nashville, TN	51	36°10'N	86°47'W
Nassau, Bahamas	44	25°04'N	77°19'W
Nasser, L., lake	91	23°00'N	33°00'E
Natal, Brazil	78	5°48'S	35°13'W
Naturaliste, C., cape	103	34°00'S	115°00'E
Nauru, country	102	1°00'S	167°00'E
Nauru, island	102	1°00'S	167°00'E
Navojoa, Mexico	76	27°04'N	109°26'W
Nayarit, state, Mex.	76	22°00'N	105°00'W
Naypyidaw, Myanmar	96	19°26'N	96°07'E
N'Djamena, Chad	90	12°06'N	15°04'E
Ndola, Zambia	90	13°00'S	28°40'E
Nebraska, state, U.S.	50	42°00'N	100°00'W
Necochea, Argentina	78	38°33'S	58°45'W
Negro, river	79	39°00'S	66°00'W
Neiva, Colombia	78	2°59'N	75°18'W
Nelson, New Zealand	102	41°17'S	173°16'E
Nelson, river	75	56°00'N	96°00'W
Nepal, country	96	29°00'N	81°00'E
Netherlands, country	84	53°00'N	5°00'E
Netherlands Antilles, dependency	44	12°10'N	69°00'W
Nettiling L., lake	75	66°00'N	71°00'W
Neuquén, Argentina	78	38°57'S	68°03'W
Nevada, state, U.S.	50	40°00'N	117°00'W
Newark, NJ	51	40°44'N	74°10'W
New Britain, island	103	6°00'S	151°00'E
New Brunswick, province, Can.	74	48°00'N	73°00'W
New Caledonia, dependency, Fr.	102	21°00'S	165°00'E
New Caledonia, island	103	21°00'S	165°00'E
Newcastle, Australia	102	33°00'S	151°44'E
Newcastle upon Tyne, United Kingdom	84	54°59'N	1°37'W
New Delhi, India	96	28°36'N	77°13'E
Newfoundland, island	75	49°00'N	56°00'W
Newfoundland and Labrador, province, Can.	74	54°00'N	59°00'W
New Glasgow, Canada	74	45°34'N	62°39'W
New Guinea, island	97	5°00'S	141°00'E
New Hampshire, state, U.S.	51	44°00'N	72°00'W

Abbreviations

Arch.	Archipelago	Den.	Denmark	Isth.	Isthmus
Austl.	Australia	Dominican Rep.	Dominican Republic	Kos.	Kosovo
Bos. & Her.	Bosnia & Herzegovina	fed. dist.	Federal District	L.	Lake
C.	Cape	Fed. States of Micronesia	Federated States of Micronesia	Liecht.	Liechtenstein
Can.	Canada	Fr.	France	Mac.	Macedonia
Cen. African Rep.	Central African Republic	Ft.	Fort	Mex.	Mexico
Czech Rep.	Czech Republic	G.	Gulf	Mont.	Montenegro
Dem. Rep. of Congo	Democratic Republic of the Congo	Gr.	Greece	Mor.	Morocco
		I.	Island	Mt.	Mount
		Is.	Islands	Mtn.	Mountain
				Mts.	Mountains
				Neth.	Netherlands

N. Korea	North Korea	Sp.	Spain		
N.Z.	New Zealand	St., St-	Saint		
Pen.	Peninsula	Ste., Ste-	Sainte		
Plat.	Plateau	Str.	Strait		
Pt.	Point	Terr.	Territory		
R.	River	U.K.	United Kingdom		
Rep.	Republic	U.S.	United States		
Rep. of the Congo	Republic of the Congo	Val.	Valley		
Res.	Reservoir				
Russ.	Russia	For U.S. two-letter state abbreviations, see pages 52–53.			
S. Africa	South Africa				
S. Korea	South Korea				

Afghanistan
Islamic republic, SW Asia

Area: 250,000 sq. mi. (647,500 sq. km.)
Population: 31,890,000
Language(s): Dari, Pashtu

Monetary unit: afghani
Economy (pre-1980): agriculture (fruits and nuts), carpets, mining, natural gas, opium

After the fall of the Taliban in 2001, the newly established Afghan Interim Authority restored, in a modified form, the national flag first introduced in 1928. Black represents the dark ages of the past; red, the blood shed in the struggle for independence; and green, hope and prosperity for the future.

Albania
Republic, S Europe

Area: 11,100 sq. mi. (28,748 sq. km.)
Population: 3,601,000
Language(s): Albanian, Greek

Monetary unit: lek
Economy: agriculture (sugar beets and grapes), mining, oil, asphalt, textiles

On Nov. 28, 1443, the flag was first raised by Skanderbeg, the national hero. After independence from Turkish rule was proclaimed on Nov. 28, 1912, the flag was flown by various regimes, each of which identified itself by adding a symbol above the double-headed eagle. The current flag, which features only the eagle, was adopted on May 22, 1993.

Algeria
Republic, N Africa

Area: 919,950 sq. mi. (2,381,740 sq. km.)
Population: 33,333,000
Language(s): Arabic, French

Monetary unit: Algerian dinar
Economy: oil, natural gas, grapes, olives, dates, livestock, mining

In the early 19th century, during the French conquest of North Africa, Algerian resistance fighters led by Emir Abdelkader supposedly raised the current flag. Its colors and symbols are associated with Islam and the Arab dynasties of the region. The flag was raised over an independent Algeria on July 2, 1962.

Andorra
Coprincipality, SW Europe

Area: 181 sq. mi. (468 sq. km.)
Population: 71,800
Language(s): Catalan, French

Monetary unit: euro
Economy: tourism, international banking, cattle, sheep

The flag may date to 1866, but the first legal authority for it is unknown. The design was standardized in July 1993. Possible sources for its colors are the flags of neighboring Spain (red-yellow-red) and France (blue-white-red). The coat of arms incorporates both French and Spanish elements dating to the 13th century or earlier.

Angola
Republic, SW Africa

Area: 481,351 sq. mi. (1,246,700 sq. km.)
Population: 12,264,000
Language(s): Portuguese

Monetary unit: kwanza
Economy: subsistence farming, iron ore, oil, diamonds

After Portugal withdrew from Angola on Nov. 11, 1975, the flag of the leading rebel group gained recognition. Inspired by designs of the Viet Cong and the former Soviet Union, it includes a star for internationalism and progress, a cogwheel for industrial workers, and a machete for agricultural workers. The black stripe is for the African people.

Antigua and Barbuda
Islands republic, Caribbean

Area: 171 sq. mi. (443 sq. km.)
Population: 69,500
Language(s): English

Monetary unit: East Caribbean dollar
Economy: tourism, light manufacturing, tropical fruits

When "associated statehood" was granted by Britain on Feb. 27, 1967, the flag was introduced, and it remained after independence (Nov. 1, 1981). Red is for the dynamism of the people, the V-shape is for victory, and the sun is for the climate. Black is for the majority population and the soil, blue is for the sea, and white is for the beaches.

Argentina
Republic, South America

Area: 1,068,296 sq. mi. (2,766,890 sq. km.)
Population: 40,302,000
Language(s): Spanish, English

Monetary unit: Argentine peso
Economy: agriculture, livestock, food processing, oil, natural gas, motor vehicles

The uniforms worn by Argentines when the British attacked Buenos Aires (1806) and the blue ribbons worn by patriots in 1810 may have been the origin of the celeste-white-celeste flag hoisted on Feb. 12, 1812. The flag's golden "sun of May" was added on Feb. 25, 1818, to commemorate the yielding of the Spanish viceroy in 1810.

Armenia
Republic, SW Asia

Area: 11,506 sq. mi. (29,800 sq. km.)
Population: 2,972,000
Language(s): Armenian

Monetary unit: dram
Economy: diamond-processing, machine tools, tires, mining, grapes

In 1885 an Armenian priest proposed adopting the "rainbow flag given to the Armenians when Noah's Ark came to rest on Mt. Ararat." On Aug. 1, 1918, a flag was sanctioned with stripes of red (possibly symbolizing blood), blue (for homeland), and orange (for courage and work). Replaced during Soviet rule, it was readopted on Aug. 24, 1990.

Australia
Continent republic, SE of Asia

Area: 2,967,893 sq. mi. (7,686,850 sq. km.)
Population: 20,434,000
Language(s): English

Monetary unit: Australian dollar
Economy: mining (gold, diamonds, uranium), gas, oil, food processing, wool, transport equipment

After Australian confederation was achieved on Jan. 1, 1901, the flag was chosen in a competition. Like the blue flags of British colonies, it displays the Union Jack in the canton. Also shown are the Southern Cross and a "Commonwealth Star." The design became official on May 22, 1909, and it was recognized as the national flag on Feb. 14, 1954.

Austria
Republic, cen. Europe

Area: 32,382 sq. mi. (83,870 sq. km.)
Population: 8,200,000
Language(s): German

Monetary unit: euro
Economy: machinery, ski equipment, motor vehicles, chemicals, mining (minerals, salt), iron, steel

The colors of the Austrian coat of arms date from the seal of Duke Frederick II in 1230. With the fall of the Austro-Hungarian Empire in 1918, the new Austrian republic adopted the red-white-red flag. The white is sometimes said to represent the Danube River. An imperial eagle, an Austrian symbol for centuries, is added to government flags.

Azerbaijan
Republic, SW Asia

Area: 33,436 sq. mi. (86,600 sq. km.)
Population: 8,120,000
Language(s): Azerbaijani

Monetary unit: Azerbaijani manat
Economy: oil, natural gas, oilfield equipment, steel, iron ore, agriculture (tea, fruit, tobacco)

In the early 20th century anti-Russian nationalists exhorted the Azerbaijanis to "Turkify, Islamicize, and Europeanize," and the 1917 flag was associated with Turkey and Islam. In 1918 the crescent and star (also symbols of Turkic peoples) were introduced. Suppressed under Soviet rule, the flag was readopted on Feb. 5, 1991.

Bahamas
Islands commonwealth, Caribbean

Area: 5,386 sq. mi. (13,950 sq. km.)
Population: 305,700
Language(s): English

Monetary unit: Bahamian dollar
Economy: tourism, banking, shellfish, pharmaceuticals, rum, fruit

The flag of The Bahamas was adopted on July 10, 1973, the date of independence from Britain. Several entries from a competition were combined to create the design. The two aquamarine stripes are for the surrounding waters, the gold stripe is for the sand and other rich land resources, and the black triangle is for the people and their strength.

Bahrain

Islamic kingdom, Persian Gulf

Area: 257 sq. mi. (665 sq. km.)
Population: 708,600
Language(s): Arabic

Monetary unit: Bahraini dinar
Economy: oil, petroleum refining, metal processing, banking, ship repairing

Red was the color of the Kharijite Muslims of Bahrain about 1820, and white was chosen to show amity with the British. The flag was recognized in 1933 but was used long before. The current flag law was adopted in 2002. The five white points represent the five pillars of Islam.

Bangladesh

Republic, S Asia

Area: 55,598 sq. mi. (144,000 sq. km.)
Population: 150,448,000
Language(s): Bengali, English

Monetary unit: taka
Economy: agriculture (rice, jute, tea), fertilizer, newsprint

The flag is dark green to symbolize Islam, plant life, and the hope placed in Bengali youth. Its original design included a red disk and a silhouette of the country. On Jan. 13, 1972, the silhouette was removed and the disk shifted off-center. The disk is the "rising sun of a new country" colored by the blood of those who fought for independence.

Barbados

Island republic, Caribbean

Area: 166 sq. mi. (431 sq. km.)
Population: 280,900
Language(s): English

Monetary unit: Barbadian dollar
Economy: tourism, sugar, molasses, rum, light manufacturing, electrical components

The flag was designed by Grantley Prescod, a Barbadian art teacher. Its stripes of blue-yellow-blue are for sea, sand, and sky. The black trident head was inspired by the colonial flag of Barbados, which featured a trident-wielding Poseidon, or Neptune, figure. The flag was first hoisted on Nov. 30, 1966, the date of independence from Britain.

Belarus

Republic, E cen. Europe

Area: 80,154 sq. mi. (207,600 sq. km.)
Population: 9,725,000
Language(s): Belarusian, Russian

Monetary unit: Belarusian ruble
Economy: machine tools, motor vehicles, mineral products, textiles, grains, flax, suger beets

In 1951 the former Soviet republic created a striped flag in red (for communism) and green (for fields and forests), with the hammer, sickle, and star of communism. In 1991–95 an older design was used, but the Soviet-era flag was then altered and readopted without communist symbols. The vertical stripe is typical of embroidery on peasant clothing.

Belgium

Constitutional monarchy, NW Europe

Area: 11,787 sq. mi. (30,528 sq. km.)
Population: 10,309,800
Language(s): Dutch, French, German

Monetary unit: euro
Economy: engineering, scientific instruments, transportation equipment, textiles, processed food

A gold shield and a black lion appeared in the seal of Count Philip of Flanders as early as 1162, and in 1787 cockades of black-yellow-red were used in a Brussels revolt against Austria. After a war for independence, the flag was recognized on Jan. 23, 1831. By 1838 the design, which was influenced by the French tricolor, became standard.

Belize

Republic, Central America

Area: 8,867 sq. mi. (22,966 sq. km.)
Population: 294,400
Language(s): Spanish, Creole, English

Monetary unit: Belizean dollar
Economy: tourism, textiles, fish, sugar, bananas, citrus fruits, timber

The flag of Belize (former British Honduras) was based on the flag of the nationalist People's United Party. Its coat of arms shows a mahogany tree, a shield, and a Creole and a Mestizo. The red stripes, symbolic of the United Democratic Party, were added on independence day (Sept. 21, 1981), when the flag was first officially hoisted.

Benin

Republic, W Africa

Area: 43,483 sq. mi. (112,620 sq. km.)
Population: 8,078,000
Language(s): French

Monetary unit: CFA franc
Economy: subsistence agriculture, textiles, food processing (palm products, cotton, cocoa)

Adopted on Nov. 16, 1959, the flag of the former French colony used the Pan-African colors. Yellow was for the savannas in the north and green was for the palm groves in the south. Red stood for the blood of patriots. In 1975 a Marxist-oriented government replaced the flag, but after the demise of communism it was restored on Aug. 1, 1990.

Bhutan

Transitional state, S Asia

Area: 18,147 sq. mi. (47,000 sq. km.)
Population: 2,328,000
Language(s): Dzongkha (Tibetan)

Monetary unit: ngultrum
Economy: subsistence farming, animal husbandry, cement, wood products, fruits

The flag of Bhutan ("Land of the Dragon") features a dragon grasping jewels; this represents natural wealth and perfection. The white color is for purity and loyalty, the gold is for regal power, and the orange-red is for Buddhist sects and religious commitment. The flag may have been introduced as recently as 1971.

Bolivia

Republic, South America

Area: 424,162 sq. mi. (1,098,580 sq. km.)
Population: 9,119,000
Language(s): Spanish, Aymara, Quechua

Monetary unit: boliviano
Economy: mining, smelting, food, beverages (soybeans, coffee), natural gas

A version of the flag was first adopted on July 25, 1826, but on Nov. 5, 1851, the order of the stripes was changed to red-yellow-green. The colors were often used by the Aymara and Quechua peoples; in addition, red is for the valor of the army, yellow for mineral resources, and green for the land. The current flag law dates from July 14, 1888.

Bosnia and Herzegovina

Republic, SE Europe

Area: 19,741 sq. mi. (51,129 sq. km.)
Population: 4,552,000
Language(s): Bosnian, Croatian, Serbian

Monetary unit: marka
Economy: mining (iron ore, lead, zinc), vehicle assembly, textiles, wood products

The medium blue field is bisected by a yellow triangle (representing equality between the three peoples of the nation) with seven full and two half stars in white along the hypotenuse, intended to represent Europe. The half stars are intended to suggest the infinity of the star pattern.

Botswana

Republic, S Africa

Area: 231,803 sq. mi. (600,370 sq. km.)
Population: 1,816,000
Language(s): English, Setswana

Monetary unit: pula
Economy: mining (diamonds, copper), tourism, food processing, financial services

Adopted in 1966, the flag was designed to contrast symbolically with that of neighboring South Africa, where apartheid was then in effect. The black and white stripes in Botswana's flag are for racial cooperation and equality. The background symbolizes water, a scarce resource in the expansive Kalahari Desert.

Brazil

Republic, South America

Area: 3,284,426 sq. mi. (8,506,663 sq. km.)
Population: 190,011,000
Language(s): Portuguese

Monetary unit: real
Economy: agriculture (coffee, soybeans), livestock, mining, aircraft, motor vehicles, machinery

The original flag was introduced on Sept. 7, 1822, when Dom Pedro declared independence from Portugal. In 1889 the blue disk and the motto Ordem e Progresso ("Order and Progress") were added. The Brazilian states and territories are symbolized by the constellations of stars. Green is for the land, while yellow is for gold and other mineral wealth.

Brunei
Constitutional sultanate, SE Asia

Area: 2,228 sq. mi. (5,770 sq. km.)
Population: 374,600
Language(s): Malay, English

Monetary unit: Bruneian dollar
Economy: oil, natural gas production and refining, agriculture, forestry, fishing

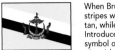

When Brunei became a British protectorate in 1906, diagonal stripes were added to its yellow flag. The yellow stood for the sultan, while white and black were for his two chief ministers. Introduced in September 1959, the coat of arms has a parasol as a symbol of royalty and a crescent and inscription for the state religion, Islam.

Bulgaria
Republic, SE Europe

Area: 42,822 sq. mi. (110,910 sq. km.)
Population: 7,323,000
Language(s): Bulgarian

Monetary unit: lev
Economy: mining (coal, copper, zinc), chemicals, machinery, textiles

The flag was based on the Russian flag of 1699, but with green substituted for blue. Under communist rule, a red star and other symbols were added, but the old tricolor was reestablished on Nov. 27, 1990. The white is for peace, love, and freedom; green is for agriculture; and red is for the independence struggle and military courage.

Burkina Faso
Republic, W Africa

Area: 105,869 sq. mi. (274,200 sq. km.)
Population: 14,326,000
Language(s): French

Monetary unit: CFA franc
Economy: subsistence agriculture, cotton, livestock, gold

On Aug. 4, 1984, Upper Volta was renamed Burkina Faso by the revolutionary government of Thomas Sankara, and the current flag was adopted with Pan-African colors. The yellow star symbolizes leadership and revolutionary principles. The red stripe is said to stand for the revolutionary struggle, while the green stripe represents hope and abundance.

Burundi
Republic, E cen. Africa

Area: 10,745 sq. mi. (27,830 sq. km.)
Population: 8,391,000
Language(s): Kirundi, French

Monetary unit: Burundi franc
Economy: subsistence agriculture, coffee, tea, hides, assembly of imported components

The flag became official on June 28, 1967. Its white saltire (diagonal cross) and central disk symbolize peace. The red color is for the independence struggle, and green is for hope. The stars correspond to the national motto, "Unity, Work, Progress." They also recall the Tutsi, Hutu, and Twa peoples and the pledge to God, king, and country.

Cambodia
Constitutional monarchy, SE Asia

Area: 69,900 sq. mi. (181,040 sq. km.)
Population: 13,996,000
Language(s): Khmer

Monetary unit: riel
Economy: subsistence farming, tourism, textiles, rice milling, wood products

Artistic representations of the central ruined temple of Angkor Wat, a 12th-century temple complex, have appeared on Khmer flags since the 19th century. The current flag design dates to 1948. It was replaced in 1970 under the Khmer Republic and in 1976 under communist leadership, but it was again hoisted on June 29, 1993.

Cameroon
Republic, W cen. Africa

Area: 183,567 sq. mi. (475,440 sq. km.)
Population: 18,060,000
Language(s): French, English

Monetary unit: CFA franc
Economy: petroleum products, aluminum, cocoa, coffee, textiles, timber, rubber

The flag was officially hoisted on Oct. 29, 1957, prior to independence (Jan. 1, 1960). Green is for the vegetation of the south, yellow for the savannas of the north, and red for union and sovereignty. Two yellow stars were added (for the British Cameroons) in 1961, but these were replaced in 1975 by a single star symbolizing national unity.

Canada
Republic, North America

Area: 3,851,809 sq. mi. (9,976,185 sq. km.)
Population: 33,390,000
Language(s): English, French

Monetary unit: Canadian dollar
Economy: motor vehicles, aircraft, industrial machinery, high-tech equipment, paper, pulp, food products

During Canada's first century of independence the Union Jack was still flown but with a Canadian coat of arms. The maple leaf design, with the national colors, became official on Feb. 15, 1965. Since 1868 the maple leaf has been a national symbol, and in 1921 a red leaf in the coat of arms stood for Canadian sacrifice during World War I.

Cape Verde
Islands republic, off W Africa

Area: 1,557 sq. mi. (4,033 sq. km.)
Population: 423,600
Language(s): Portuguese

Monetary unit: escudo
Economy: fish processing, textiles, salt mining, ship repair, sugar, fruits, coffee

After the elections of 1991, the flag was established with a blue field bearing a ring of 10 yellow stars to symbolize the 10 main islands of Cape Verde. The stripes of white-red-white suggest peace and national resolve. Red, white, and blue also are a symbolic link to Portugal and the United States. The new flag became official on Sept. 25, 1992.

Central African Republic
Republic, cen. Africa

Area: 240,534 sq. mi. (622,984 sq. km.)
Population: 4,369,000
Language(s): French, Sangho

Monetary unit: CFA franc
Economy: subsistence farming, mining (diamonds, gold), timber, vehicle assembly

Barthélemy Boganda designed the flag in 1958. It combines French and Pan-African colors. The star is a guide for progress and an emblem of unity. The blue stripe is for liberty, grandeur, and the sky; the white is for purity, equality, and candor; the green and yellow are for forests and savannas; and the red is for the blood of humankind.

Chad
Republic, N cen. Africa

Area: 495,752 sq. mi. (1,284,000 sq. km.)
Population: 9,886,000
Language(s): Arabic, French

Monetary unit: CFA franc
Economy: subsistence farming, livestock raising, oil, textiles, meatpacking

In 1958 a tricolor of green-yellow-red (the Pan-African colors) was proposed, but that design was already used by the Mali-Senegal federation, another former French colony. Approved on Nov. 6, 1959, the current flag substitutes blue for the original green stripe. Blue is for hope and sky, yellow for the sun, and red for the unity of the nation.

Chile
Republic, South America

Area: 292,258 sq. mi. (756,946 sq. km.)
Population: 16,285,000
Language(s): Spanish

Monetary unit: Chilean peso
Economy: mining (copper), timber, pulp, paper, chemicals, wine, fish processing

On Oct. 18, 1817, the flag was established for the new republic. The blue is for the sky, and the star is "a guide on the path of progress and honor." The white is for the snow of the Andes Mountains while the red recalls the blood of patriots. In the 15th century the Araucanian Indians gave red-white-blue sashes to their warriors.

China
Communist state, Asia

Area: 3,705,386 sq. mi. (9,596,960 sq. km.)
Population: 1,321,852,000
Language(s): Mandarin Chinese

Monetary unit: yuan
Economy: mining, steel, medical, high-tech equipment, textiles, consumer products

The flag was hoisted on Oct. 1, 1949. The red is for communism and the Han Chinese. The large star was originally for the Communist Party, and the smaller stars were for the proletariat, the peasants, the petty bourgeoisie, and the "patriotic capitalists." The large star was later said to stand for China, the smaller stars for minorities.

Colombia
Republic, South America

Area: 439,736 sq. mi. (1,138,910 sq. km.)
Population: 44,380,000
Language(s): Spanish

Monetary unit: Colombian peso
Economy: oil, mining (platinum, emeralds), textiles, chemicals, coffee, bananas, cocaine

In the early 19th century "the Liberator" Simon Bolivar created a yellow-blue-red flag for New Granada (which included Colombia, Venezuela, Panama, and Ecuador). The flag symbolized the yellow gold of the New World separated by the blue ocean from the red of "bloody Spain." The present Colombian flag was established on Nov. 26, 1861.

Comoros
Islands republic, off SE Africa

Area: 838 sq. mi. (2,170 sq. km.)
Population: 711,400
Language(s): Arabic, French

Monetary unit: Comoran franc
Economy: agriculture (vanilla, cloves, essential oils, copra), tourism, perfume distillation

The Comoros flag, adopted in the 1990s, contains the green triangle and crescent that are traditional symbols of Islam. The four stars and four horizontal stripes represent the country's main islands of Mwali, Njazidja, Nzwani and Mayotte, this last, a dependency of France, also claimed by Comoros.

Congo (Democratic Rep.)
Republic, Equatorial Africa

Area: 905,568 sq. mi. (2,345,410 sq. km.)
Population: 65,752,000
Language(s): French, Lingala

Monetary unit: Congolese franc
Economy: mining and processing (diamonds, copper, zinc), tobacco, palm oil, bananas, rubber

A new flag for the Democratic Republic of the Congo was unveiled on February 18, 2006, upon the adoption of a new constitution. This flag is similar in style to the one flown between 1963-1971, with a lighter blue color now used. The blue in the flag symbolizes peace; red the blood of the country's martyrs; yellow the country's wealth; and the star for the country's radiant future.

Congo (Republic)
Republic, Equatorial Africa

Area: 132,047 sq. mi. (342,000 sq. km.)
Population: 3,801,000
Language(s): French, local languages

Monetary unit: CFA franc
Economy: petroleum, diamonds, plywood, peanuts, bananas, sugarcane, coffee

First adopted on Sept. 15, 1959, the flag uses the Pan-African colors. Green was originally said to stand for Congo's agriculture and forests, and yellow for friendship and the nobility of the people, but the red was unexplained. Altered in 1969 by a Marxist government, the flag was restored to its initial form on June 10, 1991.

Costa Rica
Republic, Central America

Area: 19,730 sq. mi. (51,100 sq. km.)
Population: 4,134,000
Language(s): Spanish

Monetary unit: Costa Rican colón
Economy: tourism, textiles, plastics, electronic, medical equipment, coffee, bananas, sugar

The blue and white stripes originated in the flag colors of the United Provinces of Central America (1823–40). On Sept. 29, 1848, the red stripe was added to symbolize sunlight, civilization, and "true independence." The current design of the coat of arms, which is included on government flags, was established in 1964.

Croatia
Republic, SE Europe

Area: 21,831 sq. mi. (56,542 sq. km.)
Population: 4,493,000
Language(s): Croatian

Monetary unit: kuna
Economy: chemicals, plastics, machine tools, electronics, petroleum refining, tourism

During the European uprisings of 1848, Croatians designed a flag based on that of Russia. In April 1941 the fascistic Ustasa used this flag, adding the checkered shield of Croatia. A communist star soon replaced the shield, but the current flag was adopted on Dec. 22, 1990. Atop the shield is a "crown" inlaid with historic coats of arms.

Cuba
Island communist state, Caribbean

Area: 42,803 sq. mi. (110,860 sq. km)
Population: 11,394,000
Language(s): Spanish

Monetary unit: Cuban peso
Economy: tourism, sugar, coffee, rice, cigars, textiles, cement

In the mid-19th century Cuban exiles designed the flag, which was later carried into battle against Spanish forces. It was adopted on May 20, 1902. The stripes were for the three military districts of Cuba and the purity of the patriotic cause. The red triangle was for strength, constancy, and equality, and the white star symbolized independence.

Cyprus
Island republic, E Mediterranean

The island of Cyprus is de facto divided between predominately Greek Republic of Cyprus (internationally recognized) and the predominantly Turkish northern third of the island (Turkish republic), recognized solely by Turkey and with the economy basically dependent on Turkey.

Area: (island) 3,571 sq. mi. (9,250 sq. km.)
Population: 788,500
Language(s): Greek, Turkish

Monetary unit: euro
Economy: tourism, food, beverage processing, cement, gypsum, ship repair, textiles, clay products

On Aug. 7, 1960, the Republic of Cyprus was proclaimed with a national flag of a neutral design. It bears the island in silhouette and a green olive wreath, for peace. In 1974 there was a Turkish invasion of the island. A puppet government, which adopted a flag based on the Turkish model, was set up on the northern third of Cyprus.

Czech Republic
Republic, cen. Europe

Area: 30,450 sq. mi. (78,866 sq. km.)
Population: 10,229,000
Language(s): Czech

Monetary unit: Czech koruna
Economy: machinery, transport equipment, chemicals, coal, steel, wheat, sugar beets, fruit

When Czechs, Slovaks, and Ruthenians united to form Czechoslovakia in 1918, a simple white-red bicolor flag was chosen; in 1920 it incorporated a blue triangle at the hoist. Czechoslovakia divided into Slovakia and the Czech Republic in 1993, but the latter country readopted the Czechoslovak flag as its own.

Denmark
Constitutional monarchy, N Europe

Area: 16,639 sq. mi. (43,094 sq. km.)
Population: 5,468,000
Language(s): Danish

Monetary unit: Danish krone
Economy: metal processing, chemicals, machinery, electronics, furniture, dairy products, oil, gas

A traditional story claims that the Danish flag fell from heaven on June 15, 1219, but the previously existing war flag of the Holy Roman Empire was of a similar design, with its red field symbolizing battle and its white cross suggesting divine favor. In 1849 the state and military flag was altered and adopted as a symbol of the Danish people.

Djibouti
Republic, E Africa

Area: 8,880 sq. mi. (23,000 sq. km.)
Population: 496,400
Language(s): Arabic, French

Monetary unit: Djiboutian franc
Economy: livestock herding, hides, salt, agricultural processing, fishing

First raised by anti-French separatists, the flag was officially hoisted on June 27, 1977. The color of the Afar people, green, stands for prosperity. The color of the Issa people, light blue, symbolizes sea and sky, and recalls the flag of Somalia. The white triangle is for equality and peace; the red star is for unity and independence.

Dominica
Island republic, Caribbean

Area: 291 sq. mi. (754 sq. km.)
Population: 72,400
Language(s): English

Monetary unit: East Caribbean dollar
Economy: bananas, cocoa, coconuts, coconut oil, copra, limes; soap

The flag was hoisted on Nov. 3, 1978, at independence from Britain. Its background symbolizes forests; its central disk is red for socialism and bears a sisserou (a rare local bird). The stars are for the parishes of the island. The cross of yellow, white, and black is for the Carib, Caucasian, and African peoples and for fruit, water, and soil.

Dominican Republic
Republic, Hispaniola, Caribbean

Area: 18,815 sq. mi. (48,730 sq. km.)
Population: 9,366,000
Language(s): Spanish

Monetary unit: Dominican peso
Economy: tourism, sugar processing, mining, textiles, cigars, consumer goods, coffee

On Feb. 28, 1844, Spanish-speaking Dominican revolutionaries added a white cross to the simple blue-red flag of eastern Hispaniola in order to emphasize their Christian heritage. On November 6 of that same year the new constitution established the flag but with the colors at the fly end reversed so that the blue and red would alternate.

East Timor
Republic, Timor Island, W Pacific

Area: 5,794 sq. mi. (15,007 sq. km.)
Population: 1,085,000
Language(s): Tetum, Portuguese, Indonesian

Monetary unit: U.S. dollar
Economy: printing, soap, handicrafts, coffee, sandalwood, potential oil exports

East Timor's flag consists of two isosceles triangles, one black and one yellow, overlapping on a red background. The black stands for obscurantism that needs to be overcome; the yellow for the trace of colonialism. The red background is for the struggle for liberation. The white star is the symbol of peace.

Ecuador
Republic, South America

Area: 109,483 sq. mi. (283,560 sq. km.)
Population: 13,756,000
Language(s): Spanish, Quechua

Monetary unit: U.S. dollar
Economy: petroleum, textiles, wood products, chemicals, coffee, bananas, shrimp, cut flowers

Victorious against the Spanish on May 24, 1822, Antonio José de Sucre hoisted a yellow-blue-red flag. Other flags were later used, but on Sept. 26, 1860, the current flag design was adopted. The coat of arms is displayed on the flag when it is used abroad or for official purposes, to distinguish it from the flag of Colombia.

Egypt
Republic, NE Africa and Sinai Peninsula

Area: 386,662 sq. mi. (1,001,450 sq. km.)
Population: 80,335,000
Language(s): Arabic, English, French

Monetary unit: Egyptian pound
Economy: tourism, oil, mining, chemicals, salt, textiles, cotton, wheat, sugarcane

The 1952 revolt against British rule established the red-white-black flag with a central gold eagle. Two stars replaced the eagle in 1958, and in 1972 a federation with Syria and Libya was formed, adding instead the hawk of Quraysh (the tribe of Muhammad). On Oct. 9, 1984, the eagle of Saladin (a major 12th-century ruler) was substituted.

El Salvador
Republic, Central America

Area: 8,124 sq. mi. (21,040 sq. km.)
Population: 6,948,000
Language(s): Spanish

Monetary unit: U.S. dollar
Economy: petroleum, chemicals, fertilizer, textiles, light assembly, coffee, sugar, shrimp

In the early 19th century, a blue-white-blue flag was designed for the short-lived United Provinces of Central America, in which El Salvador was a member. On Sept. 15, 1912, the flag was reintroduced in El Salvador. The coat of arms in the center resembles that used by the former federation and includes the national motto, "God, Union, Liberty."

Equatorial Guinea
Republic, W cen. Africa

Area: 10,831 sq. mi. (28,051 sq. km.)
Population: 551,200
Language(s): Spanish, French

Monetary unit: CFA franc
Economy: oil, gas, timber, subsistence farming, cocoa, coffee, palm oil, fishing

The flag was first hoisted at independence (Oct. 12, 1968). Its coat of arms shows the silk-cotton tree, or god tree, which recalls early Spanish influence in the area. The sea, which links parts of the country, is reflected in the blue triangle. The green is for vegetation, white is for peace, and red is for the blood of martyrs in the liberation struggle.

Eritrea
Transitional state, E Africa

Area: 46,842 sq. mi. (121,320 sq. km.)
Population: 4,907,000
Language(s): Arabic, local languages

Monetary unit: nakfa
Economy: subsistence farming, herding, food processing, textiles, small manufacturing, salt

Officially hoisted at the proclamation of independence on May 24, 1993, the national flag was based on that of the Eritrean People's Liberation Front. The red triangle is for the blood of patriots, the green is for agriculture, and the blue is for maritime resources. Around a central branch is a circle of olive branches with 30 leaves.

Estonia
Republic, N Europe

Area: 17,462 sq. mi. (45,226 sq. km.)
Population: 1,316,000
Language(s): Estonian, Russian

Monetary unit: Estonian kroon
Economy: machinery, electronics, telecommunications, wood, paper, furniture, textiles

In the late 19th century an Estonian students' association adopted the blue-black-white flag. Blue was said to stand for the sky, black for the soil, and white for aspirations to freedom and homeland. The flag was officially recognized on July 4, 1920. It was replaced under Soviet rule, and readopted on Oct. 20, 1988.

Ethiopia
Republic, E Africa

Area: 435,186 sq. mi. (1,127,127 sq. km.)
Population: 76,512,000
Language(s): Amarigna, local languages

Monetary unit: birr
Economy: agriculture, food processing, hides, skins, gold, textiles, chemicals

The flag is red (for sacrifice), green (for labor, development, and fertility), and yellow (for hope, justice, and equality). Tricolor pennants were used prior to the official flag of Oct. 6, 1897, and a tricolor was flown by anti-government forces in 1991. On Feb. 6, 1996, the disk (for peace) and star (for unity and the future) were added.

Fiji
Islands republic, S Pacific

Area: 7054 sq. mi. (18,270 sq. km.)
Population: 918,700
Language(s): English, Fijian, Hindustani

Monetary unit: Fijian dollar
Economy: subsistence farming, fishing, sugar, copra, fruit, gold, tourism

The national flag, introduced on Oct. 10, 1970, is a modified version of Fiji's colonial flag. It includes the Union Jack on a light blue field. The shield has the red cross of St. George on a white background, below a yellow lion, which holds a cocoa pod. Local symbols (sugar cane, coconuts, bananas, and the Fiji dove) are also shown.

Finland
Republic, N Europe

Area: 130,559 sq. mi. (338,145 sq. km.)
Population: 5,238,000
Language(s): Finnish, Swedish

Monetary unit: euro
Economy: timber, pulp, mining, electronics, scientific instruments, shipbuilding

In 1862, while Finland was under Russian control, a flag was proposed that would have a white background for the snows of Finland and blue for its lakes. The blue was in the form of a "Nordic cross" similar to those used by other Scandinavian countries. The flag was officially adopted by the newly independent country on May 29, 1918.

France
Republic, W Europe

Area: 211,209 sq. mi. (547,030 sq. km.)
Population: 60,876,000
Language(s): French

Monetary unit: euro
Economy: machinery, automobiles, aircraft, chemicals, engineering, food processing, wine, tourism

From 1789 blue and red, the traditional colors of Paris, were included in flags with Bourbon royal white. In 1794 the tricolor was made official. It embodied liberty, equality, fraternity, democracy, secularism, and modernization, but there is no symbolism attached to the individual colors. It has been the sole national flag since March 5, 1848.

Gabon

Republic, W cen. Africa

Area: 103,347 sq. mi. (267,667 sq. km.)
Population: 1,455,000
Language(s): French

Monetary unit: CFA franc
Economy: oil, timber, mining (manganese, gold, uranium), cocoa, coffee, palm oil, ship repair

After proclaiming independence from France, Gabon adopted its national flag on Aug. 9, 1960. The central yellow stripe is for the Equator, which runs through the country. Green stands for the tropical forests that are one of Gabon's most important resources. Blue represents its extensive coast along the South Atlantic Ocean.

Gambia

Republic, W Africa

Area: 4,363 sq. mi. (11,300 sq. km.)
Population: 1,688,000
Language(s): English

Monetary unit: dalasi
Economy: agriculture (peanuts, palm kernels), hides, machine assembly, metalworking

The Gambia achieved independence from Britain on Feb. 18, 1965, under the current flag. The center stripe is blue to symbolize the Gambia River. The red stripe is for the sun and the equator. The green stripe is for agricultural produce, while the white stripes are said to stand for peace and unity.

Georgia

Republic, SW Asia

Area: 26,911 sq. mi. (69,700 sq. km.)
Population: 4,646,000
Language(s): Georgian, Russian

Monetary unit: lari
Economy: agriculture (citrus fruits, tea, hazelnuts, wine grapes), mining, chemicals, steel products

The five-cross design of the Georgian flag is believed to have been used in the Middle Ages. The central cross is the cross of St. George, the patron saint of Georgia. The red and white color is traditional, used in the flags of the independent kingdoms that eventually united to form Georgia. The current flag was adopted in 2004.

Germany

Republic, cen. Europe

Area: 137,847 sq. mi. (357,021 sq. km.)
Population: 82,401,000
Language(s): German

Monetary unit: euro
Economy: iron, steel, machine tools, electronics, wine and beer, chemicals, motor vehicles

In the early 19th century, German nationalists displayed black, gold, and red on their uniforms and tricolor flags. The current flag was used officially from 1848 to 1852 and readopted by West Germany on May 9, 1949. East Germany flew a similar flag but only the flag of West Germany was maintained upon reunification in 1990.

Ghana

Republic, W Africa

Area: 92,456 sq. mi. (239,460 sq. km.)
Population: 22,931,000
Language(s): English, local languages

Monetary unit: cedi
Economy: subsistence farming, mining (diamonds, gold), light manufacturing, cocoa, palm oil

On March 6, 1957, independence from Britain was granted and a flag, based on the red-white-green tricolor of a nationalist organization, was hoisted. A black "lodestar of African freedom" was added and the white stripe was changed to yellow, symbolizing wealth. Green is for forests and farms, red for the independence struggle.

Greece

Republic, S Europe

Area: 50,942 sq. mi. (131,940 sq. km.)
Population: 10,706,000
Language(s): Greek

Monetary unit: euro
Economy: tourism, food processing, mining, metal products, petroleum, textiles

In March 1822, during the revolt against Ottoman rule, the first Greek national flags were adopted; the most recent revision to the flag was made on Dec. 22, 1978. The colors symbolize Greek Orthodoxy while the cross stands for "the wisdom of God, freedom and country." The stripes are for the battle cry for independence: "Freedom or Death."

Grenada

Island republic, Caribbean

Area: 133 sq. mi. (344 sq. km.)
Population: 90,000
Language(s): English

Monetary unit: East Caribbean dollar
Economy: tourism, light assembly, banking, textiles, nutmeg, mace, bananas

Grenada's flag was officially hoisted on Feb. 3, 1974. Its background is green for vegetation and yellow for the sun, and its red border is symbolic of harmony and unity. The seven stars are for the original administrative subdivisions of Grenada. Nutmeg, a crop for which the "Isle of Spice" is internationally known, is represented as well.

Guatemala

Republic, Central America

Area: 42,043 sq. mi. (108,890 sq. km.)
Population: 12,728,000
Language(s): Spanish

Monetary unit: quetzal
Economy: coffee, bananas, sugar, timber, petroleum, chemicals, metals, rubber, textiles

The flag was introduced in 1871. It has blue and white stripes (colors of the former United Provinces of Central America) and a coat of arms with the quetzal (the national bird), a scroll, a wreath, and crossed rifles and sabres. Different artistic variations have been used but on Sept. 12, 1968, the present pattern was established.

Guinea

Republic, W Africa

Area: 94,926 sq. mi. (245,857 sq. km.)
Population: 9,948,000
Language(s): French

Monetary unit: Guinean franc
Economy: mining (bauxite, gold, diamonds), light manufacturing, bananas, coffee, pineapples

The flag was adopted on Nov. 12, 1958, one month after independence from France. Its simple design was influenced by the French tricolor. The red is said to be a symbol of sacrifice and labor, while the yellow is for mineral wealth, the tropical sun, and justice. Green symbolizes agricultural wealth and the solidarity of the people.

Guinea-Bissau

Republic, W Africa

Area: 13,946 sq. mi. (36,120 sq. km.)
Population: 1,473,000
Language(s): Portuguese

Monetary unit: CFA franc
Economy: cashews, peanuts, fish, seafood processing, timber, potential oil exports

The flag has been used since the declaration of independence from Portugal on Sept. 24, 1973. The black star on the red stripe was for African Party leadership, the people, and their will to live in dignity, freedom, and peace. Yellow was for the harvest and other rewards of work, and green was for the nation's vast jungles and agricultural lands.

Guyana

Republic, South America

Area: 83,000 sq. mi. (214,970 sq. km.)
Population: 769,000
Language(s): English

Monetary unit: Guyanese dollar
Economy: mining (bauxite, diamonds, gold), sugar, rum, shrimp, timber

Upon independence from Britain on May 26, 1966, the flag was first hoisted. The green stands for jungles and fields, white suggests the rivers which are the basis for the Indian word *guiana* ("land of waters"), red is for zeal and sacrifice in nation-building, and black is for perseverance. The flag is nicknamed "The Golden Arrowhead."

Haiti

Republic, Hispaniola, Caribbean

Area: 10,714 sq. mi. (27,750 sq. km.)
Population: 8,706,000
Language(s): Creole, French

Monetary unit: gourde
Economy: subsistence farming, sugar refining, flour milling, fruits, textiles, cement

After the French Revolution of 1789, Haiti underwent a slave revolt, but the French tricolor continued in use until 1803. The new blue-red flag represented the black and mulatto populations only. A black-red flag was used by various dictators, including François "Papa Doc" Duvalier and his son, but on Feb. 25, 1986, the old flag was reestablished.

Honduras
Republic, Central America

Area: 43,278 sq. mi. (112,090 sq. km.)
Population: 7,484,000
Language(s): Spanish

Monetary unit: lempira
Economy: coffee, bananas, sugar, tobacco, fishing, textiles, mining (zinc, silver)

Since Feb. 16, 1866, the Honduran flag has retained the blue-white-blue design of the flag of the former United Provinces of Central America, but with five central stars symbolizing the states of Honduras, El Salvador, Nicaragua, Costa Rica, and Guatemala. The flag design has often been associated with Central American reunification attempts.

Hungary
Republic, cen. Europe

Area: 35,919 sq. mi. (93,030 sq. km.)
Population: 9,956,000
Language(s): Hungarian

Monetary unit: forint
Economy: machinery, motor vehicles, pharmaceuticals, sugar beets, mining, textiles

The colors of the Hungarian flag were mentioned in a 1608 coronation ceremony, but they may have been used since the 13th century. The tricolor was adopted on Oct. 12, 1957, after the abortive revolution of 1956. The white is said to symbolize Hungary's rivers, the green its mountains, and the red the blood shed in its many battles.

Iceland
Island republic, off NW Europe

Area: 39,769 sq. mi. (103,000 sq. km.)
Population: 301,900
Language(s): Icelandic

Monetary unit: Icelandic krona
Economy: fishing and fish processing, aluminum, animal products, tourism, cement

Approval for an Icelandic flag was given by the king of Denmark on June 19, 1915; it became a national flag on Dec. 1, 1918, when the separate kingdom of Iceland was proclaimed. The flag was retained upon the creation of a republic on June 17, 1944. The design has a typical "Scandinavian cross".

India
Republic, S Asia

Area: 1,269,346 sq. mi. (3,287,590 sq. km.)
Population: 1,129,866,000
Language(s): Hindi, English

Monetary unit: Indian rupee
Economy: agriculture, mining, cut diamonds, crude oil, software services, textiles, machinery

Earlier versions of the flag were used from the 1920s, but the current flag was hoisted officially on July 22, 1947. The orange was said to stand for courage and sacrifice, white for peace and truth, and green for faith and chivalry. The blue wheel is a chakra, associated with Emperor Asoka's attempts to unite India in the 3rd century BC.

Indonesia
Republic, SE Asia

Area: 741,000 sq. mi. (1,919,440 sq. km.)
Population: 234,694,000
Language(s): Indonesian

Monetary unit: Indonesian rupiah
Economy: oil, natural gas, timber, plywood, rubber; tourism, cacao, nutmeg, palm oil, tea

Indonesia's red and white flag was associated with the Majapahit empire which existed from the 13th to the 16th century. It was adopted on Aug. 17, 1945, and it remained after Indonesia won its independence from The Netherlands in 1949. Red is for courage and white for honesty. The flag is identical, except in dimensions, to the flag of Monaco.

Iran
Islamic republic, SW Asia

Area: 636,296 sq. mi. (1,648,000 sq. km.)
Population: 65,398,000
Language(s): Farsi (Persian)

Monetary unit: Iranian rial
Economy: oil, natural gas, mining, metals, vegetables oils, caviar, textiles, carpets

The tricolor flag was recognized in 1906 but altered after the revolution of 1979. Along the central stripe are the Arabic words Allahu akbar ("God is great"), repeated 22 times. The coat of arms can be read as a rendition of the word Allah, as a globe, or as two crescents. The green is for Islam, white is for peace, and red is for valor.

Iraq
Republic, SW Asia

Area: 168,754 sq. mi. (437,072 sq. km.)
Population: 27,500,000
Language(s): Arabic, Kurdish

Monetary unit: Iraqi dinar
Economy: oil, natural gas, agriculture, livestock, textiles

Adopted on July 30, 1963, the Iraqi flag is based on the liberation flag first flown in Egypt in 1952. Red is for the willingness to shed blood, green is for Arab lands, black is for past suffering, and white is for purity. On Jan. 14, 1991, the Arabic inscription "God is Great" was added, and in 2008 the script was restyled.

Ireland
Republic, off NW Europe

Area: 27,135 sq. mi. (70,280 sq. km.)
Population: 4,109,000
Language(s): English, Irish Gaelic

Monetary unit: euro
Economy: engineering, machinery, tourism, brewing, distilling, mining, food products, textiles

In the 19th century various tricolor flags and ribbons became symbolic of Irish opposition to British rule. Many of them included the colors green (for the Catholics), orange (for the Protestants), and white (for the peace between the two groups). The tricolor in its modern form was recognized by the constitution on Dec. 29, 1937.

Israel
Republic, SW Asia

Area: 8,019 sq. mi. (20,770 sq. km.)
Population: 6,427,000
Language(s): Hebrew, Arabic

Monetary unit: Israeli shekel
Economy: high-technology, mining, textiles, chemicals, food processing, diamond cutting

Symbolic of the traditional tallit, or Jewish prayer shawl, and including the Star of David, the flag was used from the late 19th century. It was raised when Israel proclaimed independence on May 14, 1948, and the banner was legally recognized on Nov. 12, 1948. A dark blue was also substituted for the traditional lighter shade of blue.

Italy
Republic, S Europe

Area: 116,306 sq. mi. (301,230 sq. km.)
Population: 58,148,000
Language(s): Italian

Monetary unit: euro
Economy: iron, steel, ceramics, chemicals, fishing, textiles, automobiles, tourism, food processing

The first Italian national flag was adopted on Feb. 25, 1797, by the Cispadane Republic. Its stripes were vertically positioned on May 11, 1798, and thereafter it was honored by all Italian nationalists. The design was guaranteed by a decree (March 23, 1848) of King Charles Albert of Sardinia, ordering troops to carry the flag into battle.

Ivory Coast
Republic, W Africa

Area: 124,503 sq. mi. (322,460 sq. km.)
Population: 18,013,000
Language(s): French

Monetary unit: CFA franc
Economy: coffee, cocoa, palm oil, rubber, wood products, oil refining, diamonds, fishing

Adopted on Aug. 7, 1959, the flag of the former French colony has three stripes corresponding to the national motto (Unity, Discipline, Labor). The orange is for growth, the white is for peace emerging from purity and unity, and the green is for hope and the future. Unofficially the green is for forests and the orange is for savannas.

Jamaica
Island republic, Caribbean

Area: 4,244 sq. mi. (10,991 sq. km.)
Population: 2,780,000
Language(s): English

Monetary unit: Jamaican dollar
Economy: bauxite, alumina, tourism, tropical fruits, rum, cement, gypsum, telecommunications

The flag was designed prior to independence from Britain (Aug. 6, 1962). The black color stood for hardships faced by the nation, green for agriculture and hope, and yellow for the natural wealth of Jamaica. This was summed up in the phrase, "Hardships there are, but the land is green and the sun shineth."

Japan
Islands constit. monarchy, W Pacific

Area: 145,883 sq. mi. (377,835 sq. km.)
Population: 127,433,000
Language(s): Japanese

Monetary unit: yen
Economy: motor vehicles, electronics, optical equipment, chemicals, fishing, mining, textiles

The flag features a red sun on a cool white background. Traditionally, the sun goddess founded Japan in the 7th century BC and gave birth to its first emperor, Jimmu. Even today the emperor is known as the "Son of the Sun" and the popular name for the country is "Land of the Rising Sun." The current flag design was adopted on Aug. 5, 1854.

Jordan
Constitutional monarchy, SW Asia

Area: 35,637 sq. mi. (92,300 sq. km.)
Population: 6,053,000
Language(s): Arabic, English

Monetary unit: Jordanian dinar
Economy: phosphate mining, cement, chemicals, pharmaceuticals, wheat, fruits, olives, tourism

In 1917 Husayn ibn Ali raised the Arab Revolt flag. With the addition of a white seven-pointed star, this flag was adopted by Transjordan on April 16, 1928, and retained upon the independence of Jordan on March 22, 1946. White is for purity, black for struggle and suffering, red for bloodshed, and green for Arab lands.

Kazakhstan
Republic, W cen. Asia

Area: 1,049,155 sq. mi. (2,717,300 sq. km.)
Population: 15,285,000
Language(s): Kazakh, Russian

Monetary unit: tenge
Economy: oil, mining (manganese, titanium, gold), chemicals, agriculture, livestock, textiles

The flag was adopted in June 1992. Light blue is a traditional color of the nomads of Central Asia; it symbolizes peace and well-being. The golden sun and eagle represent freedom and the high ideals of the Kazakhs. Along the edge is a band of traditional Kazakh ornamentation; the band was originally in red but is now in golden yellow.

Kenya
Republic, E cen. Africa

Area: 224,962 sq. mi. (582,650 sq. km.)
Population: 36,914,000
Language(s): Kiswahili, English

Monetary unit: Kenyan shilling
Economy: coffee, cotton, tea, rice, mining (gold, salt), consumer goods, oil refining, tourism

Upon independence from Britain (Dec. 12, 1963), the Kenyan flag became official. It was based on the flag of the Kenya African National Union. Black is for the people, red for humanity and the struggle for freedom, green for the fertile land, and white for unity and peace. The shield and spears are traditional weapons of the Masai people.

Kiribati
Islands republic, W Pacific

Area: 313 sq. mi. (811 sq. km.)
Population: 107,800
Language(s): English, Kiribati

Monetary unit: Australian dollar
Economy: fishing, agriculture (coconuts, copra, tropical fruits), handicrafts, tourism

Great Britain acquired the Gilbert and Ellice Islands in the 19th century. In 1975 the Gilbert Islands separated from the Ellice Islands to form Kiribati, and a new flag was adopted based on the coat of arms granted to the islands in 1937. It has waves of white and blue, for the Pacific Ocean, as well as a yellow sun and a local frigate bird.

Korea, North
Communist state, E Asia

Area: 46,541 sq. mi. (120,540 sq. km.)
Population: 23,302,000
Language(s): Korean

Monetary unit: North Korean won
Economy: military products, mining (magnesite, precious metals), machinery, textiles

The traditional Korean Taeguk flag (still used by South Korea) was official in North Korea until July 10, 1948, when the current flag was introduced. Its red stripe and star are for the country's commitment to communism, while blue is said to stand for a commitment to peace. The white stripes stand for purity, strength, and dignity.

Korea, South
Republic, E Asia

Area: 38,023 sq. mi. (98,480 sq. km.)
Population: 49,045,000
Language(s): Korean, English

Monetary unit: South Korean won
Economy: electronics, motor vehicles, shipbuilding, chemicals, agriculture, mining, fishing

The flag was adopted in August 1882. Its white background is for peace, while the central emblem represents yin-yang (Korean: *um-yang*), the duality of the universe. The black bars recall sun, moon, earth, heaven and other Confucian principles. Outlawed under Japanese rule, the flag was revived in 1945 and slightly modified in 1950 and 1984.

Kosovo
Republic, SE Europe

Area: 4,203 sq. mi. (10,887 sq. km.)
Population: 2,126,708
Language(s): Albanian, Serbian

Monetary unit: euro
Economy: mining (lignite, lead, zinc, nickel, chrome, aluminum, magnesium), building materials

The flag of Kosovo, adopted at independence in February 2008, shows the shape of Kosovo in yellow on a medium blue field. Six white stars representing the country's major ethnic groups form an arc above the Kosovo silhouette. This design was chosen after a competition having nearly 1000 entries.

Kuwait
Constitutional monarchy, W Asia

Area: 6,880 sq. mi. (17,820 sq. km.)
Population: 2,506,000
Language(s): Arabic

Monetary unit: Kuwaiti dinar
Economy: oil, fishing, construction materials, industrial chemicals

The red flag of Kuwait, in use since World War I, was replaced by the current flag on Oct. 24, 1961, shortly after independence from Britain. The symbolism is from a poem written over six centuries ago. The green stands for Arab lands, black is for battles, white is for the purity of the fighters, and red is for the blood on their swords.

Kyrgyzstan
Republic, W cen. Asia

Area: 76,641 sq. mi. (198,500 sq. km.)
Population: 5,284,000
Language(s): Kyrgyz, Russian, Uzbek

Monetary unit: som
Economy: cotton, wheat, tobacco, wool, mining (gold, mercury, uranium, coal), machinery

The Kyrgyz flag replaced a Soviet-era design on March 3, 1992. The red recalls the flag of the national hero Mansas the Noble. The central yellow sun has 40 rays, corresponding to the followers of Mansas and the tribes he united. On the sun is the stylized view of the roof of a yurt, a traditional nomadic home that is now seldom used.

Laos
Communist state, SE Asia

Area: 91,429 sq. mi. (236,800 sq. km.)
Population: 6,522,000
Language(s): Lao, French, English

Monetary unit: kip
Economy: rice, corn, tobacco, fishing, timber, mining (tin, gypsum), opium

The Lao flag was first used by anti-colonialist forces from the mid-20th century. The white disk honored the Japanese who had supported the Lao independence movement, but it also symbolized a bright future. Red was said to stand for the blood of patriots, and blue was for the promise of future prosperity. The flag was adopted on Dec. 2, 1975.

Latvia
Republic, N Europe

Area: 24,938 sq. mi. (64,589 sq. km.)
Population: 2,260,000
Language(s): Latvian, Russian

Monetary unit: Latvian lat
Economy: wood, wood products, synthetic fibers, chemicals, machinery, electronics, processed foods

The basic flag design was used by a militia unit in 1279, according to a 14th century source. Popularized in the 19th century among anti-Russian nationalists, the flag flew in 1918 and was legally adopted on Jan. 20, 1923. Under Soviet control the flag was suppressed, but it was again legalized in 1988 and flown officially from Feb. 27, 1990.

Lebanon
Republic, SW Asia

Area: 4,015 sq. mi. (10,400 sq. km.)
Population: 3,926,000
Language(s): Arabic, French, English

Monetary unit: Lebanese pound
Economy: banking, agriculture (olives, tobacco), jewelry, cement, oil refining, metal fabricating

On Sept. 1, 1920, French-administered Lebanon adopted a flag based on the French tricolor. The current red-white flag was established by the constitution of 1943, which divided power among the Muslim and Christian sects. On the central stripe is a cedar tree, which is a biblical symbol for holiness, peace, and eternity.

Lesotho
Constitutional monarchy, S Africa

Area: 11,720 sq. mi. (30,355 sq. km.);
Population: 2,125,000
Language(s): Sesotho, English, Zulu

Monetary unit: loti
Economy: wool, mohair, diamonds, agriculture (corn, wheat, beans, sorghum), textiles

This flag was unfurled for the first time on October 4, 2006, to mark the occasion of Lesotho's 40th anniversary of independence from Britain. Lesotho states that the new flag shows it "at peace with itself and its neighbors". Blue signifies rain, white stands for peace, and green indicates prosperity. The black Basotho hat represents the country's indigenous people.

Liberia
Republic, W Africa

Area: ab. 43,000 sq. mi. (111,370 sq. km.)
Population: 3,196,000
Language(s): English, local languages

Monetary unit: Liberian dollar
Economy: rubber processing, rice, palm oil, coffee, cocoa, timber, iron ore, diamonds

In the 19th century land was purchased on the African coast by the American Colonization Society in order to return freed slaves to Africa. On April 9, 1827, a flag based on that of the United States was adopted, featuring a white cross. On Aug. 24, 1847, after independence, the cross was replaced by a star and the number of stripes was reduced.

Libya
Authoritarian state, N Africa

Area: 679,362 sq. mi. (1,759,540 sq. km.)
Population: 6,037,000
Language(s): Arabic, Italian, English

Monetary unit: Libyan dinar
Economy: oil, natural gas, iron, steel, textiles, barley, wheat, dates, olives, fruits

After the coup d'état of 1969, Muammar al-Qaddafi adopted a flag based on the Egyptian flag. When the Egyptian president Anwar el-Sadat made peace with Israel, however, Qaddafi broke diplomatic relations and replaced the flag. In November 1977 he established a plain green banner, symbolizing promises of agricultural wealth.

Liechtenstein
Constitutional monarchy, cen. Europe

Area: 62 sq. mi. (160 sq. km.)
Population: 34,200
Language(s): German

Monetary unit: Swiss franc
Economy: wine, dairy, textiles, pharmaceuticals, precision instruments, tourism

The blue-red flag was given official status in October 1921. At the 1936 Olympics it was learned that this same flag was used by Haiti; thus, in 1937 a yellow crown was added, which symbolizes the unity of the people and their prince. Blue stands for the sky, red for the evening fires in homes. The flag was last modified on Sept. 18, 1982.

Lithuania
Republic, N Europe

Area: 25,174 sq. mi. (65,200 sq. km.)
Population: 3,575,000
Language(s): Lithuanian, Russian, Polish

Monetary unit: litas
Economy: dairy, livestock, food products, textiles, paper, machinery

The tricolor flag of Lithuania was adopted on Aug. 1, 1922. It was long suppressed under Soviet rule until its reestablishment on March 20, 1989. The yellow color suggests ripening wheat and freedom from want. Green is for hope and the forests of the nation, while red stands for love of country, sovereignty, and valor in defense of liberty.

Luxembourg
Constitutional monarchy, W Europe

Area: 998 sq. mi. (2,586 sq. km.)
Population: 480,200
Language(s): German, French

Monetary unit: euro
Economy: wine, livestock, iron and steel, chemicals

In the 19th century the national colors, from the coat of arms of the dukes of Luxembourg, came to be used in a tricolor of red-white-blue, coincidentally the same as the flag of The Netherlands. To distinguish it from the Dutch flag, the proportions were altered and the shade of blue was made lighter. It was recognized by law on Aug. 16, 1972.

Macedonia
Republic, SE Europe

Area: 9,781 sq. mi. (25,333 sq. km.)
Population: 2,056,000
Language(s): Macedonian, Albanian

Monetary unit: Macedonian denar
Economy: wheat, corn, tobacco, iron, steel, chromium, lead, zinc

A "starburst" flag replaced the communist banner on Aug. 11, 1992. The starburst was a symbol of Alexander the Great and his father, Philip of Macedon, but its use by Macedonia was opposed by Greece. Thus on Oct. 6, 1995, the similar "golden sun" flag was chosen instead. The gold and red colors originated in an early Macedonian coat of arms.

Madagascar
Island republic, off SE Africa

Area: 226,657 sq. mi. (587,040 sq. km.)
Population: 19,449,000
Language(s): Malagasy, French

Monetary unit: Madagascar ariary
Economy: tobacco, coffee, sugar, cloves, vanilla, sisal, livestock, graphite, soap

The Madagascar flag was adopted on Oct. 16, 1958, by the newly proclaimed Malagasy Republic, formerly a French colony. The flag combines the traditional Malagasy colors of white and red with a stripe of green. The white and red are said to stand for purity and sovereignty, while the green represents the coastal regions and symbolizes hope.

Malawi
Republic, SE Africa

Area: 45,745 sq. mi. (118,480 sq. km.)
Population: 13,603,000
Language(s): Chichewa, Chinyanja

Monetary unit: Malawian kwacha
Economy: tea, tobacco, peanuts, sorghum, sugar, fishing, textiles, cement

The flag of the Malawi Congress Party was striped black for the African people, red for the blood of martyrs, and green for the vegetation and climate. The country's name means "flaming waters," referring to the setting sun on Lake Malawi. With independence on July 6, 1964, a new flag was created by adding the sun symbol to the party flag.

Malaysia
Constitutional monarchy, SE Asia

Area: 127,317 sq. mi. (329,750 sq. km.)
Population: 24,821,000
Language(s): Malay, English, Chinese

Monetary unit: ringgit
Economy: rubber, palm oil, cocoa, pineapples, natural gas, tin, electronics

The flag hoisted on May 26, 1950, had 11 stripes, a crescent, and an 11-pointed star. The number of stripes and star points was increased to 14 on Sept. 16, 1963. Yellow is a royal color in Malaysia while red, white, and blue indicate connections with the Commonwealth. The crescent is a reminder that the population is mainly Muslim.

Maldives
Islands republic, Indian Ocean

Area: 116 sq. mi. (300 sq. km.)
Population: 369,000
Language(s): Dhivehi, English

Monetary unit: rufiyaa
Economy: coconuts, millet, fishing, tourism

Maldivian ships long used a plain red ensign like those flown by Arabian and African nations. While a British protectorate in the early 20th century, the Maldives adopted a flag which was only slightly altered upon independence (July 26, 1965). The green panel and white crescent are symbolic of Islam, progress, prosperity, and peace.

Mali
Republic, W cen. Africa

Area: 478,767 sq. mi. (1,240,000 sq. km.)
Population: 11,995,000
Language(s): French; local languages

Monetary unit: CFA franc
Economy: food processing (sorghum, rice, millet), mining (phosphate, gold), livestock, leather goods

Designed for the Mali-Senegal union of 1959, the flag originally included a human figure, the Kanaga, in its center. In 1960 Senegal and Mali divided. Muslims in Mali objected to the Kanaga, and on March 1, 1961, the figure was dropped. Green, yellow, and red are the Pan-African colors and are used by many former French territories.

Malta
Island republic, Mediterranean

Area: 122 sq. mi. (316 sq. km.)
Population: 401,900
Language(s): Maltese, English

Monetary unit: euro
Economy: tourism, electronics, ship building and repair, potatoes, tomatoes, citrus fruit

The Maltese flag was supposedly based on an 11th-century coat of arms, and a red flag with a white cross was used by the Knights of Malta from the Middle Ages. The current flag dates from independence within the Commonwealth (Sept. 21, 1964). The George Cross was granted by the British for the heroic defense of the island in World War II.

Marshall Islands
Islands republic, W Pacific

Area: 70 sq. mi. (181 sq. km.)
Population: 61,800
Language(s): Marshallese, English

Monetary unit: U.S. dollar
Economy: subsistence agriculture, fishing, handicrafts, coconut products, breadfruit

The island nation hoisted its flag on May 1, 1979. The blue stands for the ocean. The white is for brightness while the orange is for bravery and wealth. The two stripes joined symbolize the Equator, and they increase in width to show growth and vitality. The rays of the star are for the municipalities; its four long rays recall a Christian cross.

Mauritania
Republic, W Africa

Area: 397,956 sq. mi. (1,030,700 sq. km.)
Population: 3,270,000
Language(s): Arabic, local languages

Monetary unit: ouguiya
Economy: mining (iron ore, copper), millet, rice, dates, livestock, fish processing

In 1958 Mauritania was granted autonomous status within the French Community. The current flag replaced the French tricolor on April 1, 1959, and no changes were made to the design at independence (Nov. 28, 1960). The green background of the flag and its star and crescent are traditional Muslim symbols that have been in use for centuries.

Mauritius
Island republic, Indian Ocean

Area: 788 sq. mi. (2,040 sq. km.)
Population: 1,251,000
Language(s): Creole, French, English

Monetary unit: Mauritian rupee
Economy: sugarcane, molasses, tea, tobacco, textiles, tourism

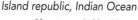

The Mauritius flag was officially adopted when the island gained independence from the United Kingdom in 1968. Designed by the College of Arms in Britain, red is symbolic of the country's struggle for independence; yellow, the bright future; green, the fertile land of the island, and blue, the Indian Ocean.

Mexico
Republic, North America

Area: 759,530 sq. mi. (1,967,183 sq. km.)
Population: 108,701,000
Language(s): Spanish

Monetary unit: Mexican peso
Economy: mining (silver, gold), oil, chemicals, motor vehicles, consumer goods, tourism

The green-white-red tricolor was officially established in 1821. Green is for independence, white for Roman Catholicism, and red for union. The emblem depicts the scene supposedly witnessed by the Aztecs in 1325: an eagle with a snake in its beak standing upon a cactus growing out of rocks in the water. The flag was modified on Sept. 17, 1968.

Micronesia
Islands federation, W Pacific

Area: 271 sq. mi. (702 sq km)
Population: 107,900
Language(s): English, local languages

Monetary unit: U.S. dollar
Economy: tourism, construction, fish processing, handicrafts (wood, pearls), bananas, black pepper

On Nov. 30, 1978, the flag of the former United States trust territory was approved by an interim congress. Based on the symbolism of the territory, the flag has stars for the four states of Micronesia. After sovereignty was granted in 1986, a dark blue background (for the Pacific Ocean) was substituted for the original "United Nations blue."

Moldova
Republic, E Europe

Area: 13,067 sq. mi. (33,843 sq. km.)
Population: 4,320,000
Language(s): Romanian, Russian

Monetary unit: Moldovan leu
Economy: food processing, cereals, fruits and vegetables, wine, sugar, machinery

By 1989, Moldovans protested against communist rule, and the traditional tricolor of blue-yellow-red, which had flown briefly in 1917–18, became a popular symbol. It replaced the communist flag in May 1990 and remained after independence in 1991. The shield has an eagle on whose breast are the head of a wild ox, a crescent, a star, and a flower.

Monaco
Constitutional principality, S Europe

Area: 0.75 sq. mi. (1.95 sq. km.)
Population: 32,700
Language(s): French, English, Italian

Monetary unit: euro
Economy: tourism

The flag of the Principality of Monaco, officially adopted in 1881, contains the heraldic colors of the ruling Grimaldi family. Those colors date to the 14th century and appear on the Grimaldi coat of arms as a series of red lozenges on a white background.

Mongolia
Republic, cen. Asia

Area: 603,909 sq. mi. (1,564,116 sq. km.)
Population: 2,952,000
Language(s): Khalkha Mongol

Monetary unit: togrog/tugrik
Economy: livestock, agriculture, animal products, cashmere, mining (coal, oil, copper, gold)

In 1945, the flag symbolizing communism (red) and Mongol nationalism (blue) was established. Near the hoist is a soyonba, a grouping of philosophical symbols (flame, sun, moon, yin-yang, triangles, and bars). Yellow traditionally stood for Lamaist Buddhism. On Jan. 12, 1992, a five-pointed star (for communism) was removed from the flag.

Montenegro
Republic, SE Europe

Area: 5419 sq. mi. (14,026 sq. km.)
Population: 684,700
Language(s): Serbian, Bosnian, Albanian

Monetary unit: euro
Economy: steelmaking, aluminum, agricultural processing, tourism

The flag of Montenegro was adopted on July 12, 2004. The flag is red with a gold coat of arms in the center. The coat of arms, based on that of the Petrović dynasty, consists of a double-headed golden eagle with a crown above its head, holding a scepter in one claw and the orb in the other, with a breast shield containing a golden lion passant over green grass with blue sky above.

Morocco
Constitutional monarchy, NW Africa

Area: 172,414 sq. mi. (446,550 sq. km.)
Population: 33,757,000
Language(s): Arabic, French

Monetary unit: Moroccan dirham
Economy: food processing, wine, leather goods, fishing, mining (phosphates, copper, silver), tourism

After Morocco was subjected to the rule of France and Spain in the 20th century, the plain red flag, which had been displayed on its ships, was modified on Nov. 17, 1915. To its center was added the ancient pentagram known as the "Seal of Solomon." The flag continued in use even after the French granted independence in 1956.

Mozambique

Republic, SE Africa

Area: 309,496 sq. mi. (801,590 sq. km.)
Population: 20,906,000
Language(s): Portuguese, local languages

Monetary unit: metical
Economy: subsistence agriculture, cashew nuts, sugar, tea, coal, bauxite, aluminum, shrimp

In the early 1960s, anti-Portuguese groups adopted flags of green (for forests), black (for the majority population), white (for rivers and the ocean), gold (for peace and mineral wealth), and red (for the blood of liberation). The current flag was readopted in 1983; on its star are a book, a hoe, and an assault rifle.

Myanmar

Military state, SE Asia

Area: 261,970 sq. mi. (678,500 sq. km.)
Population: 47,374,000
Language(s): Burmese

Monetary unit: kyat
Economy: agricultural products (rice, peanuts, sugarcane), oil, mining (silver, lead, zinc), textiles

The current flag design dates to Jan. 4, 1974. Its 14 stars, for the states and divisions of Myanmar, form a circle around a cogwheel, for industrial workers, and ears and leaves of rice, symbolizing the peasantry. Blue is for truthfulness and strength; red for bravery, unity, and determination; and white for truth, purity, and stead-fastness.

Namibia

Republic, SW Africa

Area: 318,696 sq. mi. (825,418 sq. km.)
Population: 2,055,000
Language(s): English, Afrikaans

Monetary unit: Namibian dollar
Economy: diamonds, copper, zinc, lead, salt, sheep, fishing, food processing

The flag was adopted on Feb. 2, 1990, and hoisted on independence from South Africa, March 21, 1990. Its colors are those of the South West Africa People's Organization: blue (for sky and ocean), red (for heroism and determination), and green (for agriculture). The gold sun represents life and energy while the white stripes are for water resources.

Nepal

Constitutional monarchy, S Asia

Area: 54,363 sq. mi. (147,181 sq. km.)
Population: 28,902,000
Language(s): Nepali, local languages

Monetary unit: Nepalese rupee
Economy: agriculture (rice, wheat, jute, oilseed), livestock, carpets, tourism

Established on Dec. 16, 1962, Nepal's flag consists of two united pennant shapes; it is the only non-rectangular national flag in the world. In the upper segment is a moon with a crescent attached below; in the bottom segment appears a stylized sun. The symbols are for different dynasties and express a hope for the immortality of the nation. The crimson and blue colors are common in Nepali art.

Netherlands

Constitutional monarchy, NW Europe

Area: 16,033 sq. mi. (41,526 sq. km.)
Population: 16,571,000
Language(s): Dutch, Frisian

Monetary unit: euro
Economy: farming, food processing, horticulture, natural gas, chemicals, microelectronics

The history of the Dutch flag dates to the use of orange, white, and blue as the livery colors of William, Prince of Orange, and the use of the tricolor at sea in 1577. By 1660 the color red was substituted for orange. The flag was legalized by pro-French "patriots" on Feb. 14, 1796, and reaffirmed by royal decree on Feb. 19, 1937.

New Zealand

Islands republic, SW Pacific

Area: 103,738 sq. mi. (268,680 sq. km.)
Population: 4,116,000
Language(s): English, Maori

Monetary unit: New Zealand dollar
Economy: food processing, mining (coal, gold), natural gas, manufacturing, banking, insurance, tourism

The Maori of New Zealand accepted British control in 1840, and a colonial flag was adopted on Jan. 15, 1867. It included the Union Jack in the canton and the letters "NZ" at the fly end. Later versions used the Southern Cross. Dominion status was granted on Sept. 26, 1907, and independence on Nov. 25, 1947, but the flag was unchanged.

Nicaragua

Republic, Central America

Area: 49,998 sq. mi. (129,494 sq. km.)
Population: 5,675,000
Language(s): Spanish

Monetary unit: gold córdoba
Economy: coffee, sugar, shrimp, lobster, gold, machinery, chemicals, textiles

On Aug. 21, 1823, a blue-white-blue flag was adopted by the five member states of the United Provinces of Central America, which included Nicaragua. From the mid-19th century various flag designs were used in Nicaragua, but the old flag was readopted in 1908, with a modified coat of arms, and reaffirmed by law on Aug. 27, 1971.

Niger

Republic, W cen. Africa

Area: 489,192 sq. mi. (1,267,000 sq. km.)
Population: 12,895,000
Language(s): French, Hausa

Monetary unit: CFA franc
Economy: subsistence farming, uranium mining, cement, bricks, peanuts, cotton, rice

The flag of Niger was chosen on Nov. 23, 1959. The white color is for purity, innocence, and civic spirit. The orange is for the Sahara Desert and the heroic efforts of citizens to live within it, while the orange central disk represents the sun. The green color stands for agriculture and hope; it is suggestive of the Niger River valley.

Nigeria

Republic, W cen. Africa

Area: 356,669 sq. mi. (923,768 sq. km.)
Population: 135,031,000
Language(s): English, Hausa

Monetary unit: naira
Economy: subsistence farming, oil, rubber, hides, skins, mining (tin), automobile assembly

The Nigerian flag became official upon independence from Britain on Oct. 1, 1960. The flag design is purposefully simple in order not to favor the symbolism of any particular ethnic or religious group. Agriculture is represented by the green stripes while unity and peace are symbolized by the white stripe.

Norway

Constitutional monarchy, N Europe

Area: 125,182 sq. mi. (323,802 sq. km.)
Population: 4,628,000
Language(s): Norwegian

Monetary unit: Norwegian krone
Economy: gas, oil, food processing, fishing, timber, mining, chemicals, high-tech products, tourism

The first distinctive Norwegian flag was created in 1814 while the country was under Swedish rule. It was based on the red Danish flag with its white cross. In 1821 the Norwegian parliament developed the current flag design. From 1844 to 1899, six years before independence, the official flag included a symbol of Swedish-Norwegian union.

Oman

Sultanate, SE Arabian Peninsula

Area: 82,031 sq. mi. (212,460 sq. km.)
Population: 3,205,000
Language(s): Arabic, English, Urdu

Monetary unit: Omani rial
Economy: oil, natural gas, dates, cereals, limes, fishing

The flag dates to Dec. 17, 1970, and it was altered on Nov. 18, 1995. The white is for peace and prosperity, red is for battles, and green is for the fertility of the land. Unofficially, white recalls the imamate, red the sultanate, and green Al-Jabal Al-Akhdar ("The Green Mountain"). The coat of arms has two swords, a dagger, and a belt.

Pakistan

Republic, S Asia

Area: 310,403 sq. mi. (803,940 sq. km.)
Population: 164,742,000
Language(s): Urdu, Punjabi, English

Monetary unit: Pakistani rupee
Economy: textiles, food processing, pharmaceuticals, coal, gypsum, natural gas, fertilizer, chemicals

On Dec. 30, 1906, the All India Muslim League approved this typically Muslim flag, with its star and crescent. At independence (Aug. 14, 1947) a white stripe was added for minority religious groups. Also symbolized are prosperity and peace by the green and white colors, progress by the crescent, and knowledge and light by the star.

Palau
Islands republic, W Pacific

Area: 177 sq. mi. (458 sq. km.)
Population: 20,800
Language(s): Palauan, English, Filipino

Monetary unit: U.S. dollar
Economy: tourism, subsistence farming, fishing, textiles, handicrafts

Approved on Oct. 22, 1980, and hoisted on Jan. 1, 1981, the Palauan flag was left unaltered at independence in 1994. The golden disk represents the full moon, which is said on Palau to be propitious for fishing, planting, and other activities and gives the people "a feeling of warmth, tranquillity, peace, love, and domestic unity."

Panama
Republic, Central America

Area: 30,193 sq. mi. (78,200 sq. km.)
Population: 3,242,000
Language(s): Spanish, English

Monetary unit: balboa, U.S. dollar
Economy: Panama Canal, banking, flagship registry, tourism, food processing, textiles, cement

The Panamanian flag became official on July 4, 1904, after independence from Colombia was won through the intervention of the United States, which was determined to construct the Panama Canal. The flag was influenced by the United States, and its quartered design was said to symbolize the power sharing of Panama's two main political parties.

Papua New Guinea
Islands commonwealth, W Pacific

Area: 178,704 sq. mi. (462,840 sq. km.)
Population: 5,796,000
Language(s): Melanesian pidgin

Monetary unit: kina
Economy: subsistence farming, palm oil, plywood, copper, oil, silver, coffee, tea

The formerly German-, British-, and Australian-controlled territory officially recognized its flag on March 11, 1971, and flag usage was extended to ships at independence (Sept. 16, 1975). The colors red and black are shown extensively in local art and clothing. Featured emblems are a bird of paradise and the Southern Cross constellation.

Paraguay
Republic, South America

Area: 157,047 sq. mi. (406,750 sq. km.)
Population: 6,669,000
Language(s): Spanish, Guarani

Monetary unit: guarani
Economy: food processing (meat, sugar, vegetable oils), wood products, tobacco, cotton, cement, textiles

Under the dictator José Gaspar Rodríguez de Francia (1814–40) the French colors were adopted for the flag. The coat of arms (a golden star surrounded by a wreath) is on the obverse side, but the seal of the treasury (a lion, staff, and liberty cap, with the motto "Peace and Justice") is on the reverse; the flag is unique in this respect.

Peru
Republic, South America

Area: 496,226 sq. mi. (1,285,220 sq. km.)
Population: 28,675,000
Language(s): Spanish, Quechua, Aymara

Monetary unit: nuevo sol
Economy: mining (copper, zinc, silver), oil, petroleum products, fishing, cotton, sugar, coffee, coca

Partisans in the early 19th century adopted a red-white-red flag resembling that of Spain, but they soon made its stripes vertical. In 1825, the current design was established. The shield includes figures symbolic of national wealth—the vicuna (a relative of the alpaca), a cinchona tree, and a cornucopia with gold and silver coins.

Philippines
Archipelago republic, W Pacific

Area: 115,831 sq. mi. (300,000 sq. km.)
Population: 76,498,735
Language(s): Filipino, English

Monetary unit: Philippine peso
Economy: copra, fruit, sugar, timber, iron ore, gold, nickel, textiles, electronics assembly

In 1898, during the Spanish-American War, Filipinos established the basic flag in use today; it was officially adopted in 1936. The white triangle is for liberty. The golden sun and stars are for the three main areas of the Philippines: Luzon, the Visayan Islands, and Mindanao. The red color is for courage and the blue color is for sacrifice.

Poland
Republic, cen. Europe

Area: 120,728 sq. mi. (312,685 sq. km.)
Population: 38,518,000
Language(s): Polish

Monetary unit: zloty
Economy: machine building, iron and steel, coal mining, chemicals, shipbuilding, food processing

The colors of the Polish flag originated in its coat of arms, a white eagle on a red shield, dating from 1295. The precise symbolism of the colors is not known, however. Poland's simple flag of white-red horizontal stripes was adopted on Aug. 1, 1919. The flag was left unaltered under the Soviet-allied communist regime (1944 to 1990).

Portugal
Republic, W Europe

Area: 35,672 sq. mi. (92,391 sq. km.)
Population: 10,643,000
Language(s): Portuguese; Mirandese

Monetary unit: euro
Economy: fishing, cork, oil refining, chemicals, communications equipment, shipbuilding, wine, tourism

The central shield includes five smaller shields, for a victory over the Moors in 1139, and a red border with gold castles. Behind the shield is an armillary sphere (an astronomical device) recalling world explorations and the kingdom of Brazil. Red and green were used in many early Portuguese flags. The current flag dates to June 30, 1911.

Qatar
Emirate, E Arabian Peninsula

Area: 4416 sq. mi. (11,437 sq. km.)
Population: 907,200
Language(s): Arabic, English

Monetary unit: Qatari rial
Economy: oil, natural gas, fishing, ammonia, fertilizers, cement, commercial ship repair

The 1868 treaty between Great Britain and Qatar may have inspired the creation of the flag. Qataris chose mauve or maroon instead of red (a more typical color among Arab countries) perhaps to distinguish it from the flag used in Bahrain. Passages from the Quran, in Arabic script, have sometimes been added to the flag.

Romania
Republic, E Europe

Area: 91,699 sq. mi. (237,500 sq. km.)
Population: 22,276,000
Language(s): Romanian, Hungarian

Monetary unit: Romanian leu
Economy: oil, natural gas, light machinery, motor vehicles, mining, timber, metallurgy, chemicals

In 1834, Walachia, an ancient region of Romania, chose a naval ensign with stripes of red, blue, and yellow. The modern Romanian tricolor was created in 1848 and flown for a brief time. In 1867, Romania reestablished the vertical tricolor, and with the fall of the 20th-century communist regime, it was defined on Dec. 27, 1989.

Russia
Republic, E Europe and N Asia

Area: 6,592,769 sq. mi. (17,075,272 sq. km.)
Population: 141,378,000
Language(s): Russian

Monetary unit: Russian ruble
Economy: oil, natural gas, transportation, medical, electronic equipment, chemicals, agriculture

Tsar Peter the Great visited the Netherlands in order to modernize the Russian navy, and in 1699, he chose a Dutch-influenced flag for Russian ships. The flag soon became popular on land as well. After the Russian Revolution, it was replaced by the communist red banner, but the tricolor again became official on Aug. 21, 1991.

Rwanda
Republic, E cen. Africa

Area: 10,169 sq. mi. (26,338 sq. km.)
Population: 9,908,000
Language(s): Kinyarwanda, French, English, Swahili

Monetary unit: Rwandan franc
Economy: cement, agricultural products, plastic goods, cigarettes, agriculture, minerals

In 2001, Rwanda adopted a new flag, to promote national unity after the genocide of the early 1990s. The large blue stripe represents happiness and peace, and the smaller yellow and green stripes are for economic development and for prosperity. The sun with its 24 rays stands for unity, transparency, and enlightenment.

Saint Kitts and Nevis
Islands republic, Caribbean

Area: 101 sq. mi. (261 sq. km.)
Population: 39,300
Language(s): English

Monetary unit: East Caribbean dollar
Economy: tourism, sugar processing, electronic components, banking, beverages

On Sept. 18, 1983, at the time of its independence from Britain, St. Kitts and Nevis hoisted the current flag. It has green (for fertility), red (for the struggle against slavery and colonialism), and black (for African heritage). The yellow flanking stripes are for sunshine, and the two stars, one for each island, are for hope and liberty.

Saint Lucia
Island republic, Caribbean

Area: 238 sq. mi. (616 sq. km.)
Population: 170,600
Language(s): English, French dialect

Monetary unit: East Caribbean dollar
Economy: tourism, cocoa, spices, coconuts, bananas, beverages, electronic components

The flag was hoisted on March 1, 1967, when the former colony assumed a status of association with the United Kingdom; it was slightly altered in 1979. The blue represents Atlantic and Caribbean waters. The white and black colors are for racial harmony, while the black triangle also represents volcanoes. The yellow triangle is for sunshine.

Saint Vincent and the Grenadines
Archipelago republic, Caribbean

Area: 150 sq. mi. (389 sq. km.)
Population: 118,100
Language(s): English, French

Monetary unit: East Caribbean dollar
Economy: tourism, bananas, coconuts, spices, cement, fishing

At independence from Britain in 1979, a national flag was designed, but it was replaced by the current flag on Oct. 22, 1985. The three green diamonds are arranged in the form of a V. Green is for the rich vegetation and the vitality of the people, yellow is for sand and personal warmth, and blue is for sea and sky.

Samoa
Islands monarchy, SW Pacific

Area: 1137 sq. mi. (2944 sq. km.)
Population: 214,300
Language(s): Samoan, English

Monetary unit: tala
Economy: fishing, coconut oil and cream, copra, pineapples, automotive parts, textiles, beer

The first national flag of Samoa may date to 1873. Under British administration, a version of the current flag was introduced on May 26, 1948. On Feb. 2, 1949, a fifth star, as can be seen in the sky, was added to the Southern Cross. White in the flag is said to stand for purity, blue for freedom, and red for courage. The flag was left unaltered upon independence in 1962.

San Marino
Republic, enclave in Italy

Area: 24 sq. mi. (61 sq. km.)
Population: 29,600
Language(s): Italian

Monetary unit: euro
Economy: tourism, banking, textiles, electronics, ceramics, wine and cheeses

The colors of the flag, blue and white, were first used in the national cockade in 1797. The coat of arms in its present form was adopted on April 6, 1862, when the crown was added as a symbol of national sovereignty. Also in the coat of arms are three towers (Guaita, Cesta, and Montale) from the fortifications on Mount Titano.

São Tomé and Príncipe
Islands republic, off W Africa

Area: 386 sq. mi. (1001 sq. km.)
Population: 199,600
Language(s): Portuguese

Monetary unit: dobra
Economy: cocoa and tropical fruits, some light construction, textiles, soap

The national flag was adopted upon independence from Portugal on July 12, 1975. Its colors are associated with Pan-African independence. The red triangle stands for equality and the nationalist movement. The stars are for the African population living on the nation's two main islands. Green is for vegetation and yellow is for the tropical sun.

Saudi Arabia
Islamic kingdom, Arabian Peninsula

Area: ab. 756,985 sq. mi. (2,149,690 sq. km.)
Population: 27,601,000
Language(s): Arabic

Monetary unit: Saudi riyal
Economy: oil and natural gas, gypsum, dates, wheat, commercial ship and aircraft repair

The Saudi flag, made official in 1932, but altered in 1968, originated in the military campaigns of Muhammad. The color green is associated with Fatima, the Prophet's daughter, and the Arabic inscription is translated as "There is no God but Allah and Muhammad is the Prophet of Allah." The saber symbolizes the militancy of the faith.

Senegal
Republic, W Africa

Area: 75,749 sq. mi. (196,190 sq. km.)
Population: 12,522,000
Language(s): French, local languages

Monetary unit: CFA franc
Economy: agricultural (peanuts) and fish processing, mining, petroleum refining

In a federation with French Sudan (now Mali) on April 4, 1959, Senegal used a flag with a human figure in the center. After the federation broke up in August 1960, Senegal substituted a green star for the central figure. Green is for hope and religion, yellow is for natural riches and labor, and red is for independence, life, and socialism.

Serbia
Republic, SE Europe

Area: 34,139 sq. mi. (88,361 sq. km.)
Population: 10,150,000
Language(s): Serbian

Monetary unit: Serbian dinar
Economy: machinery, electronics, chemicals, pharmaceuticals, electrical equipment, mining, agriculture

The Pan-Slavic colors (blue, white, and red) have been in the flag from Oct. 31, 1918. The coat of arms, centered vertically and shifted left of center, was added following the independence of Montenegro from the state union in 2004. On June 8, 2006, the new flag was hoisted in front of the United Nations building in New York City for the first time.

Seychelles
Islands republic, Indian Ocean

Area: 176 sq. mi. (455 sq. km.)
Population: 81,900
Language(s): Creole, English

Monetary unit: Seychelles rupee
Economy: fishing, tourism, food processing (coconuts, vanilla, cinnamon), boat building, printing

The former British colony underwent a revolution in 1977. The government was democratized in 1993, and on Jan. 8, 1996, a new flag was designed. The blue color is for sky and sea, yellow is for the sun, red is for the people and their work for unity and love, white is for social justice and harmony, and green is for the land and natural environment.

Sierra Leone
Republic, W Africa

Area: 27,699 sq. mi. (71,740 sq. km.)
Population: 6,145,000
Language(s): English, Creole

Monetary unit: leone
Economy: diamonds, small-scale manufacturing, petroleum refining, coffee, cocoa, ginger

Under British colonial control, Sierra Leone was founded as a home for freed slaves. With independence on April 27, 1961, the flag was hoisted. Its stripes stand for agriculture and the mountains (green); unity and justice (white); and the aspiration to contribute to world peace, especially through the use of the natural harbor at Freetown (blue).

Singapore
Island republic, SE Asia

Area: 267 sq. mi. (693 sq. km.)
Population: 4,553,000
Language(s): Mandarin Chinese, Malay, English

Monetary unit: Singapore dollar
Economy: banking, electronics, chemicals, oil drilling equipment, petroleum and rubber processing, shipbuilding

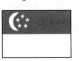

On Dec. 3, 1959, the flag was acquired, and it was retained after separation from Malaysia on Aug. 9, 1965. The red and white stripes stand for universal brotherhood, equality, purity, and virtue. The crescent symbolizes the growth of a young country, while the five stars are for democracy, peace, progress, justice, and equality.

Slovakia
Republic, cen. Europe

Area: 18,859 sq. mi. (48,845 sq. km.)
Population: 5,448,000
Language(s): Slovak, Hungarian

Monetary unit: Slovak koruna
Economy: metal products, nuclear fuel, chemicals, electrical and optical apparatus, rubber products

In 1189, the kingdom of Hungary (including Slovakia) introduced a double-barred cross in its coat of arms; this symbol was altered in 1848–49 by Slovak nationalists. After a period of communist rule, the tricolor was made official in 1989. On Sept. 3, 1992, the shield was added to the white-blue-red flag to differentiate it from the flag of Russia.

Slovenia
Republic, S cen. Europe

Area: 7827 sq. mi. (20,273 sq. km.)
Population: 2,009,000
Language(s): Slovenian, Serbo-Croatian

Monetary unit: euro
Economy: metal products, lead and zinc smelting, electronics, wood products, textiles, chemicals

Under the current flag, Slovenia proclaimed independence on June 25, 1991, but it was opposed for a time by the Yugoslav army. The flag is the same as that of Russia and Slovakia except for the coat of arms. It depicts the peaks of Triglav (the nation's highest mountain), the waves of the Adriatic coast, and three stars on a blue background.

Solomon Islands
Archipelago republic, SW Pacific

Area: 10,985 sq. mi. (28,450 sq. km.);
Population: 566,800
Language(s): Melanesian dialect, English

Monetary unit: Solomon Islands dollar
Economy: fishing, timber, copra, rice, palm oil, cocoa

The flag was introduced on Nov. 18, 1977, eight months before independence from Britain. The yellow stripe stands for the sun. The green triangle is for the trees and crops of the fertile land, while the blue triangle symbolizes rivers, rain, and the ocean. The five stars represented the original five districts of the island.

Somalia
Transitional state, E Africa

Area: 246,201 sq. mi. (637,657 sq. km.)
Population: 9,119,000
Language(s): Somali, Arabic

Monetary unit: Somali shilling
Economy: sugar refining, textiles, wireless communication, livestock, bananas, hides, fish

From the mid-19th century, areas in the Horn of Africa with Somali populations were divided between Ethiopia, France, Britain, and Italy. On Oct. 12, 1954, with the partial unification of these areas, the flag was adopted with a white star, each point referring to a Somali homeland. The colors were influenced by the colors of the United Nations.

South Africa
Republic, S Africa

Area: 471,011 sq. mi. (1,219,912 sq. km.)
Population: 44,000,000
Language(s): Afrikaans, English, local languages

Monetary unit: rand
Economy: mining (platinum, gold, chromium, diamonds), machinery, textiles, chemicals, automobiles, livestock

With the decline of apartheid, the flag was hoisted on April 27, 1994, and confirmed in 1996. Its six colors collectively represent Zulus, English or Afrikaners, Muslims, supporters of the African National Congress, and other groups. The Y-symbol stands for "merging history and present political realities" into a united and prosperous future.

Spain
Constitutional monarchy, SW Europe

Area: 194,897 sq. mi. (504,782 sq. km.)
Population: 40,448,000
Language(s): Castilian Spanish, Catalan

Monetary unit: euro
Economy: textiles, metal products, chemicals, shipbuilding, automobiles, tourism, pharmaceuticals, medical equipment

The colors of the flag have no official symbolic meaning. Introduced in 1785, by King Charles III, the flag was changed only under the Spanish Republic (1931–39). Under different regimes, however, the coat of arms has been altered. The current design dates from Dec. 18, 1981, with the death of Francisco Franco and the resurgence of democracy.

Sri Lanka
Island republic, off SE India

Area: 25,332 sq. mi. (65,610 sq. km.)
Population: 20,926,000
Language(s): Sinhala, Tamil, English

Monetary unit: Sri Lankan rupee
Economy: rubber processing, tea, telecommunications, insurance, banking, gemstones, textiles, tourism

From the 5th century BC, the Lion flag was a symbol of the Sinhalese people. The flag was replaced by the Union Jack in 1815, but readopted upon independence in 1948. The stripes of green (for Muslims) and orange (for Hindus) were added in 1951. In 1972, four leaves of the Bo tree were added as a symbol of Buddhism; the leaves were altered in 1978.

Sudan
Military state, E cen. Africa

Area: 967,500 sq. mi. (2,505,825 sq. km.)
Population: 39,379,000
Language(s): Arabic

Monetary unit: Sudanese pound
Economy: oil, cotton processing, textiles, petroleum refining, pharmaceuticals

The flag was first hoisted on May 20, 1970. It uses Pan-Arab colors. Black is for al-Mahdi (a leader in the 1800s) and the name of the country (sudan in Arabic means black); white recalls the revolutionary flag of 1924 and suggests peace and optimism; red is for patriotic martyrs, socialism, and progress; and green is for prosperity and Islam.

Suriname
Republic, South America

Area: 63,039 sq. mi. (163,270 sq. km.)
Population: 470,800
Language(s): Dutch, English, Surinamese

Monetary unit: Suriname dollar
Economy: bauxite and gold mining, alumina production, oil, food processing (fish, shrimp)

Adopted on Nov. 21, 1975, four days before independence from the Dutch, the flag of Suriname features green stripes for jungles and agriculture, white for justice and freedom, and red for the progressive spirit of a young nation. The yellow star is symbolic of the unity of the country, its golden future, and the people's spirit of sacrifice.

Swaziland
Kingdom, SE Africa

Area: 6704 sq. mi. (17,363 sq. km.)
Population: 1,133,000
Language(s): Swati, English

Monetary unit: lilangeni
Economy: mining (coal, asbestos), wood pulp, sugar, soft drink concentrates, textiles

The flag dates to the creation of a military banner in 1941, when Swazi troops were preparing for the Allied invasion of Italy. On April 25, 1967, it was hoisted as the national flag. The crimson stripe stands for past battles, yellow for mineral wealth, and blue for peace. Featured are a Swazi war shield, two spears, and a "fighting stick."

Sweden
Constitutional monarchy, N Europe

Area: 173,732 sq. mi. (449,964 sq. km.)
Population: 9,031,000
Language(s): Swedish

Monetary unit: Swedish krona
Economy: steel, chemicals, paper, tourism, precision equipments, processed foods, motor vehicles

From the 14th century, the coat of arms of Sweden had a blue field with three golden crowns, and the earlier Folkung dynasty used a shield of blue and white wavy stripes with a gold lion. The off-center "Scandinavian cross" was influenced by the flag of the rival kingdom of Denmark. The current flag law was adopted on July 1, 1906.

Switzerland
Republic, cen. Europe

Area: 15,942 sq. mi. (41,290 sq. km.)
Population: 7,555,000
Language(s): French, German, Italian, Romansh

Monetary unit: Swiss franc
Economy: machinery, watches, precisio instruments, chemicals, textiles, food products, dairy, wines

The Swiss flag is ultimately based on the war flag of the Holy Roman Empire. Schwyz, one of the original three cantons of the Swiss Confederation, placed a narrow white cross in the corner of its flag in 1240. This was also used in 1339 at the Battle for Laupen. Following the 1848 constitution, the flag was recognized by the army, and it was established as the national flag on land on Dec. 12, 1889.

Syria
Authoritarian state, SW Asia

Area: 71,498 sq. mi. (185,180 sq. km.)
Population: 19,315,000
Language(s): Arabic, Kurdish, Armenian

Monetary unit: Syrian pound
Economy: petroleum, textiles, food processing, phosphate mining, cement

In 1918 the Arab Revolt flag flew over Syria, which joined Egypt in the United Arab Republic in 1958, and based its new flag on that of the Egyptian revolution of 1952; its stripes were red-white-black, with two green stars for the constituent states. In 1961 Syria broke from the union, but it readopted the flag on March 29, 1980.

Tajikistan
Republic, W cen. Asia

Area: 55,251 sq. mi. (143,100 sq. km.)
Population: 7,077,000
Language(s): Tajik, Russian

Monetary unit: somoni
Economy: mining (aluminum, zinc), chemicals, cement, cotton, fruits, vegetable oil, textiles

Following independence from the Soviet Union in 1991, Tajikistan developed a new flag on Nov. 24, 1992. The green stripe is for agriculture, while red is for sovereignty. White is for the main crop—cotton. The central crown contains seven stars representing unity among workers, peasants, intellectuals, and other social classes.

Tanzania
Republic, E Africa

Area: 364,900 sq. mi. (945,087 sq. km.)
Population: 39,384,000
Language(s): Swahili, English, Arabic

Monetary unit: Tanzanian shilling
Economy: agriculture (coffee, sugar, cashews, cloves), food processing, mining (diamonds, coal, salt)

In April 1964 Tanganyika and Zanzibar united, and in July their flag traditions melded to create the current design. The black stripe is for the majority population, while green is for the rich agricultural resources of the land. Mineral wealth is reflected in the yellow narrow borders, while the Indian Ocean is symbolized by blue.

Thailand
Constitutional monarchy, SE Asia

Area: 198,457 sq. mi. (514,000 sq. km.)
Population: 65,068,000
Language(s): Thai, English

Monetary unit: baht
Economy: tourism, textiles, jewelry, electronic components, food processing, mining (tungsten, tin)

In the 17th century, the flag of Thailand was plain red, and Thai ships in 1855 displayed a flag with a central white elephant as a symbol of good fortune. The Thai king replaced the elephant with two white stripes in 1916 and added the blue stripe on Sept. 28, 1917. Red symbolizes the blood of patriots, white is for Buddhism, and blue is for royal guidance.

Togo
Republic, W Africa

Area: 21,925 sq. mi. (56,785 sq. km.)
Population: 5,702,000
Language(s): French, local languages

Monetary unit: CFA franc
Economy: cocoa, coffee, cotton, phosphate mining, cement, handicrafts, textiles

On April 27, 1960, Togo became independent from France under the current flag. Its stripes correspond to the administrative regions and symbolize that the population depends on the land for its sustenance (green) and its own labor for development (yellow). The red is for love, fidelity, and charity, while the white star is for purity and unity.

Tonga
Archipelago constit. mon., SW Pacific

Area: 289 sq. mi. (748 sq. km.)
Population: 117,000
Language(s): Tongan, English

Monetary unit: pa'anga
Economy: agriculture (tropical fruits, vanilla beans, coffee, ginger, black pepper), tourism, fishing

The colors red and white were popular in the Pacific long before the arrival of Europeans. The Tonga constitution (Nov. 4, 1875) established the flag, which was created by King George Tupou I with the advice of a missionary. The cross was chosen as a symbol of the widespread Christian religion, and the color red was related to the blood of Jesus.

Trinidad and Tobago
Islands republic, Caribbean

Area: 1980 sq. mi. (5128 sq. km.)
Population: 1,057,000
Language(s): English, French, Spanish

Monetary unit: Trinidad & Tobago dollar
Economy: oil, natural gas, asphalt, chemicals, tourism, fishing, citrus fruits, bananas, coffee, sugar

Hoisted on independence day, Aug. 31, 1962, the flag symbolizes earth, water, and fire as well as past, present, and future. Black also is a symbol of unity, strength, and purpose. White recalls the equality and purity of the people and the sea that unites them. Red is for the sun, the vitality of the people and nation, friendliness, and courage.

Tunisia
Republic, N Africa

Area: 63,170 sq. mi. (163,610 sq. km.)
Population: 10,276,000
Language(s): Arabic, French

Monetary unit: Tunisian dinar
Economy: petroleum, mining (phosphate, iron ore), tourism, textiles, citrus fruit, dates, almonds, olives

The Tunisian flag, established in 1835, contains the crescent and moon, a symbol used by the Ottoman Empire but dating from the ancient Egyptians and Phoenicians. More as a cultural than a religious symbol, the crescent and star came to be associated with Islam because of its widespread adoption in Muslim nations.

Turkey
Republic, SE Europe and SW Asia

Area: 301,384 sq. mi. (780,580 sq. km.)
Population: 71,159,000
Language(s): Turkish, Kurdish

Monetary unit: Turkish lira
Economy: textiles, food processing (fruit, nuts), tobacco, cotton, iron and steel, cement, chemicals

In June 1793 the flag was established for the navy, although its star had eight points instead of the current five (since about 1844). This design was reconfirmed in 1936 following the revolution led by Ataturk. Various myths are associated with the symbolism of the red color and the star and crescent, but none really explains their origins.

Turkmenistan
Authoritarian state, W cen. Asia

Area: 188,457 sq. mi. (488,100 sq. km.)
Population: 5,097,000
Language(s): Turkmen, Russian, Uzbek

Monetary unit: Turkmen manat
Economy: oil, natural gas, cotton, fruit, sheep, silk, textiles

The flag was introduced on Feb. 19, 1992. Its stripe contains intricate designs for five Turkmen tribes. Its green background is for Islam, and its crescent symbolizes faith in a bright future. The stars are for the human senses and the states of matter (liquid, solid, gas, crystal, and plasma). On Feb. 19, 1997, an olive wreath was added to the stripe.

Tuvalu
Archipelago monarchy, SW Pacific

Area: 10 sq. mi. (26 sq. km.)
Population: 12,000
Language(s): Tuvaluan, English, Samoan

Monetary unit: Tuvaluan dollar
Economy: subsistence farming (tropical fruits) and fishing, handicrafts

On Oct. 1, 1978, three years after separating from the Gilbert Islands, Tuvalu became independent under the current flag. The stars represent the atolls and islands of the country. The Union Jack recalls links with Britain and the Commonwealth. Replaced by supporters of republicanism on Oct. 1, 1995, the flag was reinstated on April 11, 1997.

Uganda
Republic, E cen. Africa

Area: 91,136 sq. mi. (236,040 sq. km.)
Population: 30,263,000
Language(s): English, local languages

Monetary unit: Ugandan shilling
Economy: coffee, tea, sugar, fish and fish products, gold, copper, cotton, flowers, cement, steel

The crested crane symbol was selected by the British for Uganda. The flag, established for independence on Oct. 9, 1962, was based on the flag of the ruling Uganda People's Congress (which has three black-yellow-red stripes), with the addition of the crane in the center. Black stands for the people, yellow for sunshine, and red for brotherhood.

Ukraine
Republic, E Europe

Area: 233,090 sq. mi. (603,700 sq. km.)
Population: 46,300,000
Language(s): Ukrainian, Russian

Monetary unit: hryvnia
Economy: coal, metals, machinery and transport equipment, chemicals, sugar, sunflowers, livestock

The first national flag of Ukraine, adopted in 1848, had equal stripes of yellow over blue and was based on the coat of arms of the city of Lviv. In 1918 the stripes were reversed to reflect the symbolism of blue skies over golden wheat fields. A red Soviet banner flew from 1949, but it was replaced by the blue-yellow bicolor on Jan. 28, 1992.

United Arab Emirates
Emirate federation, SE Arabian Peninsula

Area: about 32,000 sq. mi. (83,600 sq. km.)
Population: 4,444,000
Language(s): Arabic, Persian, English

Monetary unit: Emirati dirham
Economy: oil, fishing, aluminum, commercial ship repair, dates, vegetables, limes, textiles

On Dec. 2, 1971, six small Arab states formed the United Arab Emirates, and a seventh state joined on Feb. 11, 1972. The flag took its colors from the Arab Revolt flag of 1917. The colors are included in a 13th-century poem which speaks of green Arab lands defended in black battles by blood-red swords of Arabs whose deeds are pure white.

United Kingdom
Constit. monarchy, off NW Europe

Area: 94,526 sq. mi. (244,820 sq. km.)
Population: 60,776,000
Language(s): English, Welsh, Scottish Gaelic

Monetary unit: British pound
Economy: transportation, communications equipment, petroleum, publishing, consumer goods, food production

Within the Union Jack are combined the crosses of St. George (a symbol of England), St. Andrew (Scotland), and St. Patrick (Ireland). Its earliest form, called the "Union Flag," or "Great Union," was designed in 1606. The current flag design has been in use since Jan. 1, 1801, when Great Britain and Ireland were joined.

United States
Republic, North America

Area: 3,620,067 sq. mi. (9,375,974 sq. km.)
Population: 301,140,000
Language(s): English, Spanish

Monetary unit: U.S. dollar
Economy: transportation, communications equipment, petroleum, publishing, consumer goods, food production

The Stars and Stripes has white stars corresponding to the states of the union (50 since July 4, 1960), as well as stripes for the 13 original states. The first unofficial national flag, hoisted on Jan. 1, 1776, had the British Union flag in the canton. The official flag dates to June 14, 1777; its design was standardized in 1912 and 1934.

Uruguay
Republic, South America

Area: 68,039 sq. mi. (176,220 sq. km.)
Population: 3,461,000
Language(s): Spanish

Monetary unit: Uruguayan peso
Economy: food processing, meatpacking, electrical, transportation equipment, petroleum, textiles, chemicals

The flag adopted on Dec. 16, 1828, combined symbols of Argentina with the flag pattern of the United States. It was last altered on July 11, 1830. On the canton is the golden "Sun of May," which was seen on May 25, 1810, as a favorable omen for anti-Spanish forces in Buenos Aires, Argentina. The stripes are for the original Uruguayan departments.

Uzbekistan
Authoritarian state, W cen. Asia

Area: 172,742 sq. mi. (447,400 sq. km.)
Population: 27,780,000
Language(s): Uzbek, Russian, Tajik

Monetary unit: Uzbekistani soum
Economy: cotton, oil, natural gas, gold, copper, chemicals, machinery

The flag of the former Soviet republic was legalized on Nov. 18, 1991. The blue is for water but also recalls the 14th-century ruler Timur. The green is for nature, fertility, and new life. The white is for peace and purity; red is for human life force. The stars are for the months and the Zodiac, while the moon is for the new republic and Islam.

Vanuatu
Archipelago republic, SW Pacific

Area: 4710 sq. mi. (12,200 sq. km.)
Population: 212,000
Language(s): Bislama, local languages

Monetary unit: vatu
Economy: fishing, financial services, tourism, copra, cocoa, coffee

The flag was hoisted upon independence from France and Britain, on July 30, 1980. Black is for the soil and the people, green for vegetation, and red for local religious traditions such as the sacrifice of pigs. On the triangle are two crossed branches and a full-round pig's tusk, a holy symbol. The horizontal "Y" is for peace and Christianity.

Venezuela
Republic, South America

Area: 352,145 sq. mi. (912,050 sq. km.)
Population: 26,024,000
Language(s): Spanish

Monetary unit: bolivar
Economy: oil, natural gas, iron ore, gold, chemicals, motor vehicles, food processing, textiles

The Venezuelan flag was adopted on March 18, 1864. Yellow was originally said to stand for the gold of the New World, separated by the blue of the Atlantic Ocean from "bloody Spain," symbolized by red. The stars are for the original seven provinces. In the upper hoist corner, the national arms are added to flags which serve the government.

Vietnam
Communist state, SE Asia

Area: 127,244 sq. mi. (329,560 sq.km.)
Population: 85,262,000
Language(s): Vietnamese, English

Monetary unit: dong
Economy: rice, corn, coffee, sugarcane, fishing, textiles, rubber, coal, steel, fertilizer, cement

On Sept. 29, 1945, Vietnamese communists adopted the red flag in use today. On July 4, 1976, following the defeat of the American-sponsored government in the south, the flag became official throughout the nation. The five points of the star are said to stand for the proletariat, peasantry, military, intellectuals, and petty bourgeoisie.

Yemen
Republic, S Arabian Peninsula

Area: 203,850 sq. mi. (527,970 sq. km.)
Population: 22,231,000
Language(s): Arabic

Monetary unit: Yemeni rial
Economy: agriculture, petroleum refining, textiles, leather goods, food processing, handicrafts

Revolutions broke out in North Yemen in 1962 and in South Yemen in 1967. In 1990 the two states unified, and that May 23 the tricolor was adopted, its design influenced by the former United Arab Republic. The black is for the dark days of the past, white for the bright future, and red for the blood shed for independence and unity.

Zambia
Republic, S cen. Africa

Area: 290,586 sq. mi. (752,614 sq. km.)
Population: 11,477,000
Language(s): English, local languages

Monetary unit: Zambian kwacha
Economy: mining (copper, gold, cobalt), corn, tobacco, peanuts, cotton, livestock, textiles

Zambia separated from British rule on Oct. 24, 1964. Its flag, based on the flag of the United National Independence Party, has a green background for agriculture, red for the freedom struggle, black for the African people, and orange for copper. The orange eagle appeared in the colonial coat of arms of 1939. It symbolizes freedom and success.

Zimbabwe
Republic, S cen. Africa

Area: 150,804 sq. mi. (390,580 sq. km.)
Population: 12,311,000
Language(s): English, local languages

Monetary unit: Zimbabwean dollar
Economy: mining (coal, gold, platinum), wood products, cement, chemicals, fertilizer, textiles

On April 18, 1980, elections brought the black majority to power under the current flag. The black color is for the ethnic majority, while red is for blood, green for agriculture, yellow for mineral wealth, and white for peace and progress. At the hoist is a red star (for socialism) and the ancient "Zimbabwe Bird" from the Great Zimbabwe ruins.

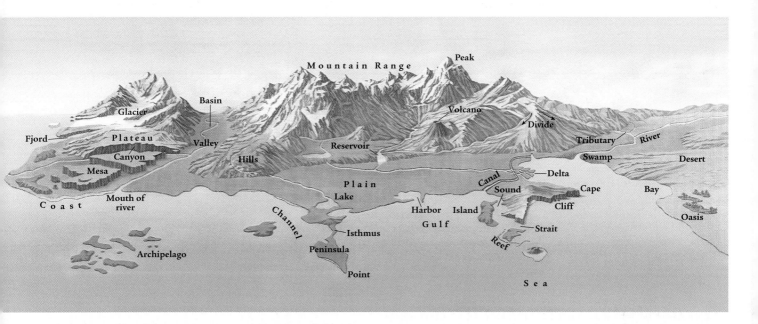

Glossary

This glossary provides brief definitions of some of the geographical terms and foreign terms used in this atlas. It does not include names of peoples, languages, religions, and geologic eras. For definitions of those terms, please refer to a standard dictionary such as *Merriam-Webster's Intermediate Dictionary* or *Merriam-Webster's Collegiate® Dictionary*.

In addition, this glossary includes information about a small set of place-names that are used in the atlas but whose meaning may not be immediately self-explanatory from the maps, graphs, or text in which they appear. More detailed information on place-names can be found in *Merriam-Webster's Geographical Dictionary*.

acid rain : rain having increased acidity caused by atmospheric pollutants

agglomeration : a cluster containing a large city and the populated areas surrounding it

alpine : of or relating to mountains

Altiplano : the region comprising a series of high plains in western Bolivia and extending into southeastern Peru

amphitheater : a flat or gently sloping area surrounded by abrupt slopes

Anatolia : the part of Turkey comprising the peninsula forming the western extremity of Asia

An Nafud : a desert in northern Saudi Arabia

aqueduct
1 : a conduit for carrying a large quantity of flowing water
2 : a structure for conveying a canal over a river or hollow

archipelago : a group of islands

arid : having insufficient rainfall to support agriculture

Arnhem Land : a coastal region of northern Australia containing a large aboriginal reservation

atoll : a coral island consisting of a reef surrounding a lagoon

bab — an Arabic word meaning "strait"

bank
1 : an undersea elevation rising especially from the continental shelf
2 : the rising ground bordering a lake, river, or sea
3 — see SANDBANK

basin
1 a : a large or small depression in the surface of the land or in the ocean floor
b : the entire tract of country drained by a river and its tributaries
c : a great depression in the surface of Earth occupied by an ocean
2 : a broad area of Earth beneath which the strata dip usually from the sides toward the center

bay — see INLET

bight : a bay formed by a bend in a coast

biodiversity : biological diversity in an environment as indicated by numbers of different species of plants and animals

Bosporus : the strait connecting the Sea of Marmara with the Black Sea

Brittany : an historical region in northwestern France

broadleaf : composed of plants having leaves that are not needles

canal : an artificial waterway for navigation or for draining or irrigating land

canyon : a deep narrow valley with steep sides and often with a stream flowing through it

cap — a French word meaning "cape"

cape : a point or extension of land jutting out into water as a peninsula or as a projecting point

cascade : one of a series of steep usually small falls of water

cataract : steep rapids in a river

causeway : a raised way across wet ground or water

cay : a low island or reef of sand or coral

Central America : the narrow southern portion of North America comprised of Guatemala, El Salvador, Honduras, Nicaragua, Costa Rica, Panama, and Belize

channel : a strait or narrow sea between two close land areas

city : an inhabited place usually of greater size or importance than a town

cliff : a very steep, vertical, or overhanging face of rock, earth, or ice

coast : the land near a shore

collectivity — see TERRITORIAL COLLECTIVITY

colony : a distant territory belonging to or under the control of a nation

coniferous : composed of plants having needle-shaped leaves

continent : one of the six or seven great divisions of land on Earth

continental shelf : a shallow submarine plain of varying width forming a border to a continent and typically ending in a comparatively steep slope to the deep ocean floor

country
1 : an indefinite usually extended expanse of land
2 : a state or nation or its territory

crown land : land belonging to a monarchy and yielding revenues that the reigning sovereign is entitled to

crust : the outer part of Earth composed essentially of crystalline rocks

current : a part of the ocean moving continuously in a certain direction

Cyrenaica : the easternmost part of Libya settled by ancient Greeks

Dalmatia : a region on the Adriatic coast

Damaraland : the plateau region of central Namibia

Dardanelles : the strait connecting the Sea of Marmara with the Aegean Sea

dasht — a Persian word meaning "desert"

deciduous : composed of plants having leaves that fall off seasonally or at a certain stage of development in the life cycle

defile : a narrow passage or gorge

deforestation : the action or process of clearing of forests

delta : the triangular or fan-shaped piece of land made by deposits of mud and sand at the mouth of a river

density : the average number of individuals per unit of space

dependency : a territorial unit under the jurisdiction of a nation but not formally annexed by it

depression : an area of land in which the central part lies lower than the margin

desert : arid land with usually little vegetation that is incapable of supporting a considerable population without an artificial water supply

diaspora : the movement, migration, or scattering of a people away from an established or ancestral homeland

division : a portion of a territorial unit marked off for a particular purpose (as administrative or judicial functions)

duchy : the territory of a duke or duchess

elevation
1 : the height above sea level
2 : a place that rises above its surroundings

eminence : a natural elevation

emirate : the state or jurisdiction of an emir (a ruler in an Islamic country)

enclave : a foreign territorial unit enclosed within a larger territory [The difference between an *enclave* and an *exclave* is one of perspective. An enclosed territorial unit is an enclave with respect to the territory that surrounds it, but it is an exclave of the country to which it belongs.]

endangered species : a species threatened with extinction

Equator : the great circle of Earth that is everywhere equally distant from the North Pole and the South Pole and divides the surface into Northern Hemisphere and Southern Hemisphere

erg : a desert region of shifting sand

escarpment : a long cliff or steep slope separating two comparatively level or more gently sloping surfaces and resulting from erosion or faulting

estuary : an arm of the sea at the lower end of a river

Eurasian : of Europe and Asia

European Union : an economic, scientific, and political organization consisting of Belgium, France, Italy, Luxembourg, Netherlands, Germany, Denmark, Greece, Ireland, United Kingdom, Spain, Portugal, Austria, Finland, Sweden, Cyprus, Czech Republic, Estonia, Hungary, Latvia, Lithuania, Malta, Poland, Slovakia, Slovenia, Bulgaria, and Romania.

evergreen : composed of plants having foliage that remains green and functional through more than one growing season

exclave : a portion of a country separated from the main part and surrounded by foreign territory — compare ENCLAVE

fjord : a narrow inlet of the sea between cliffs or steep slopes

free association : a relationship affording sovereignty with independent control of internal affairs and foreign policy except defense

geothermal : produced by the heat of the Earth's interior

geyser : a spring that throws forth intermittent jets of heated water and steam

glacier : a large body of ice moving slowly down a slope or valley or spreading outward on a land surface

Gobi : the desert in a plateau region in southern Mongolia and extending into China

Gondwana : the hypothetical land area believed to have once connected the Indian Subcontinent and the landmasses of the Southern Hemisphere

gorge : a narrow steep-walled canyon or part of a canyon

Gran Chaco : the thinly populated swampy region of South America divided between Argentina, Bolivia, and Paraguay

great circle : a circle on the surface of the Earth a portion of which is the shortest distance between any two points

grid : a network of uniformly spaced horizontal and perpendicular lines (as for locating points on a map)

gulf — see INLET

habitat : a place or environment where a plant or animal naturally or normally lives and grows

harbor : a protected part of a body of water that is deep enough to furnish anchorage; *esp* : one with port facilities

headland : a point of usually high land jutting out into a body of water

headstream : a stream that is the source of a river

hemisphere : the northern or southern half of the Earth as divided by the Equator or the eastern or western half as divided by a meridian

highland : elevated or mountainous land

hill — see MOUNTAIN

Horn of Africa : the easternmost projection of land in Africa

humid : characterized by perceptible moisture

hydroelectric : relating to electricity produced by waterpower

ice cap : an area having a cover of perennial ice and snow

ice field : a glacier flowing outward from the center of an extensive area of relatively level land

ice shelf : an extensive ice cap originating on land but continuing out to sea beyond the depths at which it rests on the sea bottom

indigenous : having originated in a particular region or environment

Indochina : the peninsula comprised of Myanmar, Thailand, Laos, Cambodia, Vietnam, and the western part of Malaysia

inlet
1 : a recess in the shore of a larger body of water [In this sense, *inlet* is a general term for *bay* or *gulf*. The chief difference between a bay and a gulf is one of size. A bay is usually smaller than a gulf.]
2 : a narrow water passage between peninsulas or through a barrier island leading to a bay or lagoon

intermittent lake : a lake that is sometimes dry

intermittent stream : a stream that is sometimes dry

intermontane : situated between mountains

International Date Line : the line coinciding approximately with the meridian 180 degrees from the Prime Meridian fixed by international agreement as the place where each calendar day first begins

island : an area of land surrounded by water and smaller than a continent

islet : a little island

isthmus : a narrow strip of land connecting two larger land areas

jebel — an Arabic word meaning "mountain"

key : any of the coral islets off the southern coast of Florida

kill : a channel — used chiefly in place-names in Delaware, Pennsylvania, and New York

kingdom : a major territorial unit headed by a king or queen

kum — a Turkic word meaning "desert"

Labrador : a peninsula divided between the Canadian provinces of Quebec and Newfoundland and Labrador

lac — a French word meaning "lake"

lagoon : a shallow sound, channel, or pond near or connected with a larger body of water

laguna — a Spanish word meaning "lagoon" or "lake"

lake : a considerable inland body of standing water

landform : a natural feature of a land surface

landmass : a large area of land

Lapland : the region north of the Arctic Circle divided between Norway, Sweden, Finland, and Russia

legend : an explanatory list of the symbols on a map or chart

Llano Estacado : the plateau region of eastern and southeastern New Mexico and western Texas

Llanos : the region of vast plains in northern South America that is drained by the Orinoco River and its tributaries

locality : a specific location

loch : a lake in Scotland

lough : a lake in Ireland

lowland : low or level country

magnetic pole : either of two small regions which are located respectively in the polar areas of the Northern Hemisphere and the Southern Hemisphere and toward which a compass needle points from any direction throughout adjacent regions

marine : influenced or determined by proximity to the sea

marsh : a tract of soft wet land

massif : a principal mountain mass

Melanesia : the islands in the southwestern Pacific northeast of Australia and south of the Equator

mesa : an isolated relatively flat-topped natural elevation usually less extensive than a plateau

Mesopotamia : the historical region between the Tigris and Euphrates rivers

metropolitan : constituting the chief or capital city and sometimes including its suburbs

Micronesia : the widely scattered islands of the western Pacific east of the Philippines

midlatitude : of the area approximately between 30 to 60 degrees north or south of the Equator

mineral : a naturally occurring crystalline element or compound that has a definite chemical composition and results from processes other than those of plants and animals

monarchy : a nation or state having a government headed by a hereditary chief of state with life tenure

mountain
1 : an elevated mass of land that projects above its surroundings [Among the many types of natural land elevations, a distinction needs to be made between *hill, mountain,* and *peak.* A hill is likely to be lower than a mountain or peak and typically has a rounded summit. A mountain is larger and projects more conspicuously than a hill, while a peak is usually a prominent type of mountain having a well-defined summit.]
2 : an elongated ridge

mouth : the place where a stream enters a larger body of water

municipality : a primarily urban political unit

narrows : a strait connecting two bodies of water

national park : an area of special scenic, historical, or scientific importance set aside and maintained by a national government

notch : a deep close pass

novaya — a Russian word meaning "new"

oasis : a fertile or green area in an arid region

occidental — a Spanish word meaning "western"

ocean : any of the large bodies of water into which the whole body of salt water that covers much of Earth is divided

Oceania : the lands of the central and southern Pacific

Okavango : a large marsh in northern Botswana

oriental — a Spanish word meaning "eastern"

Pampas : the extensive generally grass-covered plains region of South America lying east of the Andes Mountains

Pangaea : the hypothetical land area believed to have once connected the landmasses of the Southern Hemisphere with those of the Northern Hemisphere

pass : a low place in a mountain range

passage : a place through which it is possible to pass

Patagonia : a barren tableland mostly in Argentina

peak — see MOUNTAIN

peninsula : a portion of land nearly surrounded by water

per capita : per unit of population

pico — a Spanish word meaning "peak"

piedmont : the area lying or formed at the base of mountains

plain
1 : an extensive area of level or rolling treeless country
2 : a broad unbroken expanse

plate : any of the large movable segments into which Earth's crust is divided

plateau : a usually extensive land area having a relatively level surface raised sharply above adjacent land on at least one side
[Sometimes the word is used synonymously with *tableland.*]

point : a place having a precisely indicated position

polar : of or relating to the region around the North Pole or the South Pole

polder : a tract of lowland reclaimed from a body of water

pole : either extremity of Earth's axis

Polynesia : the islands of the central Pacific

pool
1 : a small and rather deep body of water
2 : a quiet place in a stream
3 : a body of water forming above a dam

Prime Meridian : the meridian of 0 degrees longitude which runs through the original site of the Royal Greenwich Observatory at Greenwich, England and from which other longitudes are reckoned

princely state : a state governed by a prince in pre-independent India

principality : the territory of a prince

profile : a drawing showing comparative elevations of land surface along a given strip

projection : an estimate of a future possibility based on current trends

promontory
1 : a high point of land or rock projecting into a body of water
2 : a prominent mass of land overlooking or projecting into a lowland

protectorate : a political unit dependent on the authority of another

punta — a Spanish word meaning "point"

race : a narrow channel through which a strong or rapid current of water flows

rain forest
1 : a tropical woodland with an annual rainfall of at least 100 inches (254 centimeters) and marked by lofty trees forming a continuous canopy
2 : woodland of a usually rather mild climatic area that receives heavy rainfall and that usually includes numerous kinds of trees with one or two types that dominate

range : a series of mountains

reef : a chain of rocks or coral or a ridge of sand at or near the surface of water

region
1 : a primary administrative subdivision of a country
2 : an indefinite area of Earth
3 : a broad geographical area distinguished by similar features

republic
1 : a political unit having a form of government headed by a chief of state who is not a monarch
2 : a political unit having a form of government in which supreme power resides in a body of citizens entitled to vote and is exercised by elected officers and representatives responsible to them and governing according to law
3 : a constituent political and territorial unit of a country

reservation : a tract of public land set aside for a special use

reservoir : an artificial lake where water is collected and kept in quantity for use

ridge
1 : a range of hills or mountains
2 : an elongate elevation on an ocean bottom

rift valley : an elongated valley formed by the depression of a block of the Earth's crust between two faults or groups of faults of approximately parallel orientation

rio — a Spanish word meaning "river"

river : a natural stream of water of usually considerable volume

roadstead : a place less enclosed than a harbor where ships may ride at anchor

Rub' al-Khali : the vast desert region of the southern Arabian Peninsula

rural : of or relating to the country

Sahel : the semidesert southern fringe of the Sahara that stretches from Mauritania to Chad

san — a Spanish word meaning "saint"

sandbank : a large deposit of sand forming a shoal

santa; santo — Spanish words meaning "saint"

são — a Portuguese word meaning "saint"

savanna : a tropical or subtropical grassland containing scattered trees

scale : an indication of the relationship between the distances on a map and the corresponding actual distances

Scandinavia
1 : the peninsula occupied by Norway and Sweden
2 : the region of northern Europe comprising Denmark, Norway, and Sweden and often including Finland and Iceland

scrubland : land covered with vegetation chiefly consisting of stunted trees or shrubs

sea
1 : a more or less landlocked body of salt water
2 : an ocean
3 : an inland body of water

semiarid : having from about 10 to 20 inches (25 to 51 centimeters) of annual precipitation

semidesert : an arid area that has some of the characteristics of a desert but has greater annual precipitation

serra — a Portuguese word meaning "mountain range"

shan — a Chinese word meaning "mountain range"

shield : the ancient mass of hard rock that forms the core of a continent

shoal : a ridge or large deposit of sand that makes the water shallow

shore : the land bordering a usually large body of water

Siberia : a vast region mostly in Russia extending from the Pacific Ocean to the Ural Mountains

sierra — a Spanish word meaning "mountain range"

site : the location of some particular thing

sound
1 : a long broad inlet of the ocean generally parallel to the coast
2 : a long passage of water connecting two larger bodies of water or separating a mainland and an island

source : the point of origin of a stream of water

spa : a town or resort with mineral springs

spring : a source of water issuing from the ground

state
1 : a sovereign politically organized body of people usually occupying a definite territory
2 : one of the constituent units of a nation having a federal government

steppe
1 : one of the vast usually level and treeless tracts in southeastern Europe or Asia
2 : arid land found usually in regions of extreme temperature range

strait : a comparatively narrow passageway connecting two large bodies of water

strata : layers having parallel layers of other kinds above or below or both

above and below

subarctic : characteristic of regions bordering the Arctic Circle

subcontinent : a major subdivision of a continent

subduction zone : an area in which the edge of one of Earth's plates descends below the edge of another

subsistence agriculture : a system of farming that provides all or almost all the goods required by the farm family usually without any significant surplus for sale

subtropical : characteristic of regions bordering on the tropics

Sudd : the lowland swamp region of southern Sudan

sultanate : a state or nation governed by a sultan

supercontinent : a former large continent from which other continents are believed to have broken off and drifted away

swamp : a tract of wetland often partially or intermittently covered with water

tableland : a broad level elevated area [Sometimes the word is used synonymously with *plateau*.]

territorial collectivity : a French overseas territorial unit enjoying some degree of local authority and having a status lesser than an overseas department but greater than an overseas territory

territory
1 a : a geographical area belonging to or under the jurisdiction of a governmental authority
b : an administrative subdivision of a country
c : a part of the U.S. not included within any state but organized with a separate legislature
d : a geographical area dependent on an external government but having some degree of autonomy
2 : an indeterminate geographical area

tidewater : low-lying coastal land

Tierra del Fuego : an archipelago divided between Argentina and Chile

time zone : a geographic region within which the same standard time is used

tract : a stretch of land

Transcaucasia : the region in southeastern Europe south of the Caucasus Mountains and between the Black and Caspian seas

trench : a long, narrow, and usually steep-sided depression in the ocean floor

tributary : a stream feeding a larger stream or a lake

Tripolitania : an historical region of northern Africa originally a Phoenician colony

tropic : either of the regions lying between the two parallels of the Earth's latitude that are approximately 23 $\frac{1}{2}$ degrees north of the Equator (Tropic of Cancer) and approximately 23 $\frac{1}{2}$ degrees south of the Equator (Tropic of Capricorn)

tundra : a treeless plain having permanently frozen subsoil and vegetation consisting chiefly of mosses, lichens, herbs, and very small shrubs

union territory : a centrally administered subdivision of India consisting of an island group, the area surrounding a city, or an area containing a linguistic minority

unitary district : one of the administrative subdivisions of Scotland since 1996

upland : high land especially at some distance from the sea

urban : of or relating to the city

valley
1 : an elongated depression of Earth's surface usually between ranges of hills or mountains
2 : an area drained by a river and its tributaries

volcán — a Spanish word meaning "volcano"

volcano : a mountain composed wholly or in part of material ejected from a vent in the Earth's crust

Wallachia : an historical region in Romania

waterway : a navigable body or course of water

wilderness : a region uncultivated and uninhabited by human beings and more or less in its natural state

woodland : land covered with woody vegetation

World's Largest Lakes

Name	Location	Area in sq. mi. (sq. km.)
AFRICA		
Victoria	Kenya—Tanzania—Uganda	26,828 (69,484)
Tanganyika	Burundi—Tanzania—Dem. Rep. of the Congo—Zambia	12,700 (32,893)
Malawi (Nyasa)	Malawi—Mozambique—Tanzania	11,430 (29,604)
Chad	Cameroon—Chad—Niger—Nigeria	6,875 (17,806)
Bangweulu	Zambia	3,800 (9,842)
Turkana (Rudolf)	Kenya extending into Ethiopia	2,473 (6,405)
NORTH AMERICA		
Superior	Canada (Ontario)—United States (Minnesota, Wisconsin, Michigan)	31,700 (82,103)
Huron	Canada (Ontario)—United States (Michigan)	23,000 (59,570)
Michigan	United States (Michigan, Wisconsin, Illinois, Indiana)	22,300 (57,757)
Great Bear	Canada (Northwest Territories)	12,275 (31,792)
Great Slave	Canada (Northwest Territories)	11,031 (28,570)
Erie	Canada (Ontario)—United States (New York, Pennsylvania, Ohio, Michigan)	9,910 (25,667)
Winnipeg	Canada (Manitoba)	9,465 (24,514)
Ontario	Canada (Ontario)—United States (New York)	7,600 (19,684)
SOUTH AMERICA		
Maracaibo	Venezuela	5,217 (13,512)
Titicaca	Peru—Bolivia	3,200 (8,288)
Poopó	Bolivia	1,000 (2,590)
Buenos Aires (General Carrera)	Argentina—Chile	865 (2,240)
Mar Chiquita	Argentina	714 (1,849)
ASIA		
Baikal	Russia	11,780 (30,510)
Aral Sea	Kazakhstan—Uzbekistan	10,263 (26,581)
Balkhash (Balqash)	Kazakhstan	6,650 (17,224)
Dongting	China	1,430 (3,704)
Tonle Sap	Cambodia	1,000 (2,590)
EUROPE		
Ladoga	Russia	6,826 (17,679)
Onega	Russia	3,753 (9,720)
Vänern	Sweden	2,156 (5,584)
Peipus (Peipsi)	Russia—Estonia	1,390 (3,600)
Vättern	Sweden	738 (1,911)
OCEANIA		
Eyre	Australia (South Australia)	3,600 (9,324)
Torrens	Australia (South Australia)	2,230 (5,776)
Gairdner	Australia (South Australia)	1,840 (4,766)
Frome	Australia (South Australia)	900 (2,331)

World's Longest Rivers

Name	Outflow	Length in miles (kilometers)
AFRICA		
Nile	Mediterranean Sea	4,160 (6,693)
Congo (Zaïre)	South Atlantic Ocean	2,720 (4,376)
Niger	Bight of Biafra	2,600 (4,183)
Zambezi	Mozambique Channel	1,700 (2,735)
Kasai	Congo River	1,338 (2,153)
Orange	South Atlantic Ocean	1,300 (2,090)
NORTH AMERICA		
Mississippi—Missouri	Gulf of Mexico	3,877 (6,238)
Mackenzie—Slave—Peace—Finlay	Beaufort Sea	2,635 (4,240)
Missouri	Mississippi River	2,466 (3,968)
Mississippi	Gulf of Mexico	2,357 (3,792)
Yukon	Bering Sea	1,979 (3,184)
SOUTH AMERICA		
Amazon—Ucayali—Apurimac	South Atlantic Ocean	4,000 (6,436)
Paraná	Río de la Plata	2,500 (4,022)
Purus	Amazon River	2,100 (3,379)
Madeira—Mamoré—Guaporé	Amazon River	2,082 (3,350)
Juruá	Amazon River	2,040 (3,282)
ASIA		
Chang (Yangtze)	East China Sea	3,965 (6,380)
Yenisey—Selenga	Kara Sea	3,442 (5,538)
Huang (Yellow)	Bo Hai (Gulf of Chihli)	3,395 (5,462)
Ob'—Irtysh	Gulf of Ob'	3,362 (5,409)
Lena	Laptev Sea	2,734 (4,399)
Mekong	South China Sea	2,600 (4,200)
Amur—Argun	Sea of Okhotsk	2,236 (3,598)
EUROPE		
Volga	Caspian Sea	2,293 (3,689)
Danube	Black Sea	1,770 (2,848)
Ural (Zhayyq)	Caspian Sea	1,575 (2,534)
Dnieper	Black Sea	1,420 (2,285)
Don	Sea of Azov	1,224 (1,969)
OCEANIA		
Darling	Murray River	1,702 (2,738)
Murray	Great Australian Bight	1,609 (2,589)
Murrumbidgee	Murray River	981 (1,578)
Lachlan	Murrumbidgee River	922 (1,483)